A general view of the rural economy
of England, 1538–1840

In rural England prior to the Industrial Revolution people generally married when they were not busy with work. Parish registers of marriage therefore form an important and innovative source for the study of economic change in this period. Professor Kussmaul employs marriage dates to identify three main patterns of work and risk (arable, pastoral and rural industrial) and more importantly to show the long term changes in economic activities across 542 English parishes from the beginning of national marriage registration in 1538. No single historical landscape emerges. Instead *A general view of the rural economy of England, 1538–1840* maps the changes in economic orientation from arable through regional specialization to rural industrialization and explores how these changes had implications for the extent of population growth in the early modern period. Professor Kussmaul's study presents a view of early modern English economic history from a unique standpoint.

Professor Ann Kussmaul is in the economics department of Glendon College, York University, Toronto. Her publications include *Servants in husbandry in early modern England* and, as editor, *The autobiography of Joseph Mayett of Quainton (1783–1839)*.

Cambridge Studies in Population, Economy and Society in Past Time 11

Series editors

PETER LASLETT, ROGER SCHOFIELD and
E. A. WRIGLEY

ESRC Cambridge Group for the History of Population and Social Science

and DANIEL SCOTT SMITH

University of Illinois at Chicago

Recent work in social, economic and demographic history has revealed much that was previously obscure about societal stability and change in the past. It has also suggested that crossing the conventional boundaries between these branches of history can be very rewarding.

This series will exemplify the value of interdisciplinary work of this kind, and will include books on topics such as family, kinship and neighbourhood; welfare provision and social control; work and leisure; migration; urban growth; and legal structures and procedures, as well as more familiar matters. It will demonstrate that, for example, anthropology and economics have become as close intellectual neighbours to history as have political philosophy or biography.

A general view of the rural economy of England 1538–1840

ANN KUSSMAUL

Glendon College, York University, Toronto

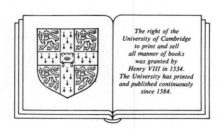

The right of the
University of Cambridge
to print and sell
all manner of books
was granted by
Henry VIII in 1534.
The University has printed
and published continuously
since 1584.

CAMBRIDGE UNIVERSITY PRESS
Cambridge
New York   Port Chester   Melbourne   Sydney

Published by the Press Syndicate of the University of Cambridge
The Pitt Building, Trumpington Street, Cambridge CB2 1RP
40 West 20th Street, New York, NY 10011, USA
10 Stamford Road, Oakleigh, Melbourne 3166, Australia

First published 1990

Printed in Great Britain at the University Press, Cambridge

British Library cataloguing in publication data
Kussmaul, Ann
A general view of the rural economy of
England, 1538–1840. – (Cambridge studies in
population, economy and society in past time; 11)
1. England, Rural regions,
Economic conditions, history
I. Title
330.942

Library of Congress cataloguing in publication data
Kussmaul, Ann.
A general view of the rural economy of England.
1538–1840 / Ann Kussmaul.
p.   cm.
Bibliography
Includes index.
ISBN 0–521–30634–5.
1. England – Economic conditions.
2. England – Rural conditions.
3. Marriage – England – Statistics.
I. Title.
HC254.5.K87   1989
330.942′009173′4–dc20

ISBN 0 521 30634 5

to the memory of
Amanda Victoria West Copley
22 April 1962–24 July 1988

Contents

Figures

Tables

Preface

It might be a peculiarly North American failing to yearn for an expansive view of the past, a view that the peculiar (from the perspective of economic history) data of marriage seasons allow. I would not have known that the economic orientations of regions in the past could be mapped so readily had I not, on a summer's day in 1979 in Cambridge, been curious about whether the changing incidence of service in husbandry in pastoral western England was reflected in changes in the strength of the springtime marriages of former farm servants there. It was not: in the sixteenth century, autumn was the dominant marriage season nearly everywhere, in the west as well as the east. This book investigates why that was so, and why regions came to differ in their marriage seasonality in the later seventeenth century.

I am indebted to so many for their help in pursuing the solution, and hope these thoughts of gratitude will be accepted by all who know the aid they gave. The Cambridge Group for the History of Population and Social Structure gave me A. N. Other's room in which to work, the marriage data from 404 parishes, and computing time to investigate them. I thank, especially, Roger Schofield, Tony Wrigley, Jim Oeppen, Ros Davies, Kevin Schurer, and Jeremy Boulton, for all the time of their own they gave to this then novice computer, for their good advice, and for good times. The last of these gifts came from Fitzwilliam College as well, in my two years as Visiting Fellow.

Explaining the method, defending the method I was devising, to the research students working with the Cambridge Group, Bridget Taylor and the late Amanda Copley, and to many others, especially John Broad, Glynis Reynolds, David Souden, Richard Wall, Chris Wilson, David Weir, and my puzzled home department was a great help in its refining. John Broad and Susan Wright, and Glynis Reynolds contri-

buted marriage data from many parishes to the data set. Meetings of
the Toronto Social History Group, the Economic History Association,
the Historical Geography Research Group, and the ESRC–Quantitative Economic History Workshop, and seminars at Cornell, Toronto,
Cambridge, London, St Andrew's, Edinburgh, Leeds, Oxford, the
L.S.E., Exeter, Hull, Warwick, York, and Queen's (Kingston) all heard
reports on this project as it unfolded, and rendered much helpful
criticism. Archivists in Norfolk, Northamptonshire, Staffordshire, and
Warwickshire were unstinting in their assistance (and occasionally in
their curiosity about my now antediluvian Tandy 100). I am grateful,
also, to the Social Science Research Council of Canada and to Glendon
College for the financial assistance that enabled me to become a
regular seasonal migrant to England for the last few years, and that
carried me through the completion of my work on servants and the
present study.

On that lazy afternoon of 1979 I was revising my thesis for publication. Readers of that first book who remember nothing about it but
the tale of the theft of the research notes in Lyons might be interested
to learn that this time I stepped on the last ice of the winter of 1986 (the
last ice of any winter in greenhoused Toronto?), and broke my fall
with my right (and writing) arm.

1

A bird's eye view of the past

Wouldn't it be nice to have a bird's eye view of the past, to grasp interrelations in the early modern economy over space and time? E. L. Jones thought so, in examining the relations between industrialization and deindustrialization in the eighteenth century.[1] But the economic history of early modern England is marked by the patchiness of its sources. Time series cannot be easily constructed, for any one variable; it is hard to map variables over space.

The challenge compounds when time and space must be considered together, to see change whole, to observe the relation of parts to the whole, over time. Linked spatial and temporal coverage is important to many historiographical pursuits, such as the investigation of the diffusion and timing of technological change, or of enclosure (on both of which the study is largely mute). Spatially wide and temporally deep coverage is decisive in other areas of exploration; regional specialization and market integration are classic problems of the relation of parts to the whole, over time; so are the temporally and spatially related processes of industrialization and deindustrialization with which Jones was concerned. It makes a difference to our interpretation of any one period within the long run to know that the transformation we are examining was concentrated in that period rather than another, or in that period alone rather than extending over the whole of the long run. As the book will show, several vital early modern changes were loaded into a shorter period than is usually thought.

The General View works through its ability to see change whole. Figure 1.1 is equivalent to a snapshot taken by a high flying (and preternaturally talented) bird, with a very long time exposure; the imaginary camera's shutter would have had to have been open for the

[1] Jones, 'Constraints', p. 424.

1

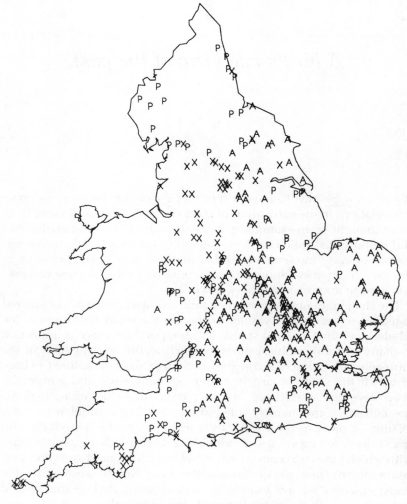

Figure 1.1 Seasonal Types, 1701–40
Key: A A-Type
P P-Type
X X-Type

first forty years of the eighteenth century. One symbol is plotted for each of the parishes of a set of 542 that (a) was not a market town and (b) recorded at least twenty-four marriages in 1701–40. Chapter 3 explains the derivation of the symbols 'P', 'A', and 'X'. I shall spend the next two chapters demonstrating that the A's represent arable practices, the P's areas of rearing, and the X's regions of rural industry.

The map is not a bad representation of the familiar, 'traditional', regions of the rural English economic landscape; the west is pastoral and industrial, the east arable, and the Midlands a heterogeneous medley of arable, pastoral, and industrial symbols. Interestingly, as most of the book will go on to argue, the regional pattern of Figure 1.1 was a creation of the late seventeenth century, replacing a far more homogeneous blanket of arable activities (see the companion map for 1561–1600, Figure 1.4, below), and was the product of regional specialization in the use of land and labour.

There is evidence here of a sharp early modern discontinuity in the English rural economy. But who would have thought that the evidence would be derived from the seasonality of marriage, the foundation of Figure 1.1? The book exploits a source that is not essentially patchy, and that contains an unparalleled length of runs and breadth of coverage, through and across early modern England. The record is, however, improbable as a source for economic history, fraught with its own difficulties, not least the one of commending its acceptance. The study is based on parish registers of marriages, used not for the occasional runs of occupations they may contain, but for the pure, quantitative, seasonality of marriage, the seasonal pattern of weddings within the year.

Lambs and calves were dropped, crops ripened for harvest, in their own seasons, different seasons. Agricultural work was seasonal, governed by the annual rhythm of growth, and marriages moulded themselves to the seasonal matrix of work. Weddings, like other celebrations, were infrequent during the months of maximum work and risk; they then clustered in the weeks immediately following the relief from work and risk. Why they clustered is probably overspecified: high harvest wages were paid to labourers; unmarried servants in husbandry were released from their annual contracts; one could posit a need to celebrate the end of a year's work; there certainly would have been a pent-up demand for weddings, strengthened by the revelation of prenuptial conceptions.[2]

There were two great agricultural seasons, the late summer, early autumn harvest, which was followed by autumn weddings, and the late winter, early spring lambing and calving of traditional animal

[2] See the discussion in Wrigley and Schofield, *Population History of England*, Chapter 8. Other influences on the timing of marriage, 'disturbances' from the instrumental point of view of this project, are discussed in this author's 'Time and Space', pp. 755–79, and below in Chapter 2.

husbandry, followed by spring and early summer weddings.[3] From this unlikely source, marriage registers, can be constructed measures of grossly arable (autumn-marrying) work, grossly pastoral (spring/summer-marrying) work, and grossly non-agricultural, rural industrial work, showing little tendency towards peaks in marriages in either of the agriculturally determined seasons.

One result of that construction was displayed in Figure 1.1; the A-Types were parishes where autumn was the main marriage season, the P-Types parishes where spring/early summer marriages (after lambing and calving) predominated, and the X-Types parishes where marriages were crowded into neither the autumn nor the spring/early summer, and which were, in the main, rural industrial places (although the next two chapters will suggest other possible meanings of non-seasonality, especially in the parishes of the northwest). The timing of weddings accommodated itself to other claims on the time of grooms and brides and other residents of the parish, work being foremost among these other claims, so the seasonality of marriage can be made into a proxy for the local pattern of work.

Why bother with so indirect a measure? If one works at a high enough level of spatial aggregation, abstraction, and inference, as in the eighteenth-century studies of Crafts, Ippolito, and Jackson, regional variations will be unimportant, and need not be measured.[4] Or one can assume away variability of change over time, and act as if the economy moved seamlessly from some late medieval state to some modern one, ever more commercial, ever more specialized. A variation on the theme of seamless progress is to appropriate all the change to the sub-period being studied (see below, Chapter 4). But if time and space are to be considered jointly, more precision is needed.

Many indicators of economic activities are more direct than are marriage seasons. Occupational designations irregularly appear in registers of baptisms, burials, and marriages, in the unusual tax record, in other occasional listings, but always erratically. There was no national directive to make census-like records of local inhabitants before the nineteenth century (and even then, as Rickman noted in his commentary on the 1821 census, local clerical pedants had balked at including shepherds and graziers in the category 'employed in agri-

---

[3] That pastoral weddings seem closely tied to the timing of the weaning of young beasts, rather than hay-making, for instance, argues for risk aversion as the influence on the timing of these weddings, in this case aversion to the risk of losing capital on the hoof. See discussion in Chapter 2.

[4] Crafts, 'Income Elasticity', pp. 153–68; Ippolito, 'Effect of the "Agricultural Depression"', pp. 298–312; Jackson, 'Growth and Deceleration', pp. 333–51.

culture', since they did not till the fields).[5] To find a number of people recorded as 'husbandmen', or 'yeomen', or later as 'farmers', tells us nothing of the cereal and animal crops they produced, although a crude breakdown between employment in agriculture and employment in crafts and trades may be possible. Even then, as Swain noted relative to cloth-working in northeastern Lancashire, many sixteenth- and seventeenth-century weavers hid from historians behind the title 'yeoman'.[6]

Identification of occupations in fiscal and other records is far from uniform over time and space. It is so much more common in the context of the varied occupations of the industrial north in the eighteenth century, for example, than in the records of the more blandly agricultural south, that one gets the impression that the record-keeper's (often the vicar's) curiosity had first to be piqued before he felt moved to record the occupation, as, in another context, one can be led to believe that most of the inhabitants of Over Areley, Worcestershire (now Staffordshire) died by hanging themselves, since that appears such a common cause of death noted in the burial register, compared to the seldom noted, presumably more tediously expected more frequent causes of death.[7] In so many otherwise promising occupational listings, a large number of people are given no occupation, leaving us with the problem of choosing one of three assumptions: (1) the record-keeper sometimes forgot, randomly, to record the occupation (so we can make inferences on the pattern of occupations based on the numbers whose work was indeed recorded), or (2) the occupation, like the other causes of death in Over Areley, was too usual to be worth noting, invalidating inferences based on the proportions recorded in the (interesting-to-the-recorder) occupations, or (3) residents in some occupations were better known to the vicar, and others less well known, again invalidating inferences based on the proportions recorded in the (known-to-the-recorder) occupations. Philip Styles felt he could estimate the occupations of 40 per cent of the adult male population of Fenny Compton, Warwickshire, from returns to the Marriage Duty Act (6 & 7 Wm. and Mary, c. 6): thirty-four were gentlemen, yeomen, husbandmen, farmers, or labourers, and nineteen were occupied in trade or crafts. But what were the other 60 per cent of the adult males doing, and what allows us to feel safe in assuming their occupations to have been distributed as were those of the registered?[8] Changes in record-keepers led to

[5] Rickman, 'Preliminary Observations', p. vii.   [6] Swain, 'Industry', p. ii.
[7] Mayo, ed., *Registers of Over Areley*.
[8] Styles, *Studies*, pp. 90–107.

changes in occupational titles, too; all the 'farmers' may appear to disappear from a parish simply because a new record-maker may have not thought an occupation as obvious as farming worth his recording.

Some candidates for sources are limited in their chronological span to a single year (such as the cross-sectional glimpse afforded by the 1801 crop returns, or by Schedule B of the 1798 income tax), or to somewhat longer periods, such as the eighteenth-century's militia lists and the settlement examinations, which abound for the eighteenth as they do not for the seventeenth or nineteenth centuries.[9] And each of these sources is also subject to problems of truncation and representativeness parallel to those mentioned above in connection with occupational listings. The crop returns, for example, asked no questions about livestock.

First hand accounts can be mined, although the biases of the observers must be taken into account. Thirsk noted the surprise expressed by continental visitors such as Friedrich, Duke of Württemberg, at the extent of English woodland, pasture, and livestock; Ashton reminded us of Defoe's eye for the striking rather than the commonplace.[10] There was no systematic attempt at national surveys until Arthur Young took his tours and the Board of Agriculture made its late eighteenth and early nineteenth century surveys, the two sets of *General Views* of each county.

A seeming patchwork of local and regional studies, patiently compiled from whatever material pertains to the place, can be gathered, but variations in sources and methods limit the stitching of the studies into one quilt. This obtains even when the principal sources are similar, and individual arguments persuasive, as in the use of probate inventories of the moveable property of dead farmers, labourers, and rural craftsmen. By no means was the moveable property of all in the locality recorded by probate. Hoskins came close to suggesting that it was lack of ambition that kept most labourers in Wigston Magna cowless, and thus lacking wills and inventories as well; Margaret Spufford wrote of the cottages the contents of which were often below the notice of the probate procedure.[11] And differences in method, between for instance Overton, Yelling, and Skipp, and in the questions asked of the inventories, complicate a clear linked perception of relations between agricultural changes in Norfolk and Suffolk, east

9 Turner, 'Arable in England and Wales', pp. 291–302; Grigg, 'Changing Agricultural Geography', pp. 73–96; Overton, '1801 Crop Returns', pp. 55–67.
10 Thirsk, 'Introduction' (1967c), pp. xxx–xxxi; Ashton, cited in Chambers and Mingay, *Agricultural Revolution*, p. 33.
11 Hoskins, *Midland Peasant*, p. 200; Spufford, *The Great Reclothing*, p. 3.

Worcestershire, and northwest Warwickshire.[12] There was no set
form for the recording of goods, as those who have used inventories
have been at pains to tell us.[13] They become consistent, comparable,
homogeneous records only to the extent that order is imposed on
them. There is, in that sense, a seeming embarrassment of national
riches, too great to be tackled by a single order-imposing researcher,
so the store has been minced into manageable sets of inventories and
other records, each subject to its own rules of consistency. Thirsk
noted a difficulty in drafting the new national map of farming types in
the fifth volume of *The Agrarian History of England and Wales*, because
the authors of the regional maps that were to be pieced together did
not always agree on their identification of farming types along the
common borders of their regions, where no difference in farming type
might have been expected.[14]

A pile of Anglican marriage registers may seem a strange perch from
which to survey change over time and space in the economy, but at
least the information drawn from the registers seems to work, in
suggesting dominant economic patterns. Consider Cowfold and
Barley, two of the parishes of Figure 1.1. Figure 1.2 plots the strength
of the tendency for the parishes' weddings to occur in the autumn
(measured on the horizontal axis), against their tendency to occur in
the spring and early summer (Chapter 3 explains the derivation of the
two indices). The points are labelled at the mid years of the contiguous
forty-year periods, and Figure 1.1's observations are italicized. The
muddied combinations of autumn and spring indices for the Interregnum (here, the points labelled '1640'), where Cowfold and Barley
almost meet, are discussed in Chapters 2 and 3.

Barley married after the grain harvest, in the autumn, and it plotted
as an 'A' on Figure 1.1. Cowfold, following a weak autumnal start,
married after calving and lambing, in the spring and early summer,
and appears in Figure 1.1 as a 'P'.

Industrial work was less seasonal than work in agriculture, and had
a lesser impact on the timing of marriages within the year, so
tendencies to marry after neither of the busy agricultural seasons of
autumn and spring/early summer can be used to root out rural
industry. Figure 1.3 shows the movement of the autumn and spring
indices of marriages for Sedgley, Staffordshire, a nail-making parish in
the Black Country. A fence enclosing predominantly non-agricultural

[12] Overton, 'Agricultural Change'; Overton, 'Estimating Crop Yields', pp. 363–78;
Yelling, 'Probate Inventories', pp. 111–26; Skipp, *Crisis and Development*.
[13] Thirsk, 'Content', p. 71; Yelling, 'Probate Inventories', p. 111.
[14] Thirsk, 'Introduction', p. xxi.

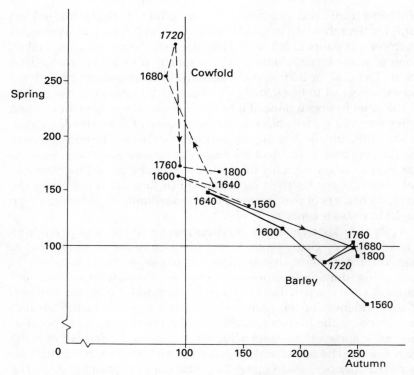

Figure 1.2 Autumn and spring/summer marriages in Cowfold (Sussex) and Barley (Herts.)

seasonal combinations of autumn and spring marriages, has been added to the figure; the fence is used in Chapter 3 to identify the non-seasonal X-Types of Figure 1.1. Sedgley enters the industrial enclosure between 1581–1620 and 1601–40; it was marked with an 'X' on Figure 1.1 (again, the observation corresponding to that map is italized).

Sedgley's rural industry hardly needs to be discovered via the seasonality of marriage, but the strong movement away from harvest-determined autumn marriages is clearly etched on the graph.[15] Asterisks indicate periods of overlap with a more conventional industry-finder, the occupational data given in Sedgly's baptism and burial registers.[16] Occupations were densely noted from 1578 to 1625, but then the vicar, Richard Browne, who had been recording the

[15] Rowlands, *Masters and Men*.   [16] Thomas, *Sedgley*.

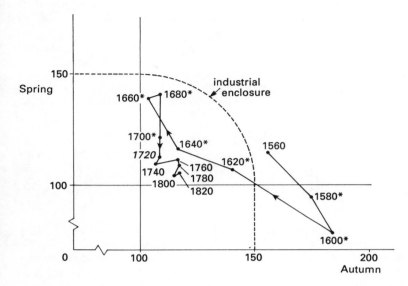

Figure 1.3 Autumn and spring/summer marriages in Sedgley (Staffs.)

occupations, died. After fifty years, occupations were once again included, from 1675 to 1685. In the late sixteenth and early seventeenth centuries, Sedgley already baptized more children of metalworkers (nailers, locksmiths or 'lockers', 'hambermen', 'bloomers', blacksmiths, and scythesmiths) than those whose fathers were given agricultural occupations, including labourers, gentlemen and their servants, and gardeners (see Table 1.1).

By the last period of the table, 1675–85, metal-workers were overwhelmingly more numerous. Agriculture was not only swamped in relative terms; it was dying out. Absolutely fewer baptisms and burials per annum in the agricultural sector were recorded in that last period. The dynamic of change is nicely caught in the disproportionately large number of burials of husbandmen, yeomen, labourers, etc., compared to the burials of the new, rising, and temporarily younger and healthier metal-workers. More farmers and labourers were buried in 1675–85 than children of farmers and labourers were baptized. The ratio of burials to baptisms in the agricultural sector was 1.33, while there were sixty-six baptisms and forty-nine burials in the metalworking sector (for a ratio of 0.74). Even in as well-documented a parish as Sedgley, the indirect evidence of marriage seasonality helps to fill in a gap in other records, in this case the run of occupations, by

Table 1.1. *Sedgley, Staffordshire: occupations from parish registers[a]*
Numbers per annum, baptisms and burials
(percentages in parentheses)

Father's occupation/ own occupation	Baptisms			Burials		
	1578–1600	1601–25	1675–85	1578–1600	1601–25	1675–85
agriculture	10.1	12.7	5.9	2.0	2.7	1.4
	(40)	(36)	(9)	(55)	(54)	(12)
metal-working	11.8	17.3	43.4	0.9	1.4	5.8
	(47)	(49)	(66)	(24)	(28)	(49)
mining	1.3	2.1	13.2	0.2	0.5	3.4
	(5)	(6)	(20)	(5)	(10)	(29)
other	2.0	3.2	3.3	5.7	0.4	1.2
	(8)	(9)	(5)	(16)	(8)	(10)
%	(100)	(100)	(100)	(100)	(100)	(100)
N in period	578	885	724	82	124	130

[a] H. R. Thomas, ed., *Sedgley, 1558–1685*, Staffordshire Parish Registers Society, 1940–1.

pointing more precisely to when change occurred, and how discontinuously, rather than leaving the answer 'at some time, at some rate, between the 1620s and the 1670s'.

The occupational registers, and the marriage seasons, can show what the probate inventories left by two groups (in this case, metal-workers and farmers) of very different wealth cannot. In 1675–85, the moveable property left by thirteen dead farmers of Sedgley was subject to the probate procedure (81 per cent of the sixteen burials of those employed in agriculture, according to the coincident burial registers), but the seven inventories pertaining to the property of dead metal-workers represent only 11 per cent of the sixty-four metal-workers buried in Sedgley in the same period.[17] Counting protoindustrialists from the number of their inventories appears, from this single test, to be equivalent to sampling from among the cow-keeping nailers and locksmiths (cows being so much more valuable than metal-working capital). Further, using inventories to study the nature of rural industry risks exaggerating the extent of dual employment, since the nailers, etc., whose inventories will be found will be the dual employed, while the great majority (in this case) not dual employed will be lost.

[17] Roper, *Sedgley Probate Inventories.*

More English marriage registers survive for more parishes over a longer period than does any more direct economic indicator. Months of marriages are simple to collect (although it would be churlish not to begin my thanks here to the Cambridge Group for the data from the majority of the parishes in my sample). The inferences that will be drawn from the seasonality of marriage will perforce be indirect, and faults can be found in the representativeness of the registers, but they hold up well against other early modern sources in cases where cross-sectional or cross-temporal comparisons are essential. They reflect the work and risks of the many, the marrying, rather than the property of the fewer. They reflect the principal employment of those marrying in the parish, without the distraction (sadly without it, in some instances) of unusual local specialties or the bold experiments of visionary farmers.

That the seasonality of marriage reflects the seasonality of work and risks would be of minor interest, if all that was shown was that Barleys married in the autumn, Cowfolds in the spring, and nail-making Sedgleys in neither of these seasons, or that the widely known pattern of regional specializations of the eighteenth century will reveal itself in the seasons of weddings.[18] England may have married according to Figure 1.1's pattern in 1701–40, but it had not 140 years earlier (Figure 1.4). The basis of the new map is the same as that of Figure 1.1, but the data is drawn from registers 140 years older. Again, twenty-four marriages had to have been recorded in the forty years of the period for the Seasonal Type to be calculated and the parish plotted.

A process of regional specialization in marriage seasonality intervened between the two mapped periods, parallel to a process of regional specialization and change in England's rural economy. In Figure 1.4, the autumn-marrying arable symbol 'A' is predominant, as it would not be by 1701–40 (Figure 1.1). Much of the northwest is once again covered with the X's of non-autumnal, non-vernal marriages; X's are dense in the Weald, as they were not in Figure 1.1; East Anglia appears more spring-marrying, pastoral, than it would be in 1701–40. Contrast the Midlands and the West Country on the two maps: the combinations of X's and P's in the west, and all three symbols in the Midlands, has only emerged in the second period. 'God [may have] made Leicestershire for grass', as a recent fox-hunting observer had it, but the map for 1561–1600 is covered with the 'A' of arable farming.[19]

---

[18] Local historians might find interest in the Appendix, where the 542 parishes are listed, by county and status as market towns, along with their Seasonal Types of 'P', 'A', or 'X' in 1561–1640, 1661–1740, and 1741–1820.

[19] *Observer*, 9 December 1984.

Figure 1.4 Seasonal Types, 1561–1600
Key: A A-Type
     P P-Type
     X X-Type

The study was feasible, in the first instance, because the data 'were there' (in the form of a machine-readable set of 404 parishes from the Cambridge Group for the History of Population and Social Structure), and secondly, because in the last stages of my earlier work on farm

servants I had uncovered a curious, tantalizing, and entirely unantici-
pated regional divergence in marriage seasonality at an intriguing time
relative to England's economic development, the later seventeenth
century.[20] I had not anticipated finding the cycle in October marriages
in the east, but, when I did, I then anticipated finding a parallel cycle
in spring marriages in the pastoral west, and did not. The east and
west both married in the autumn in the sixteenth and early seventeenth centuries, as Figure 1.4 demonstrates. So, if autumn marriages
signified arable farming in the sixteenth as they did in the eighteenth
century, indices could be developed from the marriage seasons to plot
interrelated variations in the economy over time.

And the method works; it yields a spatially and temporally specific,
if clouded, mirror of changes in early modern economic activity. Most
of the substantive interpretation of these changes will be reserved for
Chapters 4 to 7. Two of these chapters (4 and 5) will concentrate on
agriculture, investigating the east-west bifurcation of marriage
seasons and pinning down the timing of change within the 140 years
that separate Figures 1.1 and 1.4, considering productivity increase
and enclosure along the way. Chapter 6 will turn to rural industry,
treating industrialization and deindustrialization as linked processes,
and Chapter 7 will begin to sew the agricultural and industrial sectors
together again, looking at the agricultural sources of new industrial
parishes and the demographic implications of the spatial rearrangement of economic activity.

But I can not expect everyone to have been wholly convinced that so
weird a method for studying the rural economy should work. Chapter
3 explains the source (Anglican parish registers) and the method of
manipulating the dates of weddings to yield indicators of arable,
pastoral, and industrial employment. The next chapter is dedicated to
placing the connection between the seasonality of work and risks and
the seasonality of marriage on a firmer foundation; it will also concede
that there are faults with the method, finding some solace in its easier
application to the English than to the continental European rural
economy.

---

[20] Kussmaul, *Servants in Husbandry*, Chapter 6.

2

'When shall we marry?'

The timing of weddings moulded itself to the seasonality of work and risks, which varied in their seasonality. There was thus no invariant answer to the chapter's title. In 1601–1720, as Wrigley and Schofield found, marriages in regions characterized as 'open pasture' tended to have been celebrated in April, May, and June, while in 'mixed farming' regions, October and November were the popular marriage months.[1] The General View takes advantage of that plasticity, building from the marriage data proxy measures for the often hard-to-observe local economic activities. The approximations cannot be exact, however. This chapter explores the reasons behind the matching of the seasonality of weddings to the seasons of work and risks, and begins to examine the less than perfect fit. Chapter 3 will then consider the more quantitative aspects of the source and method.

Most early modern work was seasonal, more seasonal than most modern work, and different kinds of early modern work differed in their seasonality.[2] Agriculture was more seasonal than most other activities; within farming, the seasonality of arable was not that of pastoral labour. Some work in manufacturing was made seasonal by being snared within the agricultural year. Scythesmakers, for example, aimed for a summer market. Work in textiles and metalworking was sometimes slotted into slack periods in the farming year.[3] Industrial

---

[1] Wrigley and Schofield, *Population History of England*, Table 8.6, p. 304. The farming regions were identified from the map of farming regions, 1500–1640, in Joan Thirsk, ed., *Agrarian History*, p. 4. The 'mixed farming' regions over which Wrigley and Schofield calculated the marriage seasons included 'pasture farming types: stock-keeping with corn-growing, sometimes with dairying'. In Chapter 3, I look at these farming types again, using indices of marriage seasonality drawn from the period covered by Thirsk's map.

[2] Jones, *Seasons and Prices*, pp. 2–3.

[3] Hey, *Rural Metalworkers*, p. 21; Hudson, 'Proto-industrialisation', pp. 34–61; Rowlands, *Masters and Men*, pp. 41–2; Schlumbohm, 'Seasonal Fluctuations', pp. 92–123.

work often stopped for the harvest, even where the industrial workers were otherwise wholly employed in manufacturing. Other work was more directly governed by the progression of seasons; frosts stopped brick-making, and summer streams could run too sluggishly to drive waterwheels.[4]

The sun, or rather the movement of the earth relative to the sun, ran the agricultural year. Arable farming was the most seasonal; its busiest season was the grain harvest, which could begin as early as late July in the south.[5] Ploughing was a busy time, in the spring and in the autumn; threshing provided employment in the winter months. But no weeks were so greedy for the time and attention of many than the harvest itself. The demand for harvest labour was great enough to draw workers from towns and from nearby non-arable occupations; Joseph Mayett, for example, left his Buckinghamshire village for Hertfordshire's grain harvest for several years in the early nineteenth century.[6]

Market gardening was labour intensive, but its busy seasons, harvesting a variety of vegetable crops, could be spread over a longer period than the simple grain harvest. Adam Speed provided a long list of vegetable crops in 1659, with harvests stretching through the summer and autumn.[7] The rearing of cattle and sheep entailed late winter and springtime work in calving and lambing, especially up to the time of weaning. Lambing was usually managed in relation to the first flush of grass, minimizing the expense of cut hay and other fodder. In the southwest, lambing could occur in the autumn, with the combination of mild winters, water meadows, and the aseasonally breeding Dorset sheep, but lambing in late winter or spring was more common.[8] Calving also usually occurred in the spring, where beef (and tallow and hides) were the desired products, so that the new calves could be weaned onto the year's new grass. Rearing also involved work in summer hay-making, and in the harvesting of other, sown, fodder crops.[9] Breton's 'seely sheep' was 'turned out of his coat' in June; shearing was a sharp work peak, but for relatively few

---

[4] Holderness, *Pre-industrial England*, p. 3; Jones, *Seasons and Prices*, p. 23.
[5] Duckham, *Agricultural Synthesis*, p. 1; Jones, *Seasons and Prices*, p. 62; Chalklin, *Seventeenth Century Kent*, p. 84.
[6] Kussmaul, ed., *Autobiography of Joseph Mayett*, pp. 85, 92.
[7] Speed, *Adam Out of Eden*; Thirsk, 'Farming Techniques', pp. 195–7; Thick, 'Market Gardening', p. 503–32.
[8] Bettey, 'Agriculture', pp. 157–9; Duckham, *Agricultural Synthesis*, p. 264; Thirsk, 'Farming Techniques', pp. 188–91; Best, *Rural Economy*, p. 21; Breton, *The Twelve Moneths*, n.p.; Lawrence, *New Farmer's Calendar*, pp. 2–3, 519.
[9] Fussell, *English Dairy Farmer*, pp. 121–2; Mortimer, *Whole Art of Husbandry*, p. 3.

workers.[10] Two pastoral activities, dairying and fattening, were less vernal in their seasonality. Dairying, little commented upon, as Fussell noted, by the male authors of agricultural commentaries, was labour intensive, with milking, and processing the milk into cheese and butter, every day that the cows yielded milk; each day, rennet and the previous night's cream was added to the day's milk, and the resulting curd was broken and mashed by hand, packed into dishes, and then placed in a press, and sliced and repressed, four to five times on that first day, while meanwhile, the last day's cheese was salted in brine and turned during the next two or three days until the water was drawn out from the cheese.[11] Cows are aseasonal breeders, and could be made to yield milk on a year round basis, but the winter feeding of milking cows was expensive, and the cows yielded less milk. Heavily salted butter and cheese were the end products of dairying, not fast-souring liquid milk, so in traditionally managed herds the cows were dried off in the winter, and they calved in the late winter or early spring.[12] In Chartres' recent graphs of the seasonality of fairs, it is interesting that of butter and cheese, cattle, sheep, and horse fairs, only the first set peaked in the autumn, in September and October.[13]

Running a dairy to meet the luxury demand for fresh butter or veal out of season involved no single concentrated season of calving, but it increased the demand for good winter feed, and increased the derived demand for local labour in the summer and autumn's harvests, fodder being too low in price to bear transport costs. Specialized fattening, close to urban markets, of cattle reared farther afield also led to no spring work peak. Local labour would have been employed in producing fodder, and, when nature provided the bounty in the form of rich meadows and marshes, less local labour was needed.[14] Stall-feeding, which became popular only in the nineteenth century, required far more labour, producing sown fodder with an arable, not pastoral, pattern of work.[15] The specialized production of hay for urban horses and interurban road transport similarly saw most of its labour employed in the summer and early autumn.[16]

Where fishing was a major employer there was no one seasonal pattern of work, because different fish were caught at different times

[10] Breton, *The Twelve Moneths*, n.p.   [11] Fussell, *English Dairy Farmer*, pp. 223ff.
[12] Bowden, 'Agricultural Prices', 1967, p. 622; Fussell, *English Dairy Farmer*, pp. 33–6.
[13] Chartres, 'Marketing', pp. 435–6.
[14] Holderness, 'East Anglia', pp. 234–5.
[15] John Lawrence sang the praises of stall feeding at the beginning of the nineteenth century, in both *New Farmer's Calendar*, p. 523 and in *General Treatise*, p. 127.
[16] Thompson, 'Horses and Hay', pp. 50–72.

in the year. In the extreme case of the North Atlantic cod fishery, ships left the West Country in the late winter bound for Newfoundland, taking away potential grooms, and did not return until the early autumn.[17] Defoe encountered the Norfolk herring fleets on his tour, and reported that the ships set out around Michaelmas, and that the fishing, and the fishermen's absence, lasted all October.[18] Across the Channel, the July peak of weddings in a coastal parish of Normandy was explained by Lebrun with reference to the mackerel and herring seasons, which sandwiched that maximal marriage month.[19]

The timing of marriage accommodated itself to the seasonality of work. That is why the map of Figure 1.1 makes common sense. Why were weddings so accommodating? The reason is conspicuous in the case of seasonally absent fishermen. For the less obvious instances, two approaches to the question are appropriate, the first through the rational decisions of grooms and brides relative to work and risk (including the involvement of the community in the wedding celebrations), and the second through the institutionalizations of these rational decisions.

The worker in arable regions earned higher wages in the grain harvest than at any other time in the farming year. Who would sensibly lose them, by taking time off from the harvest for the wedding celebration, expecting work mates to do the same? Working through the harvest allowed the about-to-be-married to add to the savings needed for the wedding celebrations and for the formation of the new household (for the lease of a farm or a cottage, and the purchase of household furnishings and capital equipment). It would have been prudent to wait, to collect the higher wages, and only then to gather the family and community for the celebrations, marrying after the harvest.[20]

If wages were the overriding determinant of the seasonality of marriage, the single most frustrating blindness of this General View, its inability to find women's work when it differed in its seasonality from that of men, would be explained. Districts combining male day-labouring in arable farming with female employment in straw-plaiting and lace-making, in Buckinghamshire and Bedfordshire, look resolutely autumnal in their marriage seasonality, and are indistinguishable from areas without that women's industrial work. Wide-

---

[17] Innis, *Cod Fisheries*, p. 56. Chapters 4 and 5 will discuss the disappearance of autumn marriages from the southwest, however, *without* reference to the possibility that the West Country fishermen's displacement by resident Newfoundland fishermen influenced the changing pattern of marriage.

[18] Defoe, *A Tour*, p. 66.   [19] Lebrun, *La vie conjugale*, p. 40.

[20] Gillis, 'Peasant', pp. 130–6.

spread employment in spinning similarly makes no apparent impact on the seasonality of marriage. If the male workers of an area were employed in agriculture, the seasonality of marriage was agricultural. Women's wages were lower than male wages, and it would appear that the seasonality of work of the partner who had the most wages to lose determined the timing of the wedding (but see below for another explanation of the low impact of women's work on marriage seasons).

Marriages in industrial parishes were usually non-seasonal. A brief stoppage of industrial work put less at risk, compared to agricultural work. Consider the case of the bachelor farmer, combining the functions of labour and of owner of at least capital, if not also land. To stop work in the harvest to marry was not just to lose the high implicit wages as a return for his labour, but it was also to risk losing the crop itself, that is, the year's output. In the grain harvest, to delay while the sun shone meant gambling on a continuation of the good weather. In the (unlikely) event of the gamble having succeeded, having a ripe crop standing unharvested was an invitation to the 'birds and other vermine', as Barnaby Googe put it, to harvest the crop in their own fashion, and any grain that had not been so 'harvested' would soon moulder on the ground.[21]

The argument from risk is especially applicable to pastoral farming. The greatest risk fell in the season of birth of young beasts, lambs, calves, and foals. To judge from contemporary accounts, the most needful of attention were ewes and their new lambs. Googe in the sixteenth, Best and Mascall in the seventeenth, Lisle in the eighteenth, and Lawrence in the early nineteenth century all wrote of the troubles of lambing. Young ewes, wrote Googe, needed special attention: 'The Shepheard must be as careful as a midwyfe in the yeaning time, for this poore creature (though she be but a sheepe) is as tormented in her delivery, as a shrew.'[22] Lisle described the indoor care of spring lambs when the weather worsened, and Best advised not to stint on labour in early February lambing, to avoid endangering the sheep.[23] Lawrence vividly portrayed the work in lambing:

The shepherd must now watch his ewes night and day, during a succession perhaps of five or six weeks, a dreadful duty, in a rigorous climate and exposed situation. It is even necessary to visit the flock at midnight, for the purpose of arousing ewes, indolent and torpid with cold, and of obliging them

---

[21] Googe (Conradus Heresbach), *Foure Bookes*, p. 40.

[22] *Ibid.*, p. 81. Leonard Mascall echoed the image of midwife in *Government of Cattell*, p. 205.

[23] Lisle, *Observations*, p. 367; Best, *Rural Economy*, p. 81. Best also advised managing tupping to spread out the lambing, 'so that the Lambes fallinge not over thicke together', p. 3.

to stand and suckle their lambs, which might otherwise perish for want of sustenance and comfort.[24]

A late twentieth-century coda was added by composer Michael Berkeley, reflecting on the solace of the Welsh Marches:

As I arrive from a hectic tour of duty in London, a weight seems to be lifted from my shoulders and I drink in the wonderful quiet. Music has a priority in the morning (except in lambing time); then there is a long walk to mull over the day's ideas – if there have been any.[25]

Mascall also wrote of the danger to cows, in unsupervised calving, of not delivering the afterbirth, or of not casting a dead calf, and Worlidge mentioned the house-rearing of early calves as among the tasks of January and February in his calendar of the farming year.[26] Dairy farming's intensive work during so much of the year was mentioned above; Fussell noted that during calving the cowman or farmer was often up two or three times a night.[27] In lambing, calving, and foaling, most often in the early spring, the ewes, cows, and mares were at some risk, and so was that year's 'crop' of newborn beasts. It was not an appropriate season for time consuming celebrations such as marriage. Shearing a week later than usual, on the other hand, might risk only that week's interest on the wool (and, following John Lawrence, delayed the discomfort of the newly shorn sheep, 'pitiable' as they stood shivering, despite their 'flannel jackets').[28] One risk to be avoided, however, was that of missing the most convenient wool fairs.

That it was the agricultural year that drove the seasonality of marriage is strongly suggested by Figure 2.1, which asks *when* in the spring (here widely defined as April to July) the maximum numbers of marriages were celebrated in 1701–40, the period mapped in Figure 1.1. Generally speaking, spring came earlier in the south, and later in the north; calves and lambs were dropped earlier in the south, and the marriage peak, moulded to the seasonality of work and risks, came earlier there too. In parts of the southwest, lambing came so early as to make other months than in the spring or early summer the most popular time for weddings.

Risk is the strongest reason for industrial work to show less seasonality in the marriages of its workers than agriculture. All that most craftsman lost in taking a few days off for the celebration was that few days' output, no matter how uneven the pattern of production

[24] Lawrence, *General Treatise*, p. 292.   [25] Mabey, ed., *Second Nature*, p. 61.
[26] John Worlidge, *Systema Agriculturae*, p. 223.
[27] Fussell, *English Dairy Farmer*, p. 60.
[28] Lawrence, *New Farmer's Calendar*, p. 523.

Figure 2.1 Most popular spring/summer marriage months, 1701–40
Key: e =April and May
m=May and June
l =June and July

within the year.[29] Agriculture risked everything, the year's output, in a few poorly chosen days of leisure. There is some indication that the marriages of industrial workers became more seasonal in the nine-

[29] On 'the characteristic irregularity of labour patterns before the coming of large-scale machine-powered industry', see Thompson, 'Time', p. 71.

teenth century, as industrial work came to be more closely supervised and controlled. To be absent from waged factory work would have put the worker's job at risk. Marriages therefore crowded into the Christmas and the Easter holidays, shoe-horning the two celebrations into the one break from work; in a study of marriage seasonality in Shropshire, Edwards found May the most common marriage month, except in towns of more than 3,000 inhabitants (according to the 1811 census), where December was the most popular month for weddings.[30]

Risk provides another approach to the transparency of straw-plaiting, lace-making, and spinning to this study. It may simply be the fact that women in these instances were employed in the less-to-lose-in-a-day manufacturing sector and men in the everything-to-risk agricultural sector that made the seasonality of male agricultural work the dominant influence on the timing of marriage. I will return to this complication in Chapter 6, where I must concede that the General View is not at its best in spotting industrial work when it is women's work combined with (especially arable) farming.

Any disruption to the harvest risked the year's output. But the risk fell unevenly in the farming world, far more heavily on the farmer than on the worker. The latter might live to regret lost winter wages in threshing, but farmers risked a year's return on land, labour, and capital. The trick for the farmers, then, was to get the others, their harvesting labourers, to behave as if their own welfare, their livelihood, depended on their adherence to the farmers' seasonality of risk.

Paying higher wages in the harvest was the simplest method, causing labourers to lose this reward if inappropriate time was taken off from work for celebrations. But there were at least two other indirect forms of the institutionalized risk aversion of farmers with a direct bearing on marriage dates. The first is service in husbandry. This popular early modern institution employed not-yet-married workers, who were hired on annual contracts, annual contracts that terminated after the harvest.[31] In the eighteenth century, in the arable east, hirings began in the autumn, at Michaelmas or Martinmas; in the pastoral fens and the west, hirings were common in the spring, at Lady Day or May Day. While wages were sometimes paid in portions during the year, there was no legal requirement to pay them until after the harvest of grain or young beasts, at the end of the contract. Lump

---

[30] Dupree, 'Family Structure', p. 105; Trainor, 'Who Married Whom?'; Edwards, 'Marriage Seasonality', p. 23.
[31] Kussmaul, *Servants*, pp. 49–51.

sum payments, plus the legally enforceable contracts, kept servants on the farm through the harvests, and delivered some of them, newly paid-off, to the altar at the harvest's end.

The dates of taking up farms were less rigid in their seasonality than the contracts of servants, but most leases fell in after the harvest. Mortimer found September 'the most usual time for the Farmer to take possession of his new Farm'; Laurence, in a book published with a frontispiece diagram of a Herefordshire farm, discussed the competing advantages of Lady Day and May Day as times for taking up farms.[32] But the bachelor farmer posited earlier, in connection with his own wages and risks, was a useful fiction, uncommon in practice. Farms needed farmhouse managers, whom the farmer could either hire, as servants, or marry. In arable farming, leases pointed farmers-to-be, annual contracts pointed soon-to-be-former-servants, and high wages in the grain harvest pointed unmarried day-labourers towards marriage in the same season, in the autumn. In pastoral farming, by contrast, there was little part-time work in lambing, calving, and foaling, so the argument touching on day-labourers is less relevant.

Prudence, then, plus the occasional legal sanction go a long way towards explaining why marriage was seasonal, and why different patterns of seasonality were found at different times, and in different places. Not all were prudent, though; pre-marital conceptions in the spring, followed by the prudent earning of harvest wages, helped create a pent-up demand for post-harvest weddings. Not everyone in a parish married in the same season. Winter stretched ahead as a slack time in arable areas, and there was no prohibitive reason (except Advent) not to wait an extra month or two. All the General View requires is that the seasonality of work and risks was a major determinant of the seasonality of weddings.

But do I hear a faint voice, crying 'What about tradition? Where are the June brides?' The simplest finding of this study has been that there was no fixed, immutable season of English marriage, invariant over time and space; that was the hook that drew me into the project in the first place. Customary marriage seasons, though, have the institutional advantage of removing from the prospective couple the burden of sorting and measuring the costs and risks sketched above. In arable regions, for example, instead of asking 'When shall we marry?' the question becomes the easier 'After which Michaelmas (or Martinmas, further north) shall we marry?' The custom would then serve as a cultural substitute for the decisions that most couples would have made. The simple framework that Hobsbawm built in *The*

[32] Mortimer, *Whole Art of Husbandry*, p. 3; Laurence, *Duty*, p. 42.

Invention of Tradition serves well here.[33] Unlike tradition, the marriage custom was mutable, adjusting to changing circumstances. And unlike 'technical' traditions, a custom of marrying after the harvest would not have been value-free. It would have acted as an institutionalization of the risks of the fewer, the landlords and farmers, saying to their labourers 'Don't stop work to marry during my harvest.'

If economic exigencies were, in the case of marriage dates, thus operating at second hand, just how changeable were these customs over time? If they were not perfectly flexible, alterations in marriage seasonality would have lagged behind alterations in the timing of work and risks. Direct evidence is hard to find. Too often, collectors of customs took the stories told in the nineteenth and early twentieth centuries as The Past, rather as the hedges and landscaped vistas created in the later seventeenth and eighteenth centuries are taken to be The Historic Landscape. There are comprehensible aesthetic and ideological reasons for holding these positions (to demonstrate the latter was in part the objective of the Hobsbawm collection), but the positions are not useful to the historian intent on studying the sixteenth and seventeenth centuries. Can the degree of flexibility of custom instead be inferred from the evidence of marriage seasonality? Not precisely: it was not an empty claim, in the opening chapter, that other early modern sources do not easily lend themselves to the precise dating of variations in agricultural practices.

One modest chance to measure the response of marriage seasonality to external shocks arises with the implementation of the Gregorian calendar in England in 1752. Eleven days disappeared from the English autumn of that year: 2 September was followed by 14 September. Did marriage seasons adjust? The grain harvest, on average, would have happened eleven calendar days later in the autumn; the Class of 1752s lambs, dropped, for example, in late February in 1752, might have been followed by the Class of 1753, born in mid March, if farmers had let the rams in with the ewes at the same time in the solar year in both autumns. I looked at a group of autumn-marrying eastern parishes and a group of spring-marrying western ones, and calculated the weighted averages of marriage months within the autumn and the spring for each set, over the twenty years before and after the calendar change. The weights are the conventional numbers of the months (April=4, May=5, etc.). Table 2.1 displays the results; the value of 10.01 in the upper left-hand corner of the table, for example, indicates that very early October was the mean time of weddings, in the eastern set, in 1732–51. The parishes chosen for the test are not from the north,

[33] Hobsbawm, 'Introduction', pp. 2–3.

Table 2.1. *Mean marriage months, before and after the calendar change*[a]

		1732–51	1754–73
eastern set	within the autumn	10.01	10.16
	within the spring	5.32	5.37
western set	within the autumn	10.02	10.08
	within the spring	5.29	5.33

[a] The autumn months are September (9), October (10), and November (11), and the spring months April (4) through July (7).

where Martinmas (in November) was the marrying time, because the calendar change chased some post-harvest marriages into December (see below, Table 2.2.).

We would expect a higher mean value in 1754–73, and that was indeed the result, in all four rows of the table. But only in the first row, comparing the autumn values for the eastern set, is the difference significant at any acceptable level of error (the level of error of that first row is less than 0.1 per cent), and that is almost certainly accounted for by the quick adjustment in the calendar dates of hiring fairs for those marriageable young adults, servants in husbandry, in the east. There, hirings at New Michaelmas (10 October) replaced hirings at the end of September. This mediating custom, servant-hiring, adjusted quickly, where hiring fairs were the popular means of matching servants with farmers.[34]

More generally, would institutional rigidities have prevented the rapid resetting of marriage seasons from one season to another in response to more thorough changes in the seasonality of work and risks? I'm inclined to answer 'No'. Many formal statute sessions for the hiring of servants were tied to Quarter Days, at least in the eighteenth century, and there was always another Quarter Day in a newly appropriate season. Some regions had subsidiary hiring fairs. Spalding, in the Lincolnshire fens, saw most servants hired at the May Day sessions in the later eighteenth century, but a smaller hiring took place at Martinmas, in November. Had most work and risks become autumn centred there, the administrative framework already existed to hire most servants in November; the existence of the institution would indeed have facilitated the rapid shift in the dates of hirings, and therefore also of the release of some to marriage. Servants hired at Spalding at Martinmas were usually hired for six months, that is, up to

[34] Kussmaul, 'Statute Sessions'.

the main hiring session in May of the following year. Settlement examinations from many Wiltshire parishes show hirings both at Michaelmas and at Lady Day, and in at least three of the Lady Day hirings, the term was set at six months, bringing servant and master around to new hirings the following Michaelmas.[35]

The seasonality of marriage directly reflects the work of younger workers, the about-to-be-married. If the young more readily adapted their behaviour to economic change, the lag between changes in the desired-to-be-observed work and risks and the able-to-be-observed seasonality of marriage might have been short. Variations in the post-mortem inventories of the moveable possessions of usually older, recently dead farmers might then more tend to post-date changes in regional work and risks. And if there were lags in the response of marriage seasonality to economic changes, at least the bias is one-sided; the shifts in marriage seasonality indicate the latest date at which the 'real' alteration in the seasonality of work and risks could have occurred.

What patterns of work and risks do marriage seasons trace? In an earlier article, the second published instalment of the project, I presented seven stellar parishes, with very different and largely explicable patterns of seasonality.[36] Five are reproduced in Figures 2.2 and 2.4, which, like Figure 1.2's representation of Cowfold and Barley, show changes over time in the combinations of autumn and spring/summer marriages, from 1541–80 to 1781–1820. The figures are drawn as were those for Cowfold and Barley in Chapter 1; the point (100,100) is the random, non-seasonal, combination (the method is detailed in the next chapter). Arable Orwell (Figure 2.2), one of Margaret Spufford's Contrasting Communities, had severely limited pasture, and married after the grain harvest. Pastoral Alberbury, a forest parish, married in the spring/summer, and industrial Rochdale, a centre of Lancashire's textile production, in neither of the agriculturally determined seasons.[37] These three trace no directed paths of seasonal change. The variations within Figure 2.2 more resemble the Brownian motion of dust motes in narrow closed containers.

The same cannot be said of the next two figures. Willingham, another of the Contrasting Communities, shows great variability and movement, most usually with a mixture of high autumn and high

---

35 Kussmaul, *Servants in Husbandry*, p. 50; Wiltshire Record Office, Wroughton, Pewsey, and Chicklade St. Sampson.
36 Kussmaul, 'Agrarian Change', pp. 4, 5, 7. The first instalment, in order of writing, was 'Time and Space, Hoofs and Grain'.
37 Spufford, *Contrasting Communities*, p. 121.

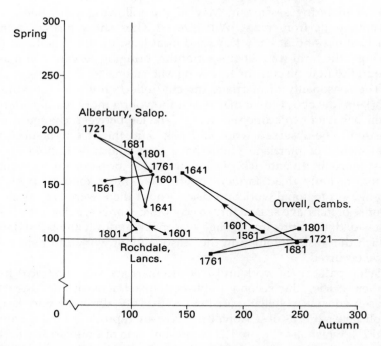

Figure 2.2 Autumn and spring/summer marriages in Alberbury (Salop), Orwell (Cambs.) and Rochdale (Lancs.)

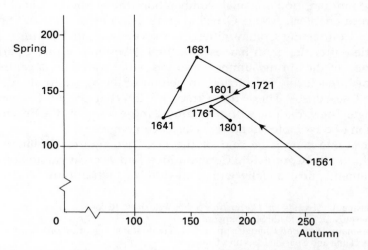

Figure 2.3 Autumn and spring/summer marriages in Willingham (Cambs.)

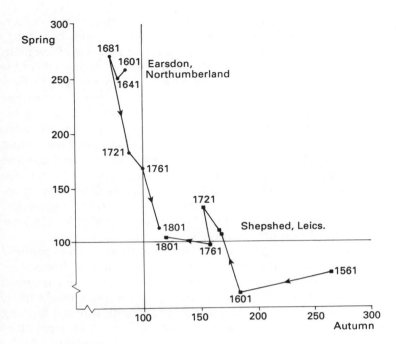

Figure 2.4 Autumn and spring/summer marriages in Shepshed (Leics.) and
Earsdon (Northumberland)

spring/summer seasonality (Figure 2.3). It was a fen parish, part able
to be ploughed, part drowned.[38]

Marriage seasons in Earsdon and Shepshed (Figure 2.4) appear, by
contrast, to move purposefully. The two parishes approach their
common late eighteenth-century fates as non-agricultural, non-
seasonal places from radically different directions, stocking-knitting
Shepshed from pronounced autumn peaks, and coal-mining Earsdon
from extraordinarily high spring/summer peaks.[39]

What patterns of work and risks are not easily found? Women's
work eludes the General View, as I have already suggested. So to the
extent that dairying was women's work, it hides from the method;
dairying is also made hard to pinpoint by its variations in seasonal
work between year-round milking, winter drying-off, and hay-

[38] Spufford, *Contrasting Communities*, p. 97; Thirsk, 'Farming Regions', p. 104 and
   Everitt, 'Farm Labourers', p. 403. Terling in Essex closely resembles Orwell in its
   marriage seasonality, an example of marriage seasonality's serving to fill a deficiency
   in other records (Wrightson and Levine, *Poverty*, pp. 23–4).
[39] Levine, *Family Formation*, pp. 16–20.

making. Convertible husbandry is importantly different from older, simpler arable rotations, but it still looks arable, autumn-marrying. This provides nice support for Jones's argument that one of the main values of animals in convertible husbandry was as dung-makers for the arable courses, but it is unfortunate that convertible practices cannot be pried loose from three-course rotations via the marriage seasons of the parish.[40] The work-risk peaks were stronger on the arable side of convertible husbandry; labour requirements were greatest in the grain harvest. Inappropriate breaks from harvesting endangered the whole crop, while inappropriate breaks from lambing risked only the loss of some lambs and ewes. Servant-hiring also mediated here, reflecting the arable farming year; there was no rotation to spring hiring with the adoption of convertible husbandry. Warwickshire's hirings, for example, remained rooted at Michaelmas throughout the eighteenth century.[41]

Farmers may have come to specialize in the production of artificial fodder, but the seasonality of that work was also harvest dominated. Specialized fattening might thus have given rise to an autumnal pattern of marriages. This appears not to have been true earlier, however, in the sixteenth- and early seventeenth-century farming regions of *The Agrarian History of England and Wales* that were characterized as 'wood pasture: stock-fattening and pig-keeping'. At the turn of the seventeenth century, in 1581–1620, 52 per cent of my sample's seasonal parishes lying within those regions would have been plotted as spring-marrying P-Types on a map similar to Figure 1.1, while less than 15 per cent of the seasonal parishes in the whole non-market set would have been so designated (see the next chapter for its discussion of the sample and the derivation of the Seasonal Types, and for further discussion of the farming regions of the fourth volume of *The Agrarian History*, and Table 3.3, below, for the breakdown by Seasonal Type for the whole sample).[42]

No one season can be made to stand as a national marker for fishing, and when fishermen returned to port at Harvest Home, it is impossible to employ marriage seasonality to differentiate between the marriages of the harvesters of fish and the harvesters of grain. In Henbury, on Gloucestershire's lower Severn, the 5 per cent of grooms who were employed in maritime occupations went to the altar overwhelmingly in October; 5.6 times the randomly expected number of

[40] Jones, 'Editor's Introduction', *Agriculture*, p. 8.

[41] Warwickshire Record Office, settlement examinations of 35 parishes.

[42] Farming types were gleaned from Thirsk, *Agrarian History*, p. 4. 'Seasonal' parishes are those marrying in the autumn and/or the spring, i.e., not the X-Types scattered on the maps of Figures 1.1 and 1.4.

their marriages was celebrated then. There was a smaller peak there in February, as if the fleet had been out from March or April until September.[43] Marske, on the North Riding's North Sea coast, registered the weddings of thirty-two fishermen and other mariners and of sixty-five agricultural workers (yeomen, husbandmen, labourers, etc.). Its fishermen married most frequently in the autumn, its farmers and labourers in the spring. The autumn marriage index for Marske's fishermen was 170; for those in agricultural occupations, the autumn index was only 93, the spring index 228.[44]

The calendar change in 1752 complicates matters as well, because it pushed some post-Martinmas marriages from November into December. The combined impact of the calendar change and the declining observance of Advent as a season in which to avoid weddings (to be discussed below) is evident in Table 2.2. Agricultural Winestead, on the peninsula of the East Riding that narrows down to Spurn Head, was within the large northeastern region of late grain harvests and post-Martinmas weddings, as the extraordinarily high November and the low October indices of marriages in the first two periods indicate. Andrew Marvell, father of the poet, was the Parson recording marriages in Winestead from 1614 to 1628, until he left to become Head of Hull Grammar School. He and his predecessor George Brooke irregularly recorded the occupations of those they buried, and agricultural occupations predominate, as they do in the burial registers of the eighteenth century (in the earlier marriage registers, the ratio of agricultural occupations to crafts and trades was 4.25 to 1).[45] December, in the earlier periods, was not a popular month for weddings (none of the forty-three weddings of 1641–80 was celebrated in that month, for example). And an index value of twenty-three, as in 1621–60, indicates that the number of weddings celebrated in December in that period was somewhat fewer than one quarter the number that would have been expected, had Winestead's weddings been evenly distributed over the days of the years. But in the forty-year period in which the Gregorian calendar was introduced, 1741–80, December became the most favoured month. By this chapter's end, however, it should have become obvious why December cannot be included in the definition of the autumn index as a proxy measure of arable work (see also Chapter 3).

The harvest of grain was so avid for labour, and offered such good wages, that it often imposed its seasonal pattern on the weddings of

[43] Phillimore, ed., *Gloucestershire Parish Registers*, pp. 1–71.
[44] Wood, ed., *Registers*.
[45] Miller, ed., *Yorkshire Parish Register Society*.

Table 2.2. *Winestead's December marriages*[a]
(indices)

Dates	Spring	October	November	December	Total marriages
1581–1620	162	62	349	39	60
(1621–60)	132	0	427	23	52
1661–1700	174	71	235	22	53
1701–40	123	40	352	116	51
1741–80[b]	140	35	179	277	34
1781–1820	106	104	251	173	34

[a] See Chapter 3 for the derivation of the indices.
[b] Calendar change in this period.

otherwise non-agricultural workers, who only temporarily left their crafts and trades for the harvest month. In Brandsburton in the East Riding, for example, the thirty-one craftsmen who married in 1754 to 1810 made October and November their favoured choices, with 2.3 and 2.8 times the randomly expected number of weddings in those two months. None of them married in September.[46] Part-time work in the harvest thus 'contaminated' what might otherwise have been a non-seasonal pattern of weddings of these craftsmen and tradesmen. This may account for Shepshed's having remained arable-looking for as long as it did (Levine never narrowly specified the timing of Shepshed's industrialization relative to the agricultural work in the parish in *Family Formation*). Part-time harvest work also enticed labour from pastoral areas for the year's highest wages; Henry Best's harvest workers came down from the moors to his East Riding farm each year.[47]

Towns were most often least seasonal in their marriages, given their heterogeneity of occupations and inmigration from potentially diverse areas (see Table 3.2 in the next chapter), and were for that reason excluded from the maps of Chapter 1. Banbury, however, does not always look like a town in its seasonality (Figure 2.5). Three good reasons account for its arable masquerade: the surrounding region offered part-time opportunities for harvest work, there was a large agricultural hamlet within the parish (Banbury itself returned 631 families in trades in the 1821 census, and only fourteen familes in agriculture, but its hamlet, Neithorp, returned 305 families in agriculture and ninety-seven in trades), and the parish was an Ecclesi-

[46] Best, *Rural Economy*, p. 115.   [47] Hicks, ed., *Parish Register of Brandsburton*.

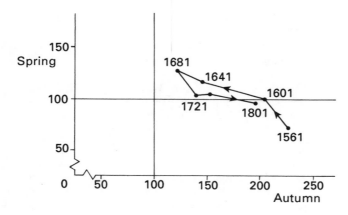

Figure 2.5 Autumn and spring/summer marriages in Banbury (Oxon.)

astical Peculiar, to which, until Hardwicke's reform of the marriage law in 1753, couples wishing to marry by licence could repair.[48]

Some non-agricultural occupations, such as building and bleaching, had natural breaks from work in the autumn, and might thus have mimicked agricultural seasonality, if a large enough group of workers with similar autumn-breaking industrial occupations had married in a parish.[49] More often, truly industrial or commercial places look arable in their marriage seasonality because of the part-time labour in the harvest by manufacturing workers. Agriculture can be mistaken for manufacturing and commerce in the cases of market gardening, very late harvests, and specialized grazing without rearing.

Agricultural orientations are also sometimes obscured by non-economic influences on the seasonality of marriage. Nearly the whole of northern Staffordshire, Cheshire, and Lancashire, for example, looks non-autumnal and non-vernal from the sixteenth through the eighteenth century, but not every parish was a textile-weaving Rochdale. Table 2.3 dissects the non-seasonality of three parishes in Staffordshire. Eccleshall is a huge parish, in which both farming and mining provided employment. The winter months of January and February became slightly more popular than autumn or spring as times of weddings. Brewood was a small market town, and its autumn marriages yielded to non-seasonality, as did marriages in

[48] Holderness, *Pre-industrial England*, p. 3.
[49] Great Britain, Parliamentary Papers, *Abstract of Answers and Returns to the 1821 Census* (1822), p. 254.

Table 2.3. *Winter marriages in three Staffordshire parishes*[a]
(indices)

Period	Eccleshall			Brewood			Audley		
	Aut	Wint	Spring	Aut	Wint	Spring	Aut	Wint	Spring
1541–80	130	138	102	154	80	117	157	66	103
1581–1620	117	91	126	129	109	107	163	67	130
(1621–60)	96	102	113	107	101	111	117	32	154
1661–1700	91	107	138	77	120	137	111	81	107
1701–40	115	125	101	99	128	112	95	111	120
1741–80	86	143	106	112	120	108	91	129	96
1781–1820	93	132	103	93	126	92	98	132	90

[a] For definitions of the autumn and spring indices, see Chapter 3. The winter index is the mean index for January and February.

Audley, which combined coal-mining for the salt pans of Nantwich and some iron-working with agriculture.[50]

I suspect that the causes for what I have been tempted to call 'cloud cover', the obscuring of my bird's-eye view of agriculture in this northwestern region, lie partly in the lateness of the harvest, pushing marriages into December (especially after the introduction of the Gregorian calendar), partly in the truly industrial nature of work in large parts of the region (less dramatic than fat Gloucestershire clothiers to contemporaries, perhaps), and partly in the very great size of some of these parishes, involving difficult journeys to the parish's church. Some of the 'cloud cover' might also have had causes unconnected to economic and geographical exigency.[51] It is to these non-economic complications that I now turn, beginning with courtship.

If time-consuming rituals preceded weddings, a gap might have existed between the cessation of work (and lowering of risks) and the marriage. The peak marriage season would then have been offset from the end of the peak work season. There are suggestions that the 'cloud-covered' region may have been a hotbed of bundling. Macfarlane, however, doubts that bundling, as a means of proving fecundity before marriage, was ever widespread in early modern England, citing first the marriage law, where the proper exchanging of vows and consummation constituted a valid marriage and barrenness was no

[50] Swain, 'Industry', p. ii.
[51] Spufford and Spufford, *Eccleshall*; Greenslade and Midgley, 'Brewood'; Speake, ed., *Audley*, pp. 54–6.

ground for the dissolution of a marriage, and secondly the random relation of the timing of marriages relative to the timing of pre-nuptial conceptions. If most English couples followed the advice 'Happy the wooing that's not long in adoing', courtship should prove no serious complication to this study.[52]

The timing of marriages, I am arguing, reflects the seasonality of work. What workers am I missing? I have already referred to the age-bias of the record; the observed seasonality is that of the about-to-be-married, usually younger, workers. The already married make no direct impression in the marriage registers, except upon their remarriage (see below). The age bias is opposite to that of probate inventories in the study of agrarian change; it could be argued that the bias of marriage seasons is less severe, because marriage customs, and mediating customs such as hiring dates, institutionalized the risk of the few in the behaviour of the many.

Not all younger workers are represented. Some never married, because they remained lifetime celibates, or formed households outside marriage. Neither of these phenomena occurred at constant rates over the otherwise gratifyingly long span of the record. Wrigley and Schofield estimated the proportions of the English population never marrying at only 4 to 8 per cent of the twenty to twenty-four year olds of the late sixteenth century; the proportion rose to 27 per cent at the Restoration, and then fell to less than 8 per cent in the second half of the eighteenth century. The rates are expressed as proportions never marrying of those who would have survived into their forties.[53]

Were soon-to-be-married young adults engaged in different occupations than were those who would remain unmarried? If they were, the marriage record would be a somewhat clearer mirror of local work and risks in the sixteenth and again in the eighteenth than in the seventeenth century. But the recorded seasonality of marriage itself argues against this; there is indeed a strong shift in the mid seventeenth century, but the new pattern is then maintained in the eighteenth century, even as more young adults again come to contribute to the record by marrying.

Clandestine marriages surged in the later seventeenth century.[54] But were the non-registered engaged in different types of work from the registered? Gillis argued that one important reason for avoiding the publicity of a church marriage was to avoid the expense of what he

[52] Wrigley and Schofield, *Population History of England*, pp. 257–65, esp. Table 7.28, p. 260. The saying was cited by Gillis, *For Better, For Worse*, pp. 43. Gillis gives examples of bundling from Cheshire and Cumberland, and also from Sussex. Cf. Macfarlane, *Marriage*, pp. 306–7.

[53] Wrigley and Schofield, *Population History of England*, p. 263.   [54] Gillis, 'Peasant'.

characterized as a 'big peasant wedding', so that the poor would be underrepresented in the marriage registers.[55] But many other motives for concealing marriages existed (too obvious bridal pregnancy, marriages which would have been within the church's prohibited degrees of 'kinship', marriages involving travellers without the weeks to spare for the reading of banns, marriages against parents' wishes, among others), and, as Gillis wrote in a more recent work, 'it was privacy rather than the savings that made clandestine marriage so attractive', although Houlbrooke found the desire of the poor to circumvent the objections of rate-payers a motive for concealment.[56]

With the introduction of a tax on weddings in 1696, a new motive arose to form a household without a (taxable) wedding, but the state also had a new motive for seeing the marriages registered. Hardwicke's Act of 1753 made only those marriages celebrated in the Anglican Church valid (excepting only the valid marriages of Quakers and Jews). Even before 1753, however, the seasonality of agricultural wages would have made the harvest a bad time for the poor to absent themselves from work to marry.

It is unlikely that changes in the incidence of clandestine marriages invalidate my use of marriage seasons as an indicator of local patterns of work.[57] One strong motive for clandestine marriage even lends support to the hypothesis of economic change that will be advanced in later chapters. Those who wished to marry during the prohibited season of Lent had either to wait until Lent was over to marry or to marry in Lent and conceal the marriage from the church.[58] A rise in clandestine marriages, such as that found in the later seventeenth century, might thus have lessened the recorded numbers marrying after Lent, in May and June, but these are months that gain recorded marriages in the later seventeenth century, as the proportion of clandestine marriages rose (see below, Table 3.2). This aspect of England's demographic past appears not to have distorted the trend in the recorded seasonality of marriage.

Real changes in the pattern of work caused changes in the seasona-

---

[55] The rates were estimated indirectly, under an assumption of no differences in mortality between the married and the unmarried (Houlbrooke, *English Family*, p. 258). I interpolated to find the rates for cohorts aged 20 to 24.

[56] Gillis, *For Better, For Worse*, p. 96; Martin Ingram, 'Spousals Litigation', p. 56; Houlbrooke, *English Family*, p. 86.

[57] Ingram, 'Spousals Litigation', p. 56.

[58] Some critics have suggested that the Cambridge Group's 404 parishes underrepresent the more unruly parishes, and that those underrepresented were less likely to have been well-ordered arable places. If this is so, the numbers of A-Type (arable and autumn-marrying) parishes, relative to the pastoral and industrial parishes, will be overrepresented.

lity of marriage, and that in turn might help account for another demographic feature of the later seventeenth century, the drop in pre-nuptial conceptions. If marriages shifted from the autumn (the 'natural' trough, that is, of pre-nuptial and second and subsequent post-nuptial conceptions, in the annual cycle of conceptions), towards the spring and early summer (the 'natural' annual peak in conceptions), marriages would then conveniently have become more nearly coincident with the conceptions, conceptions that would have been pre-nuptial had the marriages occurred months later, in the autumn.[59]

Not everyone was Anglican. Were a locality's non-conformists engaged in different types of work from its Anglicans? This is not so much a question of the regional incidence of non-conformity, but of intraregional differences between the work and risks of Anglicans and others. The survival of Roman Catholicism was also a regionally specific phenomenon. Even before Hardwicke's reform of the marriage law, though, recusants often recorded their marriage in the Anglican registers. It is possible that recusancy was in part responsible for the 'cloud cover' obscuring my view of agriculture in northern Staffordshire, Cheshire, and Lancashire, but I shall take that argument up at the end of the chapter.

Not all weddings of Anglicans appeared in the marriage registers, and not all the marriages that were recorded were of partners who had worked in the parish. Marriage by licence, rather than by banns, was possible between non-resident partners until Hardwicke's Act of 1753. Archbishops and Bishops, Chancellors and certain Archdeacons could grant licences; at a lower level, some local clergy were appointed as Surrogates, empowered to marry by licence, and some parishes were Ecclesiastical Peculiars (such as Banbury in Figure 2.5, above), where the serving clergy could sell licences.[60] Marriage by licence offered speed and concealment to a couple, at a price, so the fewer, the wealthier, absented themselves from their own parish's registers in this way. But cut-rate licences were also available from some clergy, and their parishes became the marriage shops of the later seventeenth and eighteenth century that Hardwicke's reform explicitly attacked.[61]

There were at least three marriage shops in operation in the 542 parishes of my sample. Outhwaite suspected cheap licences to have been the cause of the great increase in the number of marriages in Fledborough, Nottinghamshire after 1730.[62] Askerwell, Dorset, simi-

[59] Wrigley, 'Marriage', p. 165.
[60] See Steel, ed., *National Index*, p. 228, and Outhwaite, 'Age at Marriage', pp. 62–4. See also Gillis, *For Better, For Worse*, pp. 92ff.
[61] Outhwaite, 'Age at Marriage', p. 64.
[62] Outhwaite, 'Age at Marriage', p. 63; Elliot, 'Marriage Licenses', p. 287.

larly experienced a great increase in the number of extraparochial marriages in the decades before 1753, with the number dropping sharply after that date. In only 14 per cent of the weddings of 1661–1720 was neither partner a resident of the parish, but the extraparochial proportion exploded to 68 per cent in 1721–40.[63] Wormleighton, Warwickshire, shows a similar pattern. It was one of the depopulated Midland parishes of the fifteenth century, and became a compact and efficient sheep ranch in the sixteenth century.[64] From the start of marriage registration, a tiny number of marriages was recorded there: eleven in 1601–40, eight in 1661–1700. This changed dramatically, and briefly, in the eighteenth century. Under Vicar William Pettipher, the totals surged. Pettifer became Vicar of Wormleighton in 1726, and 198 marriages were registered in 1721–60. From 1747 to 1753, all the marriages recorded there were by licence, at fees of £1.8.0 to £1.12.0. Hardwicke's Marriage Act ended Pettipher's practice; the number of weddings subsided from fifty-two in the three years before the Act to only two in the three years that followed it. In a terrible twist of fate, the Marriage Act also marks the end of Pettipher's life; he was buried in Wormleighton in October 1754.

The marriages recorded in a marriage shop do not reflect the underlying seasonality of work and risks of the shop's parish. After Hardwicke, one partner had to be a resident of the parish in which the marriage was recorded, but this still raises the question of **which** partner. If marriage seasonality was largely determined by the work of men, and if men left their parishes to marry more than women did (before and after Hardwicke), the record of marriage seasonality would be less determined by the seasonality of work and risks of the (male) residents of the registered parish.

There remain three more serious complications to the inquiry. The most obvious motifs in early modern marriage seasonality are the dents left by Advent in December and Lent in March.[65] Marriages in Lent and Advent were not prohibited by canon law, but the practice of avoiding marriage in these periods of abstinence was fairly scrupulously observed, until the Interregnum. The religious year, not the seasonality of work and risks, caused this behaviour (although the cultural materialist would have no trouble in finding the root of the prohibition on weddings at the time of the Paschal Lamb in the seasonality of work and risks among sheep-herding peoples).[66] The

63 Phillimore and Nevill, *Dorset Parish Registers*, pp. 105–20.
64 Wrigley and Schofield, *Population History of England*, Figure 8.3, p. 299.
65 Finch, *Wealth*, pp. 40–55; Thorpe, 'The Lord'. The Wormleighton registers are in the collection of the Warwickshire Record Office.
66 See, for example, Harris, *Good to Eat*, Chapter 4 ('The Abominable Pig').

unpopularity of March and December as marriage months before the mid seventeenth century showed no regional bias. The totals of marriages in the two months first increased in the Interregnum and then subsided with the Restoration, and then both months began to fill with marriages during the late seventeenth and the eighteenth century (because marriage registration was severely disrupted during the Interregnum, the calculations that include the period will be indicated with warning parentheses in the demonstrations of the next chapters). By the nineteenth century, December had become the most popular marriage month in many manufacturing towns.

Two distortions of the General View could be caused by these changes. First, Advent may have induced a rush to marry in November, and, since November is one of the months used to define the autumn index of seasonality, perhaps autumn, so defined, was nearly everywhere the most popular marriage season in the sixteenth century for no other reason than the careful observance of Advent. At first sight, this seems to have occurred in the southwest. The mean sum of the November and December indices of marriages over twenty-four southwestern parishes is nearly constant for every forty-year period from 1561–1600 to 1801–40; the balance simply tips towards December at the turn of the eighteenth century. The mean sum of November and December indices narrowly ranges from 180 to 219 over that long run. In 1581–1620, the ratio of December to November indices was 0.203; by 1741–80, the ratio had increased to 1.15. But both the mean October and the mean November indices are higher than the means for any spring or early summer month in 1541–80 and 1561–1600, and the mean October index remains higher than any mean spring or early summer index in 1601–40. The western switch to spring/summer marriages, to be discussed in the next chapters, had economic, not ecclesiastical, roots.

Worse is the interpretative problem posed by Lent and Rogationtide, the three weeks between Rogation Sunday (the fifth Sunday after Easter) and Trinity Sunday, because they move. If the oscillation of Lent forward into April (April 25 is the latest possible Easter) and of Rogationtide back and forth through April, May, and June, chased marriages away from the spring and early summer, even when it was a true season of work and risks in a pastoral economy, the 'pastoral' marriage seasonality would have remained suppressed until Lent and Rogationtide ceased to be well-observed; only then could April, May, and June fill with marriages.

This worst case is unlikely. In the first place, marriages could have crowded into the non-prohibited weeks in the spring and early

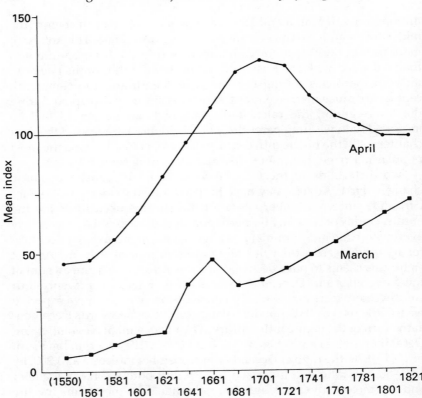

Figure 2.6 Mean indices, March and April marriages,
1538–60 to 1801–40

summer; in any year, five to thirty days of April occurred after Easter, while Rogationtide left free twenty-five to thirty days in April, ten to twenty-nine days in May, and ten to thirty days in June. The index of April marriages would have paralleled the movement of March marriages through the abrupt changes of the seventeenth century, if Lent had been preventing April marriages. The drop in the observance of Lent in the Interregnum and its modest recovery at the Restoration are clearly etched into the graph of March marriages in Figure 2.6, but April marriages show no discontinuity in their trend during the relevant periods; they simply continue their imperturbable rise. On the simplest level, marriages not occurring in March and December were being celebrated in other months, so the decline in the observance of Lent and Advent would have decreased the total of marriages in the other ten months. A mechanical solution to this problem has been forged, and is described in the next chapter.

Rogationtide creates a more difficult empirical problem; no month was affected by its three weeks as March was by Lent. A small test of the observance of Rogationtide in the period when Lent was being well observed was, however, possible. The years between 1539 and 1639 were divided into three sets. The first, late Rogationtide, set includes the eleven years in which seven days or fewer of May but fifteen or more of June were in Rogationtide (Easter having fallen between 20 and 25 April); the second set, early Rogationtide, includes the sixty-seven years in which fifteen or more May days but only seven or fewer June days were in Rogationtide (Easter, 22 March–12 April). The ratio between May and June marriages was examined in the two extreme sets (the intermediate set, the remaining twenty-three years, was ignored). If the observance of Rogationtide had had the power to mask work-induced seasonality, we would expect May marriages, as a proportion of May–June marriages, to be significantly higher in the first group of years, that is, when most of Rogationtide fell in June, than in the second group. The May proportion was indeed higher in the first set. When most of Rogationtide fell in June, 53.1 per cent of May–June marriages occurred in May; when most of Rogationtide fell in May, 45.4 per cent of May–June marriages were celebrated in May. But the small difference in proportions is not statistically significant, according to the usual standards of acceptable errors; the probability of erring in declaring the first proportion larger than the second is 0.32, or 32 per cent.[67]

There is stronger evidence that the timing of Lent affected the distribution of marriages within the spring and early summer. In Figure 2.7, squares within the grid are shaded according to then regional maximum monthly index, calculated on the basis of mean values for the region's parishes. The counties contained within the geoboxes are listed in the next chapter's Table 3.5. In the earliest forty year periods under observation, April was seldom the month with the highest spring/early summer index. One hundred years later, in the early eighteenth century, July held the maximal spring/early summer index in far fewer parishes; in general, July peaks had shifted back into June, June into May, and May into April. The evidence appears consistent with the notion that marriages before 1640 bunched both following the peak work season and in relation to the prohibited marriage seasons, and that the religious influence on the timing of marriage then fell away.

[67] Kussmaul, *Servants*, Chapter 6.

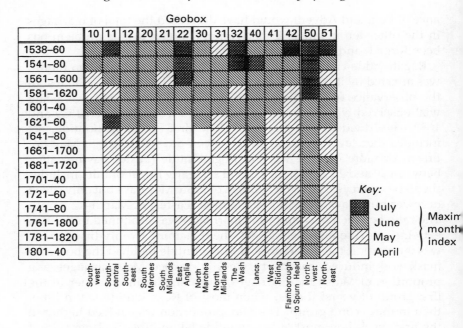

Figure 2.7 Timing of weddings within the spring/early summer by Geobox,
1538–60 to 1801–40 (non-market parishes)

The second major complication is, as it were, of my own making. In my earlier work on servants in husbandry, I argued that the most important influence on October marriages in the rural east was the changing proportion of farm servants to day-labourers. Servants there were released from their annual contracts (and their implied celibacy) each Michaelmas, and were more likely to marry then than were day-labourers, whose shorter contracts were in any case no impediment to marriage. The rise in the October index in the later seventeenth century was thus taken as a token of the increase in the proportion of young adults entering marriage from farm service, and this in turn was related to changes in the general supply of labour and relative prices.[68]

Could the changing incidence of service in husbandry account for the variations found in the seasonality of marriage? Increases in the

[68] The data were drawn from Appendix 2, Table A2.4 of Wrigley and Schofield, *Population History of England*, pp. 519–21. The number of marriages in the early Easter group was 485,879, that in the late Easter group 78,826. The Z-value for the text between proportions was 0.471 (see H. M. Blalock, *Social Statistics*, pp. 176–8).

proportion of farm servants could have intensified the existing pattern of seasonality, but could not have shifted the location of the peaks in marriage within the year, from one season to the other. The annual hiring dates of servants were not arbitrary; they located themselves in the slack season following the peak in the work year, as discussed above. Martinmas (in November), not Michaelmas, was the hiring time in arable parts of the north, with the area's later harvests. In the Lincolnshire fens, hiring fairs were held at May Day and again at Martinmas; in parts of eighteenth-century Wiltshire, Worcestershire, Dorset, Somerset, and Gloucestershire, contiguous parishes often hired most of their servants at different seasons.[69]

But the problem of the variation in the intensity of the marriage peak with the incidence of farm service remains. A very few parish registers include the occupation of the groom at marriage; unfortunately, these registers become less rare only in the later eighteenth century, and in northern, principally industrial parishes, where there were interesting occupations for vicars to note, but where the lateness of the grain harvest (especially after the mid eighteenth century's calendar change) would have pushed marriages back towards December. Brandsburton, in the agricultural East Riding, is unusual; its registers contain not only a run of marriage occupations from 1754 to 1810 but also a large enough number of recorded weddings to yield reliable estimates of marriage seasonality by groom's occupation. Advantage has already been taken of the register in connection with part-time work (see above). Forty-six of Brandsburton's grooms entered marriage directly from service, almost certainly from service in husbandry, for twenty-two of them (5.8 times the randomly expected number) married in November, after Martinmas. Brandsburton's yeomen, husbandmen, and farmers also married in the late autumn, but at only 1.6 times the expected rate for October and November; that ratio for the husbandmen, farmers, and yeomen, however, is still high enough for the seasonality of their marriages to appear to have been influenced by the seasonality of arable work (see Chapter 3).[70]

Those whose marriages were recorded in the Anglican registers changed in one final respect. Over time, the incidence of remarriage fell. Very few registers recorded the marital status of brides and grooms, but the fragmentary evidence suggests that later in the long span of registration, first marriages formed the great majority of marriages.[71] Beccles, Suffolk, provides one of those fragments.

[69] Kussmaul, 'Statute Sessions'.
[70] Hicks, ed., *Parish Register of Brandsburton*.
[71] Wrigley and Schofield, *Population History of England*, pp. 258–9.

The underlying number of events in the parish is large (365 weddings of single grooms, 146 of widowed grooms in 1661–1700, and 259 single, 173 widowed in 1568–1640), but Beccles would not have been my first choice as a test, from the point of view of this study. It was a market town; its main non-mercantile activity appears to have been fishing, and tides, currents, and the reproductive cycles of fish are beyond the scope of this study; finally, as the note on p. 258 of Wrigley and Schofield, 1981, reveals, remarriages did not decline in Beccles.

First marriages there had somewhat sharper seasonal peaks than did subsequent marriages. In 1568–1640, both groups failed to register as seasonal; the marriages of single grooms in 1661–1700 were just enough clustered in October and November to look influenced by arable work, while marriages of remarrying males were more non-seasonal. This is not surprising; the evidence from the sporadically recorded occupations at marriage had exhibited a similar difference between the marriage seasonality of (usually not widowed) farm servants and that of (more often widowed) farmers.[72]

The seasonality of second marriages would have been influenced by the seasonality of deaths (of first spouses), as well as by the seasonality of work and risks. Burials were most frequent in late winter.[73] The seasonality of marriage was very occasionally also driven by the seasonality of baptisms. In large parishes, especially, parents sometimes brought several children to be baptized in one trip to the church, and even more occasionally, as long as they were there, married. In Yorkshire's Horbury, for example, a clothier married and baptized a daughter on the same January day of 1722.[74] The parishes of the 'cloud-covered' northwest were large, but I suspect this to be the least of the reasons for the obscuring of agriculture there.

But at least this study is free from the complications that would have been encountered on the Continent. When I began the project, I had hopes for the method's proving useful in cross-country comparisons. But English marriage dates seem to have been largely free of three influences on continental marriage seasonality, two of which float free from economic exigency. First, there is the curious case of the aversion to marry in May. I leave the dilemma to others of finding a common

[72] Wrigley and Schofield, *Population History of England*, p. 293.
[73] The sum of the monthly deviations of the indexes from the non-seasonal 100 (divided by 12) for first marriages (both spouses single) in Beccles, 1568–1640, was 35.9, that for remarriages (at least one spouse widowed) only 24.4. The register is in the Suffolk Record Office, Ipswich.
[74] Charlesworth, ed., *Registers of the Chapel of Horbury*.

cause (if common cause there can be) for a dearth of May marriages in the Midi and Massif Central in France (which some ascribed to May's being the month of the Virgin) and in Calvinist Geneva, where the aversion to May was not caused by the immigration to Geneva of Italian Catholics, for it was the native Genevois craftsmen who most avoided May marriages.[75] In no large area of England was May rigorously avoided as a marriage month; it became the most popular marriage month in the later seventeenth and eighteenth centuries in many parishes.[76] There is the mystery of several coastal Cornish parishes with low, consistently low, totals of May marriages, but I suspect this to have been a reflection of the local seasonality of fishing, or wrecking. In St Just-in-Penwith, for example, the May marriage index is lower than 40 from 1581–1620 until 1741–80.

Secondly, January and February were important marriage months in much of France. Croix explained the popularity of these months in sixteenth-century Nantes, and of October and November, by the liturgical year; marriages were bunched into the period between Advent and Lent, and couples rushed to the altar to beat the Advent deadline. Blayo and Henry also found a pre-Lenten peak of marriages in Brittany and Anjou in 1740–1829.[77] But Advent and Lent were scrupulously observed as prohibited marriage seasons in England, too, at least before the mid seventeenth century, **without** January and February being noticeably popular as marriage months in most of England.

So the explanation for the peak of marriages in January and February cannot be mechanical, of the form 'so few marriages were celebrated in December and March that January and February had to be popular'. I should like (moving well out of my field) to hazard a modest hypothesis of Carnival Culture to account for the differences in January and February marriage. What delineates the Carnival, Carneval, or Faschung is indeed its bracketing by Advent and the looming abstinence of Lent, but the meaning of the revelries was radically secular. They marked Our Time, as distinct from The Church's Time. The only area in England where January and February

---

[75] Perrenoud, 'Calendrier du Mariage', pp. 926–30; Lebrun, *La Vie Conjugale*, p. 40. Dupaquier argued that May **became** unpopular in the nineteenth century (Dupaquier, 'Le Mouvement Saisonnier', p. 138).
[76] In Scotland, however, May was considered to bring bad luck to couples choosing it for their marriage. See the letter of Smith in *Local Population Studies*, p. 67. See Figure 3.1, below, for the popularity of May as a marriage month in many English parishes.
[77] Croix, 'La Démographie', p. 109; Blayo and Henry explained the low May marriage total by the large numbers of marriages celebrated in January, February, and November ('Donées Démographique', p. 109).

were popular marriage months was northern Staffordshire, Cheshire, and Lancashire, which I described above as 'cloud-covered', in the sense that its agricultural parishes did not celebrate many marriages in the autumn and the spring. This was the English stronghold of Roman Catholicism in post-Reformation England. Perhaps recusancy, and local Carnival Culture, is yet another candidate to add to the list for that region to explain the unusual (for England) seasonality of marriages there, but it is interesting in this respect that January and February only become modestly popular marriage months there during the eighteenth century (see Table 2.3, above). Eighteenth-century settlement examinations from the region show Christmas hirings of farm servants.[78]

I am loathe to return to England, so I shall add a third continental influence early modern England seemed largely free of, seasonal migration. Transhumance, like fishing on the coasts, could have separated potential marriage partners and so left marks on recorded marriage seasonality. Transhumance was not completely unknown in England, and the practice did not always separate males and females. In the extreme north, near the border with Scotland, transhumance was practised in the sixteenth century, with the whole community moving up into the high pasture region, but it died out in the seventeenth century.[79] But on both the French and Swiss Alps, there were great troughs in marriage totals while the flocks (and the men) were up in the summer pasture. The maximum marriage month there was April, before the men and sheep left.[80] The seasonal separation of potential marriage partners was of course also behind the autumn marriage peak in otherwise non-agricultural towns in England, as many left for a month in the country to earn high harvest wages.

The book rests on the answers given to this chapter's title. In the main, the replies were 'not until these next months of good wages and/or high risks are over'. Only the changing incidence of farm service and remarriage, and the possibility of Carnival-like behaviour in parts of the northwest, pose irremediable problems to the method, and farm service and remarriage only affected the peakedness of the tendency to marry in the autumn or in the spring/summer, not the

---

[78] See, for example, the examinations for Handforth, Lymm, Tattenhall, and Wilmslow in the Cheshire Record Office. See also Hole, *Traditions*, p. 28.

[79] Thirsk, 'Farming Regions', p. 22, and 'Farming Techniques', p. 182, and Paul Brassley, 'Northumberland and Durham', p. 34.

[80] Perrenoud, 'Calendrier du Mariage'. On the edge of the Massif Central, seasonal migrants married on their return from the hills (Ogden, 'Patterns of Marriage Seasonality', p. 62).

location of the seasonal peaks in marriages within the year. The next chapter, 'Source and method', has to be tedious at first. But in it I present more evidence of directed changes in marriage seasonality, to which meaning will be given in the chapters that follow.

3

Source and method

Changes in English marriage seasonality reflect, imperfectly, changes in rural economic activity. The great advantage of the method is the extent of the early modern marriage record, a quantitative source continuous over both time and space. The seasonal indices are derived from 542 Anglican marriage registers, roughly 5.4 per cent of English parishes (roughly 5.4 per cent, because of changes in parish boundaries); the proportion of this sample to the *surviving* total of registers is of course far higher. The sample's foundation is the set that Wrigley and Schofield employed in *The Population History of England*; I added to it 138 parishes, from original registers and transcripts and gifts from other workers. I employed the raw totals of registered marriages, uncorrected for underregistration. The method of correction employed by Wrigley and Schofield, the application of a national template of monthly seasonality of events,[1] would have served to dampen the regional variations in seasonality that are of interest in this study.

I cannot pretend that the 542 represent a randomly drawn sample of English parishes. To begin with, the Cambridge Group's set is not a random sample; multiple, sometimes mutually inconsistent, guidelines were given to the volunteers who collected the data. Parishes with larger recorded numbers of baptisms, marriages, and burials, for instance, were initially to be preferred to the smaller, to increase the possibility of record-linkage needed to calculate, for example, ages at marriage and age-specific fertility.[2] Some volunteers may have had their own interests and agendas in collecting the data. None of the fourteen Gloucestershire parishes in the Cambridge Groups's set, for example, is in the six most agricultural Hundreds of the county as

---

[1] Wrigley and Schofield, *Population History of England*, p. 31.   [2] *Ibid.*, pp. 5–6.

measured by Tawney and Tawney from the 1608 Muster Roll.[3] Any random selection of volunteers would have produced more from larger places, and, since volunteers usually included their own parish in their submission, parochial loyalty compounded the selection's bias towards places with larger numbers of recorded demographic events.[4] The less seasonal industrial parishes were generally more densely settled than the more seasonal agricultural ones, so the Cambridge Group's large contribution to the 542 parish set leans towards the less agricultural end of the spectrum of rural seasonality. Spatial variations in cooperation existed as well, producing a set with twenty-nine parishes from both Kent and Suffolk, twenty-eight from Bedfordshire, twenty-six from the West Riding of Yorkshire, and twenty-five from Leicestershire, but only three from Buckinghamshire and from Wiltshire, two each from Northamptonshire and Worcestershire, and none at all from Cornwall or Westmorland.[5]

I intended, in supplementing this 404 parish sample, to compensate for its biases and spatial lacunae. I therefore added seven Gloucestershire parishes from the more agricultural Hundreds, and parishes from Cornwall, the East Riding, Worcestershire, and Wiltshire, among others. But in accepting, most gratefully, the gift of marriage data drawn from a well-stratified sample of parishes in the Home Counties and the South Midlands, I compounded one of the biases of the 404, rather than compensating for it.[6] This region, broadly speaking, was already represented by forty-nine parishes in the Cambridge Group's sample (including Bedfordshire's twenty-eight). The addition of twenty-nine Northamptonshire parishes, among others, made the counties running north from Hertfordshire and Buckinghamshire to Leicestershire and Northamptonshire amply represented, over-represented compared to other parts of the country (see Table A.1 for the number of parishes in each county in my set, relative to the county totals). In calculating aggregate statistics for the whole sample, a process of weighting was adopted to counteract the regional bias of the sample (see below).

My primary methodological goal was to observe the use of land, the changing use of land, at two removes, by gauging the seasonality of

[3] The 6 Hundreds with at least two-thirds of their males reported as employed in agriculture in the Muster Roll of 1608 are Tewkesbury, Henbury, Deerhurst, Rapsgate, Crowtherne and Minty, and Tyboldstone. Tawney and Tawney, 'An Occupational Census', p. 64.
[4] I am grateful to Tony Wrigley for having pointed out this bias.
[5] See discussion of sampling problems in Wrigley and Schofield, *Population History of England*, pp. 45–51.
[6] I am indebted to John Broad and Sue Wright for the use of marriage data collected for their study.

work on that land through the seasonality of marriage. The parish, not the individual, is the basic unit of observation. This raises the problems of very small numbers of weddings in some parishes, very different numbers of events in different parishes, and also the ecological fallacy. Parishes did not make decisions about marriage months based on the seasonality of work and risks; individuals did, possibly with the nudging of local customs. But, even if the use of land had not been the initial object, some way of ordering the information about the 989,729 weddings whose months are contained in the 542 parish set would have been needed.

I elected not to sum marriages over larger regions than the parish, for two reasons. First, I would have to have had an *a priori* definition of regional boundaries, and one of the possibilities I wished to investigate was the malleability of regions over time.[7] Second, amalgamating less densely populated agricultural places with more densely populated commercial or industrial ones would have biased any measure towards the industrially and commercially employed. Even if I had chosen the county as the unit of observation, or the historiographically arbitrary, rectilinear 'geoboxes' used above in Figure 2.7, the problem of the swamping of agriculture's seasonality by the larger number of events in non-agricultural places would have remained. And amalgamating spring-marrying places with autumn-marrying ones would have produced muddled observations, appearing either heterogeneous to an unusual degree or, more likely, non-seasonal.

The raw number of weddings per month in each parish is not the best measure of the seasonality of marriage; not only did parishes vary greatly in the number of recorded marriages, but months have different numbers of days. Indices of monthly marriages were therefore constructed:

$$I_{(month,\ period)} = [(T_{month} \ / \ T_{period})/(D_{month}/365.25)] * 100$$

I is the index for the month and period, T the total of marriages, and D the number of days in the month. The indices would take the value of 100 were weddings evenly strewn over all the days of the year; an index of 200 for any month would indicate that twice the expected random number had occurred in that month, an index of 50 that half the expected number had.

The more than 300 years covered by the data set were sliced into fifteen forty-year periods, each one overlapping the previous period by twenty years (the truncated first period, 1538–60, begins at the start of nationwide parochial registration under Henry VIII). For some

---

[7] See discussion in Grigg, 'Regions', p. 471 and in Everitt, 'Country', p. 80.

Table 3.1. *Parishes and periods*[a]

Period	Dates	Parishes in observation[b]	Of which non-market[c]	market
1	1538–60	111	71	40
2	1541–80	327	229	98
3	1561–1600	407	294	113
4	1581–1620	477	355	122
5	1601–40	500	372	128
6	(1621–60)	507	375	132
7	(1641–80)	511	376	135
8	1661–1700	519	385	134
9	1681–1721	528	393	135
10	1701–40	531	395	136
11	1721–60	534	398	136
12	1741–80	537	401	136
13	1761–1800	536	401	135
14	1781–1820	533	398	135
15	1801–40	513	378	135

[a] See Appendix for the names of the parishes, by county and market status.
[b] Parishes, that is, with at least 24 recorded marriages in the period.
[c] These are parishes not listed in Adams, *Index Villaris*, as market towns. See below for the reasons for excluding market towns from many runs.

purposes, it proved useful to combine the forty-year periods into longer ones, but any span **shorter** than forty years would have intensified the problem of small numbers. Some parishes in the sample, like sheep-ranching Wormleighton before William Pettipher, had very few recorded marriages in a year; many parishes have gaps in their registration. Small numbers lead to large swings in the calculated indices; one marriage per period would score c. 1200 for the month in which it occurred, and 0 for the other eleven months. I decided to eliminate from observation, for any period, all parishes in which fewer than twenty-four marriages were recorded in the forty years, but not to attempt to amalgamate parishes to boost the total number of marriages in a period; I would have eliminated real diversity between the parishes if any had existed. Over the course of my research, the arbitrary number dropped from ninety-six to forty-eight to its present twenty-four; readers can trace this process in the two articles that preceded this book.[8] Table 3.1 lists the numbers of non-market parishes and market towns that passed the hurdle of twenty-four marriages, for each of the fifteen overlapping periods.

[8] Kussmaul, 'Agrarian Change'; Kussmaul, 'Time and Space'.

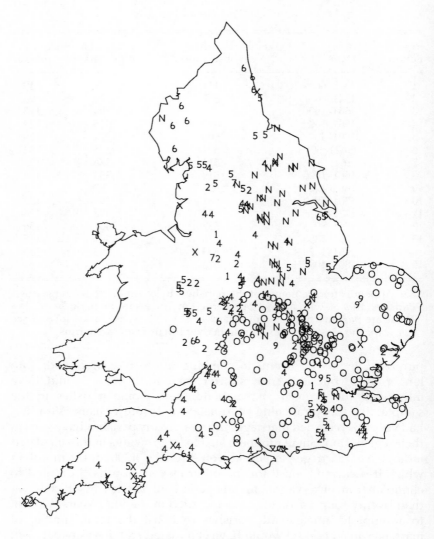

Figure 3.1 Maximum marriage month, 1701–40

Key: 1 January   5 May   9 September
     2 February   6 June   0 October
     3 March   7 July   N November
     4 April   8 August   X December

There is a necessary asymmetry of error in adhering to the parish as the unit of observation. Densely settled parishes, with larger numbers of marriages, yield more reliable estimates of seasonality than would any single less densely settled place, simply because of the larger number of underlying events. The seasonality indices for any single small place might fluctuate wildly, by chance. But none of the major empirical findings underpinning the book's arguments rests on the evidence of a single small place; the maps of Chapter 1 (Figures 1.1 and 1.4) showed a large number of small places simultaneously changing their seasonality, in a directed fashion. Working with forty-year periods and a minimum of twenty-four marriages in the period represents a joint compromise. Had I lengthened the periods, to increase the number of marriages per period, I would have lost some ability to locate changes in time; if I had instead increased the minimum number from twenty-four, I would have lost from observation many agricultural parishes.

There are twelve months in which marriages could have occurred, in each of the 542 parishes, in fifteen periods. Collapsing the 300 years of the record into forty-year periods still leaves twelve awkward months to manipulate. Figure 3.1, which maps the parishes according to their maximal marriage month in 1701–40, speaks, most inarticulately, for itself. The twelve months were abandoned in favour of the two main periods of agriculturally determined seasonality, autumn and spring.

No single months within autumn or spring can be usefully made to serve as national indicators of seasonal marriages. Since the peak in marriages could easily span two months, the means of monthly indices in contiguous pairs of months were used in deriving the working indices. In addition, although one of the nicest things about this odd method is its consistency with logic, that consistency occasionally played havoc with the method. If peaks in spring marriages, for example, were really tied to the seasonality of work in lambing and calving, then the peak in spring marriages should occur earlier in the spring in the milder south and west than in the colder north and east, since lambs were dropped later in the season where the winter lasted longer and the first growth of new grass came later. And, as Figures 2.1 and 2.7 showed, this was indeed the case. Because the spring month of interesting pastoral seasonality could be as early as February, or as late as July, depending on whether the lambs were being dropped in the southwest or the north, no unique pair of months can be isolated as representative of spring work, in all of England. A similar argument applies to autumn seasonality; the grain harvest happened within a general range of several months, south to north. The timing of the harvest also varied within single places; Jones reported harvests starting at dates between 27 July and 6 September on a Gloucestershire farm.[9]

A set of compromises was adopted. The autumn (AUT) and spring (SPR) indices, for every parish (p) in every period (t), choose themselves, as it were. The spring index is based on the maximum of the sum of the indices of marriages in the pairs of months from April and May through June and July, and the autumn index on the maximum of the sum of the September and October or October and November indices:

$$AUT_{pt}=MAX \; [of \; (SEPT_{pt}+OCT_{pt}), \; (OCT_{pt}+NOV_{pt})]/2$$
$$SPR_{pt}=MAX \; [of \; (APR_{pt}+MAY_{pt}), \; (MAY_{pt}+JUNE_{pt}),$$
$$(JUNE_{pt}+JULY_{pt})]/2$$

The random index is still 100, but the maximum attainable value has dropped from 1200 to 600; if all marriages had occurred in October and November, for example, the sum of the indices would have been c. 1200, but c. 1200/2=c. 600.

The very early lambing of the southwest is now unfortunately hidden from view, but to allow any winter month into the definition of the spring index would have led to a greater distortion; the winter marriages of the 'cloud-covered' northwest would have resembled the pattern generated by very early lambing in the southwest. The lateness of the grain harvest in the north, coupled with the calendar change in the mid eighteenth century, would make December a candidate for inclusion in the autumn index. But widening the definition of the autumn index would have introduced new confusions as Advent came to be less observed and as December became a popular marriage month in industrial towns (see above, Chapter 2).

Basing the autumn index on the maximum of double-month indices from September to November and the spring index on the maximum double-month combination from April to July has the advantage of resolving one of the puzzles mentioned in the last chapter. Spring and autumn marriages came to be celebrated at earlier dates within the seasons, well before the adoption of the new calendar (see above, Figure 2.7). Why the seasonal peaks regressed is something of a mystery. The changing observance of Advent, Lent, and Rogationtide was advanced as an explanation in Chapter 2. Of course, had all England grown warmer between 1580 and 1680, the earlier growth of grass would eventually have prodded farmers into procuring earlier

[9] Jones, *Seasons and Prices*, pp. 62–3.

lambing and calving, and pulled the pastoral work peak back in the calendar year, but this is hardly likely; the period is generally characterized as a Little Ice Age.[10] Perhaps the increasing appreciation of sheep as mutton-producers led farmers to maximize the weight-gain of sheep with earlier lambing.[11] In any case, the method that adjusts for the variation of the timing of marriages within seasons over **space**, using the maximum sum of two monthly indices within the seasons, also automatically corrects for short-term and long-term variation over **time**, including the regression towards marriages earlier in the seasons (whatever its cause).

A simple mechanical solution was found for the changing observance of Lent and Advent. Marriages that were barred from March and December had to have occurred in one or more of the ten remaining months, inflating their totals, and the inflation ended as Lent and Advent ceased to be closely observed. Earlier in the series, the autumn and spring indices could have been higher than the later indices, for this reason alone. I therefore took the sum of March and December indices, in each parish, in each period, subtracted that sum from 200 (the sum that would have resulted if marriages had been evenly strewn into March and December as into other months), divided by ten (for the remaining ten months), and subtracted the result from the index for that parish, in that period, to yield the final indices (it is these corrected indices that were used in the maps and figures of Chapters 1 and 2). The method of correction does not admit the possibility of clandestine marriages in March and December.

$$AUT_{pt} = AUT_{pt} - [200 - (MARCH_{pt} + DECEMBER_{pt})]/10$$
$$SPR_{pt} = SPR_{pt} - [200 - (MARCH_{pt} + DECEMBER_{pt})]/10$$

No adjustment was made for the possibility that tenacious customs slowed the response of marriage seasonality to changes in the seasonality of work and risks. The meaning of a shift between marriage seasons can therefore be taken (if the argument of Chapter 2 has been swallowed) as the latest possible dating for the economic changes.

The autumn and spring indices, already used in the first chapters, have now been defined. How does the whole sample behave, statistically speaking? Two modifications to the meaning of 'whole sample' are employed in answering this question. Where rural change was the object of investigation, parishes lying within market towns were dropped from the sample. Towns, with their diverse occupational blend, were in any case places of muted marriage seasonality, as Table

[10] See, for instance, Bayson and Padoch, 'On the Climates', pp. 583–98.
[11] Conversation with Tony Wrigley.

3.2 will show, whether or not they were industrial.[12] In the Northamptonshire Militia Lists of 1777, while six crafts occupations were
common in rural parishes (tailor, blacksmith, carpenter, shoemaker,
weaver, wheelwright), there were seventy-four others, almost all in
towns.[13]

Secondly, I have reason to regret the spatial non-randomness of the
set of 542 parishes. Fully one-quarter of Bedfordshire's parishes is in
the set, along with nearly 20 per cent of Hertfordshire's parishes and
more than 10 per cent of the totals of Leicestershire, Northamptonshire, Staffordshire, and Warwickshire, while less than 2 per cent of
the totals of parishes in Berkshire, Derbyshire, Huntingdonshire,
Middlesex, and Westmorland are (see Appendix for the numbers of
parishes by county). This makes little difference to the mapping of the
parishes (by Seasonal Type, for example, in Figures 1.1 and 1.4,
above), where readers will have performed their own visual sampling
in taking in the pictures, except where the clumping of Bedfordshire's
parishes nearly defied the eye.

But in calculating the aggregate statistics that follow, some correction for the imbalances in representation was warranted. I chose a
simple method, based on the area of each parish's county (drawn from
the 1831 census) and the number of non-market parishes from the
county in the sample.[14] The fewer the sample's non-market parishes
or the larger the county's area, the greater are the weights. Area was
chosen as a basis for the weights in preference to population because
the relative areas of the counties remained largely unchanged from the
beginning of the registration of marriages to 1831, but the relative size
of the county populations changed over that long span. The first
weights I could have relied on, based on county populations, would
have had to come from the 1801 census, far too late for appropriate
sixteenth and seventeenth century weights. Table 3.2 applied the
weights, which are based on the area in observation by county. The
table displays the means for the autumn and spring indices and a
measure of dispersion about the means, the Coefficient of Variability
(C.V.) for the non-market parishes, using the weights, and the means
and C.V.'s for the market towns, appropriately unweighted.

In the non-market portion of the table, AUT begins at its maximum,
but the C.V. does not attain its maximum until 1681–1720. The autumn

12 Market towns were identified from Adams, *Index Villaris*. There are 136 market towns
   in the 542-parish sample, and a maximum of 401 non-market parishes in observation
   in any forty-year period.
13 Everitt, 'Country', p. 99.
14 The WEIGHT option was invoked in SAS, with WEIGHT set by the ratio of the
   country's area to the number of the country's non-market parishes in the sample.

Table 3.2. *Mean and C.V., autumn and spring indices, market towns and non-market parishes*

Period	Non-market[a]				Markets[b]			
	Mean autumn	CV autumn	Mean spring	CV spring	Mean autumn	CV autumn	Mean spring	CV spring
1538–60	186	38	123	36	165	36	117	32
1541–80	185	33	117	32	166	26	109	23
1561–1600	179	33	116	31	159	28	108	19
1581–1620	164	33	120	31	152	26	112	18
1601–40	156	31	124	29	145	26	114	17
(1621–60)	140	32	134	31	137	27	118	20
(1641–80)	133	35	141	34	131	28	122	18
1661–1700	135	40	143	33	135	27	122	20
1681–1720	134	43	143	33	138	29	120	23
1701–40	134	41	140	35	141	29	116	25
1721–60	136	39	130	35	139	28	110	23
1741–80	138	37	123	35	138	27	107	21
1761–1800	140	36	121	35	139	25	107	21
1781–1820	141	36	119	34	139	25	105	21
1801–40	137	35	123	37	136	25	105	22

[a] See Table 3.1 above for the numbers of parishes in observation (that is, having recorded at least 24 weddings) in each period.
[b] The means for the market towns are not weighted by area; it would have been inappropriate to do so.

index declines to its minimum during the disrupted record-keeping of the Interregnum, and then largely levels off, at mean index values narrowly ranging from 134 to 141; its C.V. declines somewhat from its late seventeenth-century maximum, but never again drops to the minimum recorded in 1601–40. The non-market mean spring index begins and ends at the same mean value, with a maximum in the late seventeenth century. Its C.V., after a moderately high start, ranges from 29 to 32 before the Interregnum, and afterwards rises to between 33 and 37.

Until the later seventeenth century, the mean non-market autumn index is higher than the corresponding index for the market towns; thereafter, the two means are nearly identical, but at very different C.V.'s. That difference indicates the contrast between the generally low seasonal indices of market towns and the splitting of the rural subset into high autumn and low autumn (high or low spring) parishes. The rural mean spring index is always higher than the index

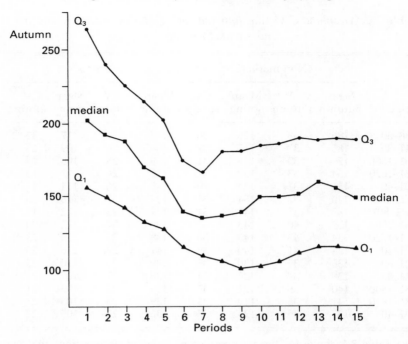

Figure 3.2 Medians and quartiles, autumn index (non-market parishes)

for market towns; the difference widens in the later seventeenth century. Again, the C.V.'s are uniformly lower in the urban subset.

Figures 3.2 and 3.3 present graphic non-parametric alternatives to the means and C.V.'s of Table 3.2.[15] The new figures show the aggregate behaviour of the non-market portion of the sample via medians and quartiles: 50 per cent of observations of the autumn and spring indices fell within the bands of Q1 and Q3. The median autumn index, like the mean, begins at its maximum in the first period, falls to its minimum in the Interregnum, and then recovers somewhat by the end of the eighteenth century.

Figure 3.3 repeats the exercise for the spring index. Here, the median rises to a maximum in the later seventeenth century, and then subsides. The spring index generally does not attain the high levels possible with the autumn index. Through most of the series, autumn's Q3 indicates that a minimum of one quarter of the rural parishes saw twice the randomly expected number of weddings clustered in the

[15] See Figure 3, 'Clouds', in Kussmaul, 'Time and Space', p. 761, for another way of demonstrating the increasing dispersion of the observations.

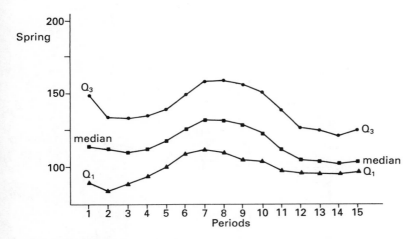

Figure 3.3 Medians and quartiles, spring index (non-market parishes)

autumn. By contrast, spring's Q3 indicates that over most of the series, three-quarters of rural parishes celebrated fewer than one and one half times the expected number of weddings in the spring and early summer.

The means and medians cannot show the combinations of autumn and spring indices that were evident in the graphs for individual parishes in the first two chapters. Two hybrid variables can be generated from the autumn and spring indices to show the degree of agricultural seasonality (SEAS) and the tendency towards marriage in the autumn or the spring (ANG). Figure 3.4 illustrates the derivation of ANG and SEAS. Three hypothetical parishes (X, Y, and Z) are graphed. Y is autumn-marrying, like Orwell and Barley; Z is spring-marrying, like Cowfold or early Earsdon; X is not very seasonal at all.

SEAS is the length of the vector (RX, RY, or RZ) drawn out from the non-seasonal point R (100,100) to the observation. In Figure 3.4, RY=RZ, so the SEAS index for the two parishes Y and Z are identical, and much greater than SEAS for parish X. ANG is the angle formed by the SEAS vector (RY, for example) and the line RA. ANG was chosen in preference to the simple ratio of autumn to spring, or spring to autumn indices. ANG is symmetrical about the value of ANG for autumn index=spring index (45°); the ratios are not. Where the autumn index is 100 and spring index 300, for example, ANG is 90°; where the spring index is 100 and autumn 300, ANG is 0°. The corresponding simple ratios of spring to autumn indices would have been 0.33333 and 3. When the spring index is less than 100, ANG is

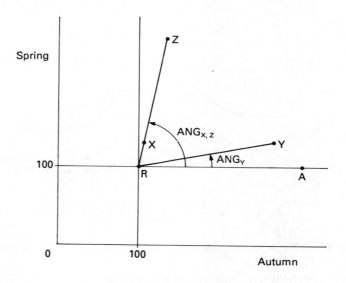

Figure 3.4 Defining SEAS and ANG

negative; when the autumn index is less than 100, ANG is greater than 90°. In Figure 3.4, ANG is far higher for parish Z than for parish Y; as sketched, the ANG for parish X is identical to that of parish Z. ANG can thus show the dominant season for weddings, but not how seasonal the parish's marriages were; SEAS can show how seasonal, but not the season.

Figure 3.5 displays the movements of mean ANG and SEAS for the non-market sample. A trap is built into the calculation of mean ANG, using SEAS, to snare non-seasonal mimics like parish X. The decline of SEAS reflects both the disappearance of the sixteenth-century's nearly uniform blanket of very high autumn seasonality, the subject of the next two chapters, and the growth of rural manufacturing, the concern of Chapter 6. ANG is at its (high autumn, low spring) minimum in the second and third periods, and then climbs steeply to its maximum in the later seventeenth century before regaining autumn and losing (some) spring weddings. But the post-Interregnum minimum, at the close of the eighteenth century, is still higher than the low values recorded in the later sixteenth century.

A last demonstration with the continuous variable ANG shows the sample stretching apart with respect to the autumn and spring indices in the later seventeenth century (Figure 3.6). ANG is measured on the horizontal axis, and the cumulative frequencies of parishes at values of

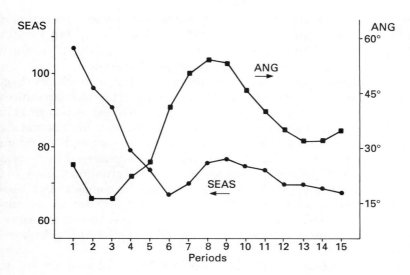

Figure 3.5 Mean SEAS and ANG
(non-market parishes, 1538–60 to 1801–40, weighted)

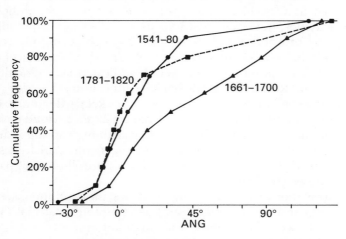

Figure 3.6 Cumulative frequency, ANG
(non-market parishes)

ANG on the vertical axis. In 1541–80 (period 2) the distribution is positively skewed at the low mean value of ANG that was shown in the previous figure. By 1661–1700 (period 8) the distribution has been flattened by the movement of so many parishes into the high spring, high ANG camp. The distribution then retreats to positive skewness at a lower mean value of ANG by 1781–1820 (period 14). But English marriage seasonality had not simply retreated to its sixteenth-century starting position, as Figure 3.12 will (eventually) show.

The moment of the emergence of this study from my earlier work on farm servants came when I realized that looking at low October indices of marriages told me only that the grain harvest was probably unimportant as an employer of servants in husbandry, but not that the parish was pastoral. It is in tandem that the two measures, the autumn and spring indices, convey their greater information. The hybrid measures ANG and SEAS indicate movement between autumn and spring seasonality (ANG), and between non-seasonality and agriculturally influenced seasonality (SEAS). They are continuous variables, but each loses information; ANG cannot reveal non-seasonality, and SEAS cannot differentiate between varieties of agricultural influences.

A non-continuous variable, Seasonal Type (plotted above on Figures 1.1 and 1.4), was therefore devised. The sketches of stellar individual parishes in the last chapter used the autumn and spring indices together. A high autumn index, by itself, indicated arable activities, as in Orwell; a high spring index, by itself, indicated pastoral activities, especially rearing, as in Alberbury (specialized fattening was probably not characterized by high spring indices of marriage, as the next chapter will argue). The combination of low autumn with low spring indices generally indicated non-agricultural activities, as in Rochdale or late eighteenth-century Earsdon and Shepshed (the combination also arises with market gardening, exceptionally early lambing, and with what Chapter 2 called 'cloud cover'); the least common association, high autumn with high spring indices, occurred especially in topographically heterogeneous parishes, such as half-drowned, half-dry Willingham. But a portfolio of 542 parish graphs would be cumbersome.

More information can be gained by sacrificing the continuous nature of the autumn and spring indices, and defining four Seasonal Types (Figure 3.7): Orwell-like Type A, with high autumn and low spring indices (arable); Alberbury-like Type P, with high spring but low autumn indices (pastoral); Rochdale-like Type X, with both low autumn and low spring indices (non-agricultural); and Willingham-like Type H, with both high autumn and high spring indices ('mixed', not in the sense that Thirsk, for example, employed, but instead 'heterogeneous').

But how high is high, how low is low? This is a question with a

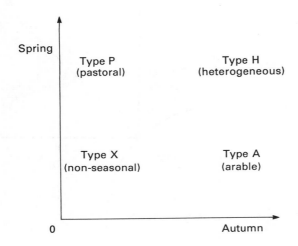

Figure 3.7 Towards Seasonal Types

wider application than to Seasonal Types alone. It is the dread question of scale, affecting the reading of the single-parish diagrams of Chapter 2 and the aggregate means and medians of this chapter. I needed a shorter title than 'PALEONTOLOGIST' for a computer file name for 'Agrarian Change in Seventeenth-Century England: The Economic Historian as Paleontologist', and 'SCALES' it was, for the vexing problems of scale, and for the resistance of fishing to identification.

Here I am hoist on the petard I constructed with some care in the first chapter. Against what comparable early modern source can I calibrate my measures? There is a lively debate among readers of English probate inventories over how to judge the mix between arable and pastoral practices from valuations of moveable property alone, and, as I mentioned in that first chapter, great problems exist in judging the mix between agriculture and industry because of the low value of fixed capital in much rural manufacturing. Occupational listings, including the broad categories of early nineteenth-century censuses, may give an indication of the blend between agriculture and manufacturing, but not that between arable and pastoral farming. Estate maps, where they exist, may indicate the balance between ploughland and pasture or meadow, but are silent on manufacturing.[16]

[16] Techniques such as discriminant analysis would have been no help here: I would have to have had a known set of arable and pastoral parishes (or irises, or male and female skulls, to use the standard examples).

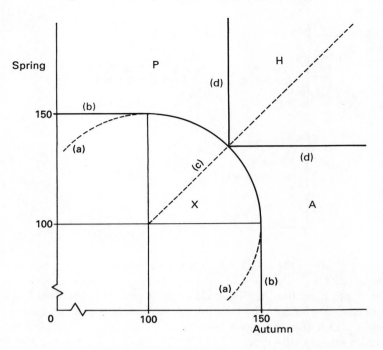

Figure 3.8 Defining Seasonal Types

Where are the boundaries to be placed between Seasonal Types? I decided to use arbitrary delineators between the four types. They are sketched in Figure 3.8. My defence for them rests on aesthetic appeals to round numbers and symmetry:

(a) if the SEAS index, the distance of the observation from (100,100) was less than 50 (arc (a)), or

(b) if the autumn (or spring) index was less than 100 while the spring (or autumn) index was less than 150 (lines (b)), the parish was assigned to Type X (non-seasonal).

The remaining (seasonal) parishes were then labelled:

(c) as Type A (arable) if the autumn index was higher than the spring index (vector (c), autumn index=spring index),

(d) as Type P (pastoral) if the spring index was higher than the autumn index,[17] and

---

[17] I elected to accept the simple symmetrical definition of A- and P-types, despite the likelihood of arable's stronger seasonal peak in work.

Table 3.3. *Frequency by Seasonal Type*
(non-market parishes, period percentages in parentheses)[a]

	Period	A-Type		P-Type		X-Type		H-Type		Missing
1	1538–60	45	(63.4)	8	(11.3)	4	(5.6)	14	(19.7)	335
2	1541–80	150	(65.5)	9	(3.9)	32	(14.0)	38	(16.6)	177
3	1561–1600	186	(63.3)	24	(8.2)	48	(16.3)	36	(12.2)	112
4	1581–1620	206	(58.0)	43	(12.1)	66	(18.6)	40	(11.3)	51
5	1601–40	200	(53.8)	44	(11.8)	79	(21.2)	49	(13.2)	34
6	(1621–60)	138	(36.8)	69	(18.4)	122	(32.5)	46	(12.3)	31
7	(1641–80)	113	(30.1)	95	(25.3)	119	(31.6)	49	(13.0)	30
8	1661–1700	131	(34.0)	96	(24.9)	109	(28.3)	49	(12.7)	21
9	1681–1720	139	(35.4)	102	(26.0)	103	(26.2)	49	(12.5)	13
10	1701–40	175	(44.3)	77	(19.5)	101	(25.6)	42	(10.6)	11
11	1721–60	179	(45.0)	66	(16.6)	124	(31.2)	29	(7.3)	8
12	1741–80	198	(49.4)	54	(13.5)	134	(33.4)	15	(3.7)	5
13	1761–1800	210	(52.4)	51	(12.7)	123	(30.7)	17	(4.2)	5
14	1781–1820	206	(51.8)	47	(11.8)	132	(33.2)	13	(3.3)	8
15	1801–40	176	(46.6)	44	(11.6)	144	(38.1)	14	(3.7)	28

[a] See text for the definition of the Seasonal Types.

(e) as Type H if both the autumn and spring indices were greater than (the exceedingly unround) 135.355339 (where the autumn index=spring index vector (c) cuts the SEAS arc (a)).

These are razor-edge boundaries between Seasonal Types, where a marriage celebrated on 31 August instead of 1 September could shift a parish from A-Type into X-Type. But I accepted the risk, after considering 'tertiles', in which I might have dropped the middle third of parishes, as insufficiently differentiated. If the middle third had been dropped with reference to both the autumn and the spring indices, though, I might have lost at least 5/9 of the possible observations (and that under the assumption that the observations were evenly distributed in autumn–spring space, and not bunched near the medians).

Table 3.3 shows the sharing out of the samples' parishes among these four Seasonal Types, for each of the fifteen overlapping forty year periods (the two periods 'contaminated' by the disturbed record-keeping of the Interregnum are indicated with parentheses in the table). The seasonally heterogeneous H-Type becomes increasingly rare over time, as the specialized pastoral, spring marrying P-Type emerges. Characterizations as H-Type were also the least consistent over time. H-typing will therefore be dropped from many of the applications, and the parishes that would have been so typed assigned to the P- and A-Types, according to whether the spring or the autumn index was higher. P-Types are most common, comprising 25 to 26 per cent of the total in observation, in the later seventeenth and early eighteenth centuries; their share then halves during the later eighteenth and early nineteenth centuries. The number of non-seasonal X-Types more simply grows, from only 6 per cent of the total to a maximum in the last period of 38 per cent. The autumn-marrying arable A-Type is dominant at the start and the finish of the series, and only in the Interregnum's disrupted record-keeping does it fail to capture the largest number of parishes. The number of A-Types drops in the last period, partly because of the disappearance of most of Bedfordshire, arable Bedfordshire, from the sample (the collectors for Bedfordshire for the Cambridge Group stopped their reporting at 1812).

No one pitch is correct for all music; the early modern note A is lower than the modern 440 + cycles per second, as lonely owners of Baroque recorders with piano-owning friends learn. No one classific scheme serves all purposes equally well, as Grigg reminded us (1976b, p. 468), and felicitously, the arable Type A is 'tuned' too high to detect some interparochial differences in the earliest periods of marriage registration, for, as Figure 1.4 and Table 3.3 may have suggested, nearly all English parishes were Type A (arable) or Type H (hetero-geneous) then. It proved helpful in some instances to define relative Seasonal Types, with the mean spring and autumn indices for each period used as simple (but mobile, period to period) differentiators between types for each period, as illustrated in Figure 3.9 for 1561–1600. The figure plots mean autumn against mean spring indices for contiguous periods from 1561–1600, and adds dotted lines as differen-tiators between a new set of relative Seasonal Types in 1561–1600. That period sets both the strictest standard of the plotted series for the relatively arable a-Type (in which the autumn index for 1561–1600 would have to be greater than the mean autumn index for that period) and the laxest standard for the relatively pastoral p-Type.

There are those who have approached the subject of regional specialization, the concern of Chapter 5, as if it involved answers to questions such as 'From where did London get its beef – from region A?' If the answer is 'Not from everywhere, but from region A', they find region A to exhibit regional specialization. That sort of 'regional specialization', the existence of marketed specialties, can easily be found before the middle of the seventeenth century. Palliser, follow-ing Thirsk, found pastoral specialization in upland areas in the

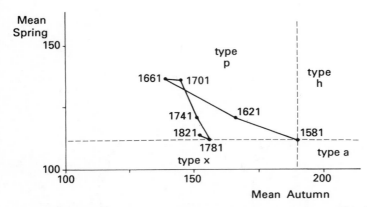

Figure 3.9 Mean autumn and spring indices, 1561–1600 to 1781–1820
(non-market parishes)
(dates are mid-points of the 40-year periods)

sixteenth century; they produced 'only enough grain for their own needs'; it is the marketed specialties of regions that Clay may have had in mind in maintaining that 'the geographical distribution of various forms of agricultural production was not fundamentally different in 1700 from what it had been in 1500'.[18]

For reasons that will be clearer in the next chapters, I am more interested in answers to questions like 'What was most of the labour (and, by extension, land and capital) of region A (and B, and C) tied up in – was it, for example, in the rearing and/or fattening of cattle?' But the marketed specialties of sixteenth-century regions can be glimpsed using the relative tuning of Seasonal Types. Parishes can be placed in the new classes a, p, h, and x according to whether their autumn and spring indices were both greater than the mean autumn and spring indices for the whole non-market sample in that period (h-Type), or both less than the mean autumn and spring indices (x-Type); if either the autumn or the spring index was above the period mean, and the other index below the mean, then the parish was typed as either a-Type or p-Type. Figure 3.9 sketches these mean differentiators for the period 1561–1600. Figure 3.10 maps the relative types of parishes for that period; it can be compared with Figure 1.4, the Seasonal Type map for 1561–1600.

There is a symmetry of bias between the absolute Seasonal Types of Figure 3.8 and other records. Marriage seasonality cannot help but be

[18] Palliser, *Age of Elizabeth*, p. 162; Thirsk, 'Farming Regions', p. 14; Clay, *Economic Expansion*, p. 56.

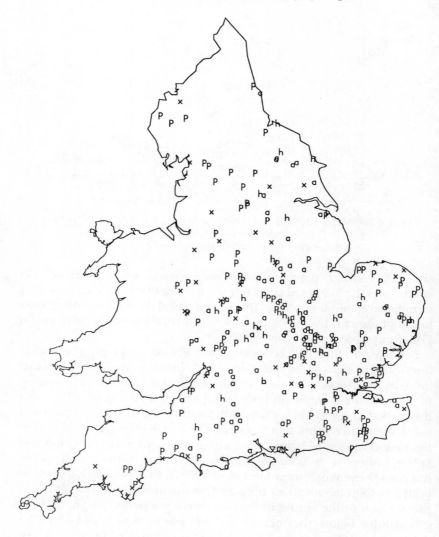

Figure 3.10 Relative types, 1561–1600
(non-market parishes)
Key: a AUT≥mean AUT, SPR<mean SPR
     h AUT≥mean AUT, SPR≥mean SPR
     p AUT<mean AUT, SPR≥mean SPR
     x AUT<mean AUT, SPR<mean SPR

dominated by the dominant activity, even if it is 'only' subsistence farming, while unusual goods catch the eye in inventories and records of trade. Tuning the seasonal boundaries of the types to an Elizabethan pitch makes East Anglia appear less arable (and incidentally finally allows some relative non-seasonality to emerge there); there is now no national blanket of grain harvesting, but widespread symbols for relative pastorality and heterogeneity. The marketed specialties of Elizabethan England have thus been encouraged to appear.

The finding of the study, however, is for regional specialization in the later seventeenth century in the employment of land and labour, and for enough coordination of regional markets at that time for the west to begin to marry in the spring. What would otherwise be a fault with this indirect method, that the grain harvest makes a stronger dent in marriage seasonality than does any other economic activity (save only the seasonal absence of marriage partners in fishing or transhumance), allows me to conclude that large portions of England had stopped producing their own grain by the end of the seventeenth century. I shall therefore prefer the absolute Seasonal Types of Figure 3.8 (often exploding the increasingly rare H-Types into A-Types and P-Types depending on whether the autumn or the spring index was the larger) to the relative types of Figure 3.9.

With the Seasonal Types now generated, their relation to the farming types mapped by Joan Thirsk in *The Agrarian History of England and Wales*, volume 4, *1500–1640* can be reinvestigated, using marriage data drawn from the late sixteenth and early seventeenth centuries (Table 3.4).[19] All of the Farming Types that involve dairying have here been extracted to form a separate category.[20] 'Mixed' parishes are grain-growing; 'wood pasture' are the three remaining wood pasture categories and 'open pasture' the four remaining open pasture categories.[21]

The expected values, shown under the observed values for each of the four Seasonal Types, are those that would have resulted if the sizes of the cells had been determined by the observed proportions of Farming Types and Seasonal Types, shown in the margins of the table. Thus, the upper left-hand corner of the table shows that while 71.5

[19] See above, Chapter 2. Wrigley and Schofield used the marriage seasonality of 1601–1720 for their contrast with the Thirsk farming types of 1500–1640 in *Population History of England*, Table 8.6, p. 304.

[20] They are parishes mapped into the first and last of the pasture farming types on the key of Figure 1 of Thirsk, 'Farming Regions', p. 4.

[21] I am indebted to the Cambridge Group for their mapping of their 404 parish sample onto the map of farming types; the parishes contained in Table 3.4 are the non-market portion of the 404 parish set.

Table 3.4. *Farming types (1500–1640) and Seasonal Types (1581–1620)*
(non-market parishes, 404 parish set)

Farming Types[a]	Seasonal Types				Totals	row %
	A-Type	P-Type	H-Type	X-Type		
mixed	97	7	17	17	138	55.4
(expected)	(71.5)	(18.8)	(15.0)	(32.7)		
dairy	11	1	6	7	25	10.0
(expected)	(13.0)	(3.4)	(2.7)	(5.9)		
wood pasture	12	11	3	13	39	15.7
(expected)	(20.2)	(5.3)	(4.2)	(4.2)		
open pasture	9	15	1	22	47	18.9
(expected)	(24.3)	(6.4)	(5.1)	(11.1)		
totals	129	34	27	59	249	
column %	51.8	13.7	10.8	23.7		100

[a] See text for the combinations of Farming Types.

parishes might have been expected to have been both autumn-
marrying A-Types and 'mixed', in fact ninety-seven parishes met both
criteria. This is just the direction of difference we would have
expected, since 'mixed' is used by Thirsk to mean grain-growing,
whatever else the parishes might have been doing. 'Mixed' regions
were not spring-marrying, as the junction of the 'mixed' row and the
'P-Type' column shows, with less than half the expected number
actually filling that cell.

'Wood pasture' and 'open pasture' regions were both less likely to
have contained autumn-marrying A-Types, and very much more
likely to have included non-seasonal, probably industrial, X-Types.
Both the 'open pasture' and the 'wood pasture' regions contain more
than twice their expected number of spring-marrying P-Type
parishes. The small number of H-Types is randomly associated with
'mixed' and 'wood pasture' farming types, unlikely to have been
found in open-pasture areas, but twice as likely as expected to have
been in one of Thirsk's dairying regions. The overall fit between the
two classifications is far from perfect, with a Cramer's V of 0.321, but at
least the directions of the imbalances between observed and expected
frequencies accord with the arguments advanced in defence of the
Seasonal Types. Chi-square for the comparison is 76.9, significantly
non-random somewhat unsurprisingly, given the large number of
observations.

Table 3.5. *Parishes by geobox*

Geobox/ number of parishes	Counties
10/24	Southwest: all of Cornwall, Devon and Somerset, and part of Dorset, Wiltshire, and Gloucestershire
11/15	Southcentral: all of Hampshire, and part of Wiltshire, Surrey, Sussex, Berkshire, Oxfordshire, and Buckinghamshire
12/44	Southeast: all of Kent, and part of Surrey, Sussex, Middlesex, Essex, Hertfordshire, and Buckinghamshire
20/11	South Marches: all of Herefordshire, and part of Gloucestershire, Worcestershire, Shropshire, and Staffordshire
21/30	South Midlands: part of Warwickshire, Gloucestershire, Oxfordshire, Northamptonshire, Buckinghamshire, Leicestershire, Worcestershire, and Staffordshire
22/53	East Anglia: all of Suffolk, Rutland, and Huntingdonshire, and part of Norfolk, Cambridgeshire, Bedfordshire, Hertfordshire, Essex, Middlesex, Buckinghamshire, and Northamptonshire
30/11	North Marches: part of Staffordshire, Shropshire, Cheshire, Lancashire, and Derbyshire
31/28	North Midlands: part of Leicestershire, Staffordshire, Lincolnshire, Nottinghamshire, Derbyshire, the West Riding, Warwickshire, Cheshire, and Lancashire
32/10	The Wash: part of Lincolnshire, Norfolk, Cambridgeshire, and Northamptonshire
40/10	Lancashire: part of Lancashire, Cumberland, Westmorland, the West Riding, and Derbyshire
41/27	West Riding: part of the West Riding, the North Riding, the East Riding, Lincolnshire, Nottinghamshire, and Cheshire
42/4	Flamborough to Spurn Head: part of Lincolnshire and the East Riding
50/4	Northwest: part of Cumberland, Westmorland, Northumberland, Durham, and the North Riding
51/8	Northeast: part of Durham, Northumberland, and the North Riding

Half the parishes represented in Table 3.4 were autumn-marrying A-Types, less than a quarter were non-seasonal X-Types, and only 14 per cent spring-marrying P-Types. As the earlier Table 3.3 indicated, these proportions changed, radically, over the seventeenth century. One hundred years on from Table 3.4, the proportion of A-Types had

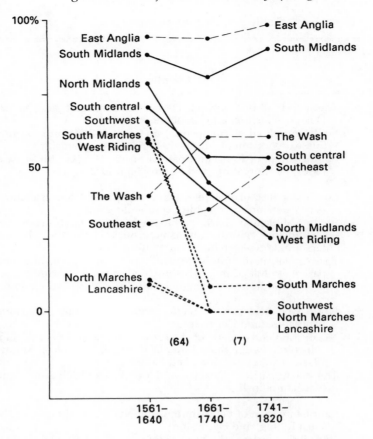

Figure 3.11(a) The proportion of parishes that were A-Type by geobox

dropped to a third, and those of P- and X-Types to 27 to 28 per cent each. But it was not just the relative numbers that changed. There was a strong spatial component to the shift as well, as the Seasonal Type maps of Chapter 1 (Figures 1.1 and 1.4) implied. The meaningfully jumbled Figure 3.11 (a–c) illustrates the spatial rearrangement. In each part of the figure, the percentage of non-market parishes falling into the A-Type (Figure 3.11a), P-Type (Figure 3.11b), and non-seasonal X-Type (Figure 3.11c) is graphed, for each 'geobox', rectilinear subdivisions of England along Ordnance Survey coordinates ending in (000). To help with following the fates of the Seasonal Types, the paths traced by the eastern geoboxes (southeast, East Anglia, and The Wash) are shown with long dashes, those of the western geoboxes

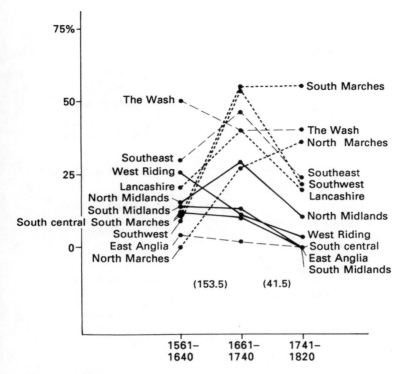

Figure 3.11(b) The proportion of parishes that were P-Type by geobox

(southwest, south and north Marches, and Lancashire) with short dashes, and the middle set (south central, south and north Midlands, and the West Riding) with solid lines. Table 3.5 shows the number of parishes in observation in each geobox, along with the counties contained within the geobox's boundary. Three northern geoboxes had fewer than eight parishes in observation, and are not included in Figure 3.11.

Each part of Figure 3.11 contains three observations for the eleven geoboxes, showing the proportions for 1561–1640 (early), 1661–1740 (middle), and 1741–1820 (late). Beneath the panels are simple measurements of rearrangements in ranking of the geoboxes, the sum of the squared differences in rank. Consider the change among the autumn-marrying A-Types (Figure 3.11a). Four geoboxes show very little variation over time, at the top and the bottom of the graph. East Anglia and the south Midlands head the list throughout, and the 'cloud-covered' (see Chapter 2) and industrial mid northwest (the

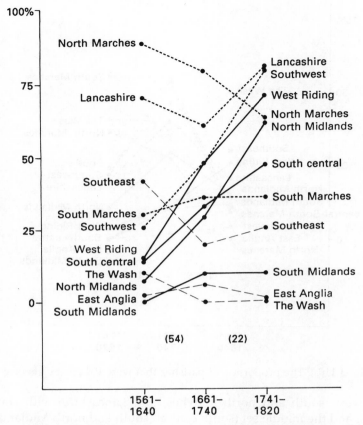

Figure 3.11(c) The proportion of parishes that were X-Type by geobox

north Marches and Lancashire) are consistently averse to autumn marriages. Four geoboxes decline in their proportion of A-Types. Two of them (the southwest and the south Marches) plummet between 1561–1640 and 1661–1740; by the second of the two long periods virtually every western parish had stopped marrying in the autumn. The proportion of A-Types in the north Midlands and the West Riding steadily declines (see Figure 3.11c for the coincident increase in the proportion of X-Types there). Only two of the eleven geoboxes buck the general trend and increase in their tendencies towards autumn marriages: the southeast, because it was deindustrializing (see Figure 3.11c), and The Wash, possibly reflecting the drainage of the fens (see Figure 3.11b for the decline in the percentage of P-Types there).

The crowded second part of the figure (3.11b) traces the proportions of P-Types. None of the percentages ever exceeds 55 per cent. There is little doubt that recognition of a parish as P-Type was more difficult than characterization as A-Type; Lent cut into spring marriages in the sixteenth and early seventeenth centuries, and there was little part-time work in lambing and calving. The figure is marked by an increase in the proportion of P-Types from 1561–1640 to 1661–1740, followed by a decline, with much rank-switching. Three western geoboxes (the southwest, and the south and north Marches) behave differently, moving from the bottom of the ranks (8, 9, and 11 of 11) to the top (1, 3, and 5); the proportion in the West Riding more simply declines, as had its proportion of A-Types in Figure 3.11a.

X-Types became more common over time (Figure 3.11c): six of the eleven geoboxes never saw a decline in the proportion of the parishes with non-seasonal marriages. The proportions of X-Types in the 'cloud-covered' geoboxes (North Marches and Lancashire) are high at the start, and some marriages were beginning to be celebrated in the spring (see Figure 3.11b). There is a sharp increase in the proportion of X-Types in the southwest, and the north Midlands and the West Riding are also shown to have been exchanging autumn-marrying A-Types (Figure 3.11a, above) for non-seasonal X-Types. Only two geoboxes (other than the North Marches and Lancashire) exhibit a decline in the proportion of X-Types from 1561–1640 to 1661–1740 (the Southeast and the Wash).

Most of the interregional rearrangement occurred between 1561–1640 and 1661–1740, as is shown by the decline in the sum of the squared differences in ranks below each panel. Interestingly, Cramer's V, here a measurement of the association between Seasonal Types and geoboxes, is stronger in each of these three long periods than it was for the Farming Types of Table 3.4, rising from 0.483 in 1561–1640 to 0.594 in 1741–1820.

The spatial variations can be condensed onto one graph, Figure 3.12; it demonstrates the changes over time and space through the movements of the mean east and mean north map coordinates (centroids) of non-market parishes in the three main Seasonal Types. The H-Type has been dropped, and H-Type parishes distributed to Types P and A, according to whether the spring index was greater than the autumn index; in Figure 3.8, imagine that lines (d) have vanished (and with them, the H-Type), leaving vector (a) as the differentiator between A- and P-Types. The non-seasonal industrial X-Type moves away from the southeast, towards the north and west. More surprisingly, the pastoral P-Type starts to the **east** of the arable A-Type; it then moves

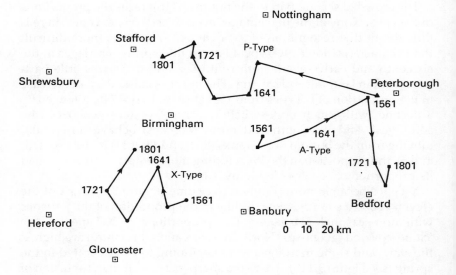

Figure 3.12 Centroids by Seasonal Types

strongly westwards, as the A-Type centroid moves more weakly east. Something drove the centroids apart, and upset the rankings by geobox. I shall be arguing, in the next chapters, that the driver was temporally and spatially specific changes in the seasonality of work.

Viewing work through the lens of marriage seasonality is an indirect method, fraught with difficulties that threaten its consistency over time and space. To use the method is implicitly to assume that Anglican registers of marriages recorded the decisions of labour in the eighteenth century as they had in the sixteenth century. I throw up my hands over the problem of the Interregnum, and its disruption to record keeping, fatally contaminating two of the forty year periods (1621–60 and 1641–80).

The autumn and the spring indices drawn from the Anglican registers are the foundations of the quantitative estimates that form this General View. Do the autumn and spring indices mean the same things, regardless of whether the parish is in the east or west, north or south? Is an autumn index of 200 in 1561–1600 equivalent to an autumn index of 200 in 1781–1820? Service in husbandry delivered many single young adults to the altar in the same month, but the proportion of young adults who were servants in husbandry changed over time; no adjustment can protect the method from this. Lent and Advent were less and less observed as periods inappropriate to weddings, but at least the remedy of subtracting the difference between the randomly expected sum of indices for March and December and the actual sum of indices for those two months from the autumn and spring indices is a crude correction. I rest happier with the accommodation to the differences over space in the timing of the harvest and of lambing and calving, the movable indices. I have retreated into the metaphor of 'cloud cover' to apologize for the impenetrable pattern of winter weddings in northern Staffordshire and Cheshire. For the rest of England, however, it is manifest that no inflexible traditions dictated the seasonality of marriages, because marriage seasons changed. If less than perfectly flexible customs intervened between the seasonality of work and the seasonality of marriage, the worst possible outcome would be a lag in the response of wedding customs to changing economic exigencies.

What caught and held my interest in marriage seasonality, after all, was not the snapshot of marriage seasons in Figure 8.4 of *The Population History of England*, so like a schoolbook picture of a pastoral west and arable east, but the realization that the seasonal pattern was not static, fixed. The north Midlands, the West Riding, and the west had all married in the autumn in the sixteenth century, the Weald only began to marry in the autumn and the spring in the later seventeenth century. The causes were spatially specific changes in the seasonality of work. I would hope that by this time that it is unsurprising that the map of Figure 1.1, Seasonal Types in 1701–40, made some sense. Making sense of the changes in ANG, in the centroids of the Seasonal Types, and in the changing proportions of Seasonal Types are the tasks of the next three chapters. Chapters 4 and 5 investigate the divergence of the paths carved by the arable and pastoral centroids of Figure 3.12, and Chapter 6 explores the industrialization and deindustrialization that combined to move the X-Type's centroid.

4

Agrarian change: the evidence

The evidence of the last chapter, introduced as if in demonstration of method, began to make a case for interrelated changes over time and space in agriculture and industry, and to locate the interlocked changes more strongly in the seventeenth than in its flanking centuries. But in the interest of best comprehending the early modern restructuring of the rural economy, the agricultural and industrial sectors will be conditionally sundered in the next three chapters, before returning to synthesis in Chapter 7. Chapter 6 will investigate rural industry, but this and the next chapter examine agriculture. What happened that the centre of pastoral marriage seasonality moved to the west and north in Figure 3.12, while that of arable seasonality moved eastward? What happened that in parishes in many parts of England (Figures 1.1 and 1.4), marriages ceased to cluster in the weeks after the grain harvest?

First, consider the timing of the change. The regionally specific switch from arable to pastoral seasonality did not occur at a constant rate over the long span of the marriage record. Table 4.1 compares the Seasonal Types, autumn-marrying (A), spring-marrying (P), non-seasonal (X), or heterogeneous (H), of parishes in 1661–1700 (the rows) with their typing in the next adjacent forty year period, 1701–40 (the columns). The expected frequencies are given in parentheses, under the observed frequencies; they would have resulted had the size of the sixteen cells been determined by the row and column totals (displayed in the table's margins). Thus, twenty-six of the 127 A-Types of 1661–1700 might have been expected to have become spring-marrying P-Types by 1701–40. But only three of those 127 turned from A-Type to P-Type; the switch from arable to pastoral seasonality had already occurred.

A set of twelve similar tables, comparing typing in all adjacent

Table 4.1. *Seasonal Type in 1701–40 by Seasonal Type in 1661–1700*[a]
(expected numbers in parentheses)

		Seasonal Type in 1701–40				
		X	A	P	H	n
Seasonal Type in 1661–1700	X	57	31	16	5	109
		(29)	(48)	(22)	(11)	
	A	17	92	3	15	127
		(34)	(55)	(26)	(12)	
	P	21	17	50	7	95
		(25)	(41)	(19)	(9)	
	H	6	25	7	10	48
		(13)	(21)	(10)	(5)	
	n	101	165	76	37	379

[a] Non-market parishes; see Chapter 3 for definition of Seasonal Types.

periods from 1541–80 to 1801–40, would disclose, clumsily, the timing of the change. Figure 4.1 instead compresses their message into a single set of values, Cramer's V, representing the independence (Cramer's V=−1.0) or dependence (Cramer's V=1.0) of seasonal typing on the seasonal typing of the parishes in the preceding period; Cramer's V for the comparison in Table 4.1 is 0.38. Since the number of H-Types becomes very small by the later comparisons, H-Type parishes have been reclassified, in many subsequent demonstrations (as they were in Figures 1.1 and 1.4 above), into A-Type and P-Type according to whether the AUT or the SPR index was larger. Cramer's V among these three types A, P, and X for the periods used in Table 4.1 is 0.42.

The figure confirms the changing constancy of seasonal typing over time. The instability of seasonality at first increased, and then diminished from the late seventeenth century; Cramer's V climbs to its maximum in the final comparison. Four of the comparisons are indicated by parentheses. Each involves the Interregnum, when the combination of temporary changes in marriage registration and general disorder in record keeping casts doubt on the accuracy of measurements of marriage seasons. But a pairing of periods that skips 1641–60 is indicated on the vertical axis, 1621 (1601–40) to 1681 (1661–1700), along with two measurements of change over earlier and later periods. The latest comparison of the three, 1681 (1661–1700) to 1741 (1721–60), stands alone, above the other two; the measure for

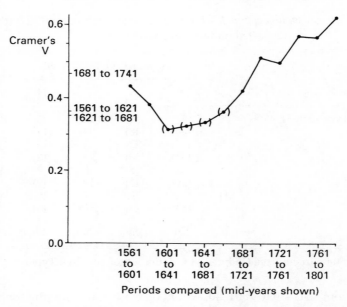

Figure 4.1 Cramer's V of interperiod Seasonal Types (A-Type, P-Type and X-Type)

change over the century before the Interregnum and the century that spans it are nearly identical, and below the measure for the century that followed. The value of Cramer's V for the latest possible (ungraphed) sixty-year comparison, 1761 (1741–80) to 1821 (1801–40), is 0.534.

That more changes in agricultural orientations were happening in the seventeenth than in the eighteenth century can also be inferred from eight maps, Figures 4.2 to 4.9. They display change over time and space, using the three longer periods: Early (1561–1640), Middle (1661–1740), and Late (1741–1820). The initial year of the Middle period is offset by twenty years from the end of the Early period in order to avoid the Interregnum. Four of the maps pick out the seasonal precursors of the arable and pastoral parishes of a period (Figures 4.4, 4.5, 4.8, and 4.9), and four their seasonal fates in the following period (Figures 4.2, 4.3, 4.6, and 4.7). The first four maps survey the eighty years before and after the Interregnum, the second four 1661–1740 and 1741–1820. A parallel exercise, showing the agricultural sources of rural industry, is reserved for Chapter 7.

The first two figures map the fates, in 1661–1740, of the A-Type (Figure 4.2) and P-Type (Figure 4.3) parishes of 1561–1640. That so

Figure 4.2 Fate of 1561–1640s A-Types in 1661–1740
Key: . still A-Type in 1661–1740
P new P-Type
X new X-Type

many English parishes had high autumnal seasonality of marriage in
the earlier period is evident from the density of Figure 4.2. Its symbols
represent the A-Type parishes of 1561–1640, the dots consistent
A-Types, the X's losers of agricultural seasonality, and the P's switchers

Figure 4.3 Fate of 1561–1640s P-Types in 1661–1740
Key: . still P-Type in 1661–1740
      A new A-Type
      X new X-Type

to vernal, pastoral, seasonality. Note the conjunction of P's and X's in the West Country and the Midlands: 1661–1740 will find the West Country nearly devoid of arable A-Types, and the Midlands a mixture of A-, P-, and X-Types.

That so few parishes achieved high spring seasonality in 1561–1640

Figure 4.4 Source in 1561–1640 of 1661–1740s A-Types
Key: . was A-Type in 1561–1640
P was P-Type in 1561–1640
X was X-Type in 1561–1640

is reflected in the sparseness of Figure 4.3, the seasonal fates in 1661–1740 of the very few P-Type parishes of the Early period. A's are converts to autumnal seasonality, as in northern Norfolk; X's, again, are industrializing, and dots are in the constant P-Types.

Figures 4.4 and 4.5 find the seasonal precursors, in 1561–1640, of the

Figure 4.5 Source in 1561–1640 of 1661–1740s P-Types
Key: . was P-Type in 1561–1640
A was A-Type in 1561–1640
X was X-Type in 1561–1640

A- and the P-Types of 1661–1740. The maps are more equally dense than were the first two, because there were many more P-Type parishes (and fewer A-Types) in 1661–1740 than in 1561–1640. Figure 4.4, mapping 1661–1740s A-Types, reveals some recruitment to that arable pattern of seasonality, in south central parishes and Norfolk.

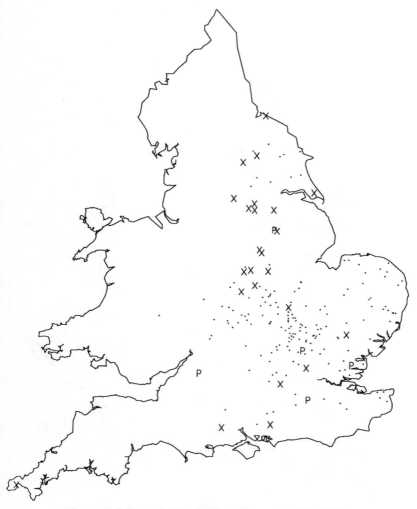

Figure 4.6 Fate of 1661–1740s A-Types in 1741–1820
Key: . still A-Type in 1741–1820
      P new P-Type
      X new X-Type

Far more recruitment into the P-Type is indicated by Figure 4.5. The Weald is contributing mainly via deindustrialization, as are pockets in the west; in the West Country and the Midlands, 'dearablization' is the principal source.

The next four maps repeat the exercise for 1661–1740 and 1741–1820.

Figure 4.7 Fate of 1661–1740s P-Types in 1741–1820
Key: .   still P-Type in 1741–1820
A new A-Type
X new X-Type

The first two present the fates in 1741–1820 of the A- and P-Types of
1661–1740. If the A-Types of 1661–1740 were going anywhere by
1741–1820 (Figure 4.6), it was towards the loss of agricultural seasonality, mapped as 'X', especially in the northeast Midlands and the West
Riding of Yorkshire.

Figure 4.8 Source in 1661–1740 of 1741–1820s A-Types
Key: . was A-Type in 1661–1740
P was P-Type in 1661–1740
X was X-Type in 1661–1740

In Figure 4.7, a depiction of the seasonal fates of the spring-marrying parishes of 1661–1740, a reversion to arable (mapped as 'A') is obvious, especially in the southeast and the Midlands.

Finally, Figures 4.8 and 4.9 give an impression of the spatial spread of the A- and P-Types of 1741–1820. The reversion to A-Type (mapped

Figure 4.9 Source in 1661–1740 of 1741–1820s P-Types
Key: . was P-Type in 1661–1740
A was A-Type in 1661–1740
X was X-Type in 1661–1740

as 'P'), and deindustrialization to A-Type (mapped as 'X'), are both
represented on Figure 4.8.

Figure 4.9, the seasonal sources of 1741–1820s P-Types, has grown
sparse again, as was Figure 4.3, which had displayed the seasonal
fates of 1561–1640s P-Types, but here the impression is somewhat
formed by the wide spacing of the self-effacing dots, marking consist-

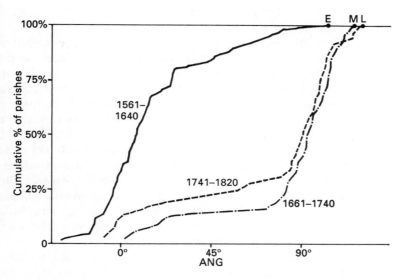

Figure 4.10 Cumulative frequency of ANG, early, middle and late: west

ently spring-marrying parishes, many more of which are present than were on the earlier figure. Boundaries of regions to be discussed in the next pages are marked on the map.

Several areas of interesting agricultural change emerge from the eight maps. ANG, the variable that measured the relative strength of spring to autumn marriage seasonality in the last chapter, can be applied to them. The greater the value of ANG, the higher is the spring index relative to the autumn index; a value of 45° indicates equality between the two indices (Chapter 3 discussed the derivation of the variable ANG; it is the angle formed at the intersection of the vector drawn from (100,100) to the (autumn, spring) combination and the line where the spring index=100). Regions, in the next figures, are large boxes conveniently defined using Ordnance Survey map coordinates (I took advantage of the sparseness of Figure 4.9 to sketch the boundaries of the regions). Three of the large (mostly) rectilinear 'Regions' will be considered here (I shall return to the southeast in the next chapter); for each, the cumulative frequency distribution of ANG, by parishes and periods, is presented. The computation of the measure ANG involved dropping non-seasonal X-Type parishes from the sample in each period; market towns are also excluded. Arbitrary in outline, the regions illustrate competing models of homogeneity, East Anglia uniformity of seasonality and constancy over time, but the west uniformity of change. The Midlands, homogeneous at first, became heterogeneous with time.

Figure 4.10 begins with the most dramatic change, the inversion of the distribution of the west, which contains all the non-market parishes in the 542-parish set in Cornwall, Devon, Somerset, Gloucestershire, Herefordshire, Shropshire, Cheshire, and Lancashire, and in the westernmost parts of Yorkshire's West Riding, Worcestershire, Staffordshire, Dorset, and Wiltshire. The west was a nearly homogeneous autumn-marrying region in the sixteenth and early seventeenth centuries; most of its parishes are then bunched to the left of the figure, indicating a low ratio of spring to autumn indices. In 80 per cent of the parishes of 1561–1640, ANG was 30° or lower. But by 1661–1740, the parishes crowd to the right of the figure; only 12 per cent of parishes had ANGs of less than 30° then, indicating a wholesale shift from arable employment to employment in rearing as the main agricultural determinant of marriage seasonality.

Over the past few centuries, only the Common Agricultural Policy succeeded in making the west look arable. Hoskins pointed to the difficulty of imagining an arable west in the grassland Devon of the mid twentieth century.[1] But Norden had described in 1618 the arable techniques of the southwest as if entirely unremarkable, and an impression of declining arable, consistent with Figure 4.10, is conveyed by a dispute over Gloucestershire land described as 'old tyme arable' in 1631.[2] Yarranton in 1677 was looking back to the time when Hereford, adopting clover in his time, had been an exporter of grain to Wales, and the theme of declining exports of grain from the west has been taken up in this century by Chartres and Everitt.[3]

The change undergone in East Anglia is more subtle, in part because observing it involves one of the blind spots of the method (the region contains all the sample's non-market parishes in Bedfordshire, Cambridgeshire, Huntingdonshire, Norfolk, and Suffolk, in southern Northamptonshire, and in northern Essex and Hertfordshire). In Figure 4.11, the distribution of the parishes is always gathered at the arable left (high autumn, low spring indices). Over time, the distribution just succeeds in becoming even more bunched, with the pastoral tail of the sixteenth and early seventeenth century (in 1561–1640, 12 per cent of the region's parishes had ANG's greater than 30°) disappearing, absorbed into the regionally homogeneous mass of the

[1] Hoskins, *Devon*, pp. 95–7.
[2] Norden, *Surveyors*, pp. 192–3; Finberg, *Gloucestershire*, pp. 70–1.
[3] Yarranton, *England's Improvement*, p. 157; Chartres, *Internal Trade*, p. 15; Everitt, 'Marketing', p. 526.

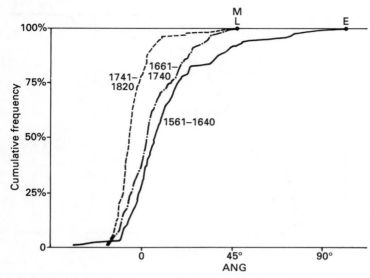

Figure 4.11 Cumulative frequency of ANG, early, middle and late: East Anglia

later eighteenth century. The earlier period's spring-marrying parishes were in Norfolk, Suffolk, and Essex; only one of East Anglia's ninety-five sampled parishes registered enough spring weddings in 1741–1820 for ANG to reach the moderate standard of 30°.

Pastoral activities had not disappeared from the area (although complaints about the quality of the region's cheeses had increased), but the great sheep walks of the fifteenth and sixteenth centuries had yielded to the specialized fattening of cattle and sheep bred in (spring-marrying) western and more northern areas. Without the supervision needed in lambing and calving, no reason remained for the region to show a seasonal pattern of marriage influenced by anything but the harvest of fodder crops (and of course of wheat, and of barley for the brewers of England and the Netherlands).[4]

The Midlands had already distinguished itself in Figure 1.1 by its late seventeenth- and eighteenth-century heterogeneity. Non-seasonal X-Types, autumn-marrying A-Types, and spring-marrying P-Types crowded together there in a patchwork of regional seasonality. Calculating the relative strength of autumn and spring indices

[4] Reyce and Defoe commented on the cheese (Reyce, *Suffolk*, p. 40 and Defoe, *A Tour*, p. 74); Jones, *Season and Prices*, p. 78; Holderness, 'East Anglia', pp. 227, 234–6; Bowden, 'Agricultural Prices', 1967, p. 644; Overton, 'Diffusion', pp. 205–21.

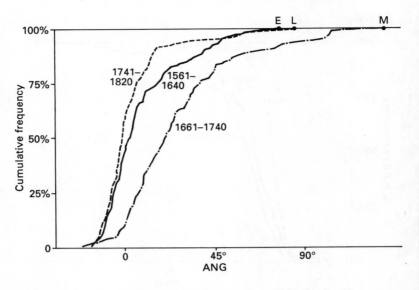

Figure 4.12 Cumulative frequency of ANG, early, middle and late: Midlands

with ANG involved dropping a period's X-Types from the region's sample for that period, but, as Figure 4.12 discloses, the region is still interestingly different (the region contains all the sample's non-market parishes in Nottinghamshire, Leicestershire, Warwickshire, Derbyshire, and Oxfordshire, in southwestern Lincolnshire, and in the southernmost West Riding). Instead of the unidirectional (if opposing) change exhibited by the East Anglian and western regions, the Midlands region first sends a number of its parishes out to the green pastures of spring seasonality in 1661–1740, but then calls them back to the autumn, with even greater positive skewness in 1741–1820 than the region had managed in 1561–1640.

That most of the Midlands appears so arable in the earliest period graphed (1561–1640) would have come as no surprise to some English contemporaries, although any permanent grass seemed to fill Continental visitors with wonder.[5] Blith, writing in 1649, described the 'gallant corn counties' in western Warwickshire, northern Worcestershire, and Staffordshire, among others, that had formerly been wooded.[6] Plattes found 'the best, and purest Wheate in Europe' (or so he claimed) growing in the Vale of Belvoir in Leicestershire.[7] Leland had described a southeastern Warwickshire that was 'plentifull of

[5] Thirsk, 'Introduction' (1967c), pp. xxix–xxxii.   [6] Blith, *English*, p. 40.
[7] Plattes, *A Discovery*, p. 47.

corne' in the second quarter of the sixteenth century, while pasture reigned there by the end of the eighteenth century.[8]

That most of the Midlands appears to arable in that earliest period the General View can discern is also a minor trick of the light. More's early sixteenth-century criticism of enclosures for pasture had stressed their low opportunities for employment, and thinly settled, recently depopulated parishes did not witness enough weddings (twenty-four) in most forty year periods to come into observation at all.[9] Wormleighton, Warwickshire, mentioned above in Chapter 2, is an example of an early enclosed parish with a tiny number of marriages. And Skipp described the farmers of the Forest of Arden as producing grain on a subsistence basis in the later sixteenth and early seventeenth centuries.[10] Grain produced for the farming family's own use was harvested in the same season as grain produced for more distant markets, so no distinction in marriage seasonality would be expected between subsistence and commerical orientations of the area.

Skipp found greater commercial output of grain in the second half of the seventeenth century,[11] but this is not at all inconsistent with the stretching out of the distribution of ANG over the whole of the Midlands region in 1661–1740; the distribution still retained a heavy low ANG (high autumn) anchor. In south Staffordshire, Frost noted a decline in the value of livestock in probate inventories of farmers of the late seventeenth and early eighteenth centuries.[12] It is a subset of the parishes of the Midlands region that made the excursion into spring seasonality, and that subset's behaviour is more than a little consistent with Broad's analysis of agrarian change in the region. He found widespread alternate husbandry, with grain grown on a semi-subsistence basis, before the mid seventeenth century, followed by a reversion to permanent grass in the south and east Midlands in the later seventeenth century.[13] Permanent pasture, if not used only for fattening beasts reared elsewhere, would have given rise to vernal weddings, which we find in the high ANG subset of Figure 4.12, while the earlier alternate husbandry would have looked arable, autumn-marrying, the grain harvest's labour peak being sharper than that of lambing and calving. Defoe captured the patchwork in the 1720s, finding Leicestershire and Northamptonshire both vast maga-

[8] John Leland, cited in Slater, *English Peasantry*, p. 205; Wedge, *A General View*, p. 8.
[9] On the region's cattle ranching, see also Alcock, *Warwickshire Grazier*.
[10] Skipp, 'Economic and Social Change', p. 91.
[11] *Ibid.*, p. 91.   [12] Frost, 'Yeoman and Metal Smiths', p. 33.
[13] Broad, 'Alternate Husbandry', p. 78.

zines of wool and major suppliers, with Bedfordshire, of wheat for the mills of Hertfordshire.[14]

That most of the inhabitants of the agricultural Midlands married in the autumn in the last of the periods graphed on Figure 4.12 is perhaps more surprising. Much of the region, it should be remembered, had remained autumn-marrying through the three long periods. But I find myself making excuses for this indirect method in accounting for the apparent reblanketing by autumn weddings of nearly the whole of the region (only 6 per cent of the ninety-two seasonal parishes in observation there in 1741–1820 has a higher spring than autumn index of marriages, compared with 19 per cent in 1661–1740). This is no mere trick of the light, but a combination of three of the most regretted blindnesses of the method.

One was alluded to above. Convertible husbandry, the very substance of the Agricultural Revolution, may have been slower in penetrating the heavy clay of the region than it was the chalk lands, but there is no reason to doubt that the grain harvest was the greediest time for employment in convertible husbandry, and thus the major determinant of the seasonality of weddings (and the hiring of farm servants), no matter how intricate the rotation.[15] Secondly, one need only dip into accounts of the agriculture of the region in the later eighteenth century to find references to dairying.[16] As discussed in Chapter 2, dairying is resistant to identification via marriage seasonality. Milking and cheese- and butter-making could be year-round occupations, and, if not year-round, the slack time for work began in the autumn, as it did with grain production. Hay-making at mid summer and again in late summer was labour-using, and reinforced the sensible choice of autumn as a time for weddings. And calving was not restricted to the spring; Fussell noted that only better fodder than hay was necessary for winter milk.[17]

'Better fodder' is the third and last of the complications posed by the Midlands in the eighteenth and early nineteenth centuries. As already noted in connection with the ever more congested low ANG of East Anglia, artificial fodder was harvested in the same general season, late summer and early autumn, as was the grain grown for more direct human consumption. Lawrence praised the stall feeding of animals, warning that folding, one alternative, endangered the delicate

---

14 Defoe, *Compleat English Tradesman*, volume 2 (part 2), pp. 32, 136.
15 Jones, 'Agriculture and Economic Growth', pp. 1–18.
16 See for example Wedge, 'A General View', p. 34.
17 Fussell, *English Dairy Farmer*, p. 65. Fussell gives a good description of the time-consuming work in hay-making, with the cut hay spread to dry on the ground each morning, and cocked each night.

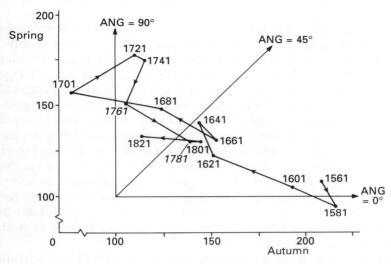

Figure 4.13 Autumn and spring/summer indices in Bottesford, Leics.

sheep.[18] Edward Laurence found that clover trebled the number of cows that could be carried on a given amount of land, compared with natural grass; Mortimer went further, claiming one acre of clover the equal of five to six acres of common grass.[19] And the dairying of the previous paragraph was by no means the only reason for producing sown fodder; cattle reared in the southwest and Wales were 'finished' in, among other regions, the Midlands.[20]

One of the Midland parishes in the sample is Bottesford, Leics., the agricultural foil for protoindustrial Shepshed in Levine's *Family Formation*. Figure 4.13 finds it an exemplar of the region's tendency to forsake autumn marriages as the seventeenth century progressed (reference lines have been included showing values of ANG, for comparison with the preceding figures). Levine traced the agrarian changes in the parish, from the cultivation of wheat in the sixteenth and early seventeenth centuries, through increased pastoral farming over the later seventeenth century, to dairying and the making of Stilton in the first half of the nineteenth century.[21] Bottesford's marriage seasons reflect the shift to pastoral farming in the swing

[18] Lawrence, *General Treatise*, p. 127; Lawrence, *New Farmer's Calendar*, p. 523.
[19] Laurence, *Duty*, p. 184; Mortimer, *Whole Art*, p. 30.
[20] Fussell and Goodman, 'Eighteenth Century Traffic', p. 216.
[21] Levine, *Family Formation*, pp. 89–90.

towards spring marriages; the pattern then loses its specificity with the shift to less seasonal dairying.

Botteford was enclosed by Act in 1770 (the two observations containing that year are italicized in Figure 4.13); 89 per cent of the parish's land was involved in its Parliamentary Enclosure. Debates over enclosure surface several times over the span of the marriage record, and have continued into the present day. Were the hedges of new enclosures shelter for livestock, for example, or havens for birds 'and other vermine'?[22] One abiding issue has been the association of enclosure with depopulation, from More's sheep 'so wild they devour human beings themselves' in the early sixteenth century (just before the start of marriage registration), through the reminders by Hartlib (1655) and Yarranton (1677) of the argument that enclosure saw a 'Boy and his Dog' displacing ten ploughteams and forty workers, to the twentieth-century's debates.[23] Another issue has been the flexibility or rigidity of open-field practices. Marriage seasons can be made to make a small contribution to these debates.

In my sample of 542 parishes are twenty-four other Leicestershire and thirty-one Northamptonshire parishes. Nine of the fifty-six have no record of Parliamentary Enclosure; they form an Old Enclosed group, enclosed by agreement before the parliamentary era, some like Courteenhall, Northants., within the span of the marriage series (a transcript of the Courteenhall enclosure agreement of 1650 is in the Northamptonshire Record Office (86P/32, 33)). The other Old Enclosed parishes, from the perspective of the eighteenth century, are Fotheringay, Little Billing, Loddington, Marholm, and Sywell in Northamptonshire and Enderby, Kirby Muxloe, and Wymondham in Leicestershire.[24] Fifteen of the fifty-six, Bottesford among them, have a very different history of enclosure; they all meet an arbitrary standard of having been enclosed by Act of Parliament with an enclosure award of arable land amounting to at least 75 per cent of the parish's acreage in the 1831 census. The parishes of Parliamentary Enclosure (with dates of enclosure Acts/Awards in parentheses) are Ashfordby (1761/62), Bottesford (1770/72), Great Bowden (1776/77), Husbands Bosworth (1764/65), Kibworth Beauchamp (1779/80), Long Clawson (1779/80), Market Harborough (1776/77), Medbourn

---

[22] Worlidge, *Systema Agriculturae*, pp. 10–13; Nourse, *Campania Foelix*, p. 27.
[23] More, *Utopia*, p. 24; Hartlib, *His Legacie*, p. 45; Yarranton, *England's Improvement*, p. 50; Johnson, *Disappearance*; Gonner, *Common Land*; Chambers, 'Enclosure and Labour Supply', pp. 391–43; Mingay, *Enclosure*; Neeson, 'Common Right'; Turner, *Enclosures in Britain*.
[24] Tate, *A Domesday*. On the extent of enclosure before the eighteenth century see Wordie, 'Chronology', pp. 494–5.

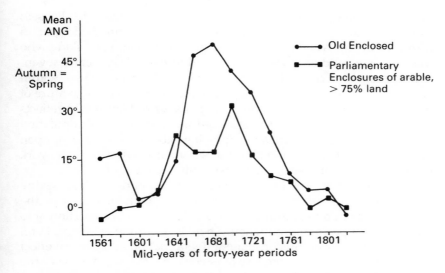

Figure 4.14 Enclosure and seasonality
ANG by enclosure, 24 Leics. and Northants. parishes

(1842/44), Saddington (1770/71), and Wigston Magna (1764/66) in Leicestershire and Earls Barton (1771/72), East Farndon (1780/81), Naseby (1820/22), Raundes (1797/1800), and Winwick (1794/97) in Northamptonshire (Tate, 1978).

What, then, do marriage seasons reveal about enclosure? Figure 4.14 plots ANG over time for the two sets of parishes, the Old Enclosed and the Parliamentary Enclosures. Both sets trace an inverted U over the later seventeenth and early eighteenth centuries (as would have ANG for the whole Midlands region of Figure 4.12), but the rise in ANG is stronger for the Old Enclosed group. A higher value of ANG indicates greater vernal, pastoral, seasonality, so the figure gives support both to the notion of some flexibility of practice within the open fields of the parishes of Parliamentary Enclosure in the century **before** their enclosure, as argued, for example, by Havinden, and for the still greater flexibility of farming practice in severalty.[25] Alternately, the figure might be more simply interpreted as showing that the land relatively better suited to pasture (or less suited to grain production) was enclosed first.

Ernle had categorically asserted that agricultural improvements awaited enclosure; in a sense, McCloskey followed, by finding the risk-aversion met by scattered strips a compensating advantage to

[25] Havinden, 'Agricultural Progress', pp. 74–82.

open fields, given the otherwise rigid practice they entailed.[26] Fussell, though, argued against what he felt to be a convention of agrarian history, the impossibility of altering open-field rotations, asking who the Improvers audience was, and indeed Robert Loder's early seventeenth-century account had implied some flexibility, even within two-field systems.[27] It is possible, of course, that the vernal venture of marriage seasonality in the still open parishes of Figure 4.14 reflects nothing more than the ability of closed parishes to resist population increase (see below), instead employing labour from nearby open parishes, and thereby imposing the seasonal rhythm of their work upon the pattern of marriages in their still open neighbours.

Over the eighteenth century, both sets of parishes lose spring marriages to the autumn, and ANG drops, with increases in the relative price of grain pointing farmers either to grain production or to more efficient pastoral production. There is no strong evidence, here, for permanent grass and consequent depopulation as a general effect of either the state or the process of enclosure, after the middle of the eighteenth century.[28] Dairying (as in Bottesford), the new rotations of convertible husbandry, and the cultivation of artificial fodder for stall feeding could all have made autumn the sensible marriage season, but all are labour using, far from the domain of the Boy and his Dog.

The next figure (Figure 4.15) plots mean totals of marriages in the Old Enclosed and the Parliamentary Enclosed groups over time (the number of Acts of enclosure per period are shown above the horizontal axis). Nearly identical in the first plotted period (1541–80), when many of the Old Enclosed parishes were still open, the mean totals then separate, with the parishes of Parliamentary Enclosure thereafter registering more marriages, on average, than the Old Enclosed group. The difference widens abruptly in the eighteenth century. Industrialization within the open parishes of the set cannot account for the rapid increase in marriages there; rural industrial parishes should have been non-seasonal X-Types, and parishes drop out of these samples whenever they lose enough autumn or spring weddings to fall into the X-Type's trap.

The graph suggests instead that not only was sixteenth and seven-

---

[26] Ernle, *English Farming*, p. 103; McCloskey, 'Enclosure', pp. 15–35, and McCloskey, 'English Open Fields', pp. 124–70.

[27] Fussell, *Robert Loder's Farm Accounts*; Fussell, *Old English Farming Books*, p. 73.

[28] Cf. the complaint reported in Hoskins, that the immediate effect of Parliamentary Enclosure in Leicestershire was conversion to permanent pasture, with insufficient grain grown for local needs (*Midland Peasant*, pp. 261–2). Permanent grass should have led to spring marriages, except where the grass was used mainly for fattening, with little rearing.

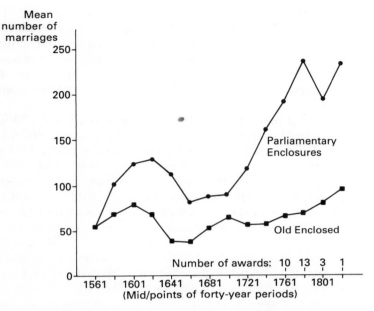

Figure 4.15 Enclosure and mean marriage totals
24 Leics. and Northants. parishes

teenth-century enclosure depopulating, the Old Enclosed parishes continued to resist population increase within their boundaries, by denying space for the settlement of newly formed couples, whatever the prevailing agricultural practice, and very nearly whatever the national rates of population increase. Palliser noted that 98 per cent of the sixteenth-century complaints about depopulating enclosures came from ten Midlands counties, including Northamptonshire and Leicestershire.[29] The curve for the parishes of Parliamentary Enclosure may well have been reflecting that set's function as open parishes, supplying residence for labour employed in both the Old Enclosed and industrializing parishes. The mean marriage total for the parishes being enclosed does dip once, in 1781–1820; all but two of the fifteen parishes in that group had been enclosed by 1820, but it would take a braver writer than I to find evidence for further depopulation in that dip.

Seventeenth-century enclosures in this region, however, *were* associated with the laying down of permanent grass, and one worry registered by opponents of enclosure in that century was 'If every one

[29] Palliser, *The Age of Elizabeth*, p. 181.

should lay sward that would, how shall we do for bread?'[30] The patchwork of A-Type, P-Type, and X-Type parishes that characterizes the Midlands in the late seventeenth and early eighteenth centuries (and at that time no other large English region) suggests an answer: supplies of grain and other foodstuffs were being assured through intraregional specialization, of which the enclosures for pasture were a part.

But the national pattern suggests increasing specialization *between* larger regions, only possible when a supply of basic foodstuffs can be organized and distributed to the specialized producers of other things. As De Vries put it, 'one cannot live on butter, cheese, and cabbage alone; and one cannot live on hemp, madder, flax, and coleseed at all'.[31] That supplies of grain were reaching more distant consumers, discontinuously more distant consumers, is ultimately the message of Figure 4.16. The parishes in the 542-parish national sample that were not market towns were divided into two groups for each forty year period from 1541–80 to 1801–40 on the basis of their indices of autumn marriages. The first group, the putative grain harvesters, were those parishes that registered an autumn index of at least 150 in the relevant period. The rest of the parishes in observation in that period were presumed to be eaters of bread and drinkers of ale made from the first group's grain. Next, the straight-line distance of each of the consuming parishes to its nearest harvesting 'neighbour' was found, and finally the means of these minimum distances between consumers and harvesters were calculated over all the consuming parishes (the unreliable computations involving the Interregnum are isolated in parentheses).

At first, the minimum distance falls, but this is in large part caused by the sample's becoming denser over time. In 1541–80, for example, there are only 229 parishes in observation (fifty-nine consumers seeking among 170 harvesters for a nearest neighbour). So, despite this being the highest ratio of harvesters to consumers in the series, the 170 harvesting parishes are relatively thinly spread over the map. The mean minimum distances are thus without doubt greater than they would have been with more surviving registers among the sample's parishes. By 1581–1620, the number of parishes in observation grows to 355 (227 harvesting targets), and from 1601–40 the sample size is almost steady, between 372 and 401 parishes (square

---

[30] Atwell, *Faithfull Surveyour*, p. 101. Broad noted that the stagnation in rents after 1660 encouraged enclosure for permanent pasture, since pasture rents remained higher than arable ('Alternate Husbandry', p. 82).
[31] De Vries, *Dutch Rural Economy*, p. 164.

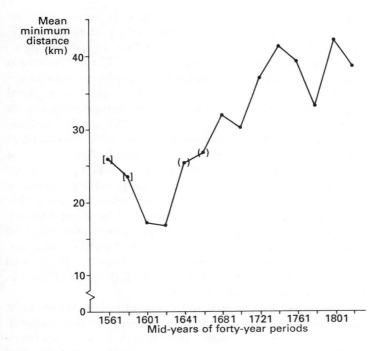

Figure 4.16 Mean minimum distance of consuming from harvesting parishes

brackets indicate the period of growth in the size of the sample). The sample size stabilizes in the early seventeenth century. The mean minimum distance to the nearest harvesting parish was then only 17 km, and it remained low until the beginning of the Interregnum.[32] But by 1721–60 the mean distance had increased to 42 km. There is thus a discontinuity in the series, and the break occurred in the second half of the seventeenth century.

Given that discontinuity, and the change and consolidation of Seasonal Types (Cramer's V, Figure 4.1), and the partitioning of England into regions of seasonality between 1561–1600 (Figure 1.4) and 1701–40 (Figure 1.1), can it come as any surprise that the agricultural manuals and farming books of the seventeenth century are full of turmoil and change, while those of the consolidating eighteenth century are models of placidity? In the vivid writing of

[32] The finding accords well with Kerridge, who found tillage everywhere in the sixteenth and seventeenth centuries. Kerridge, *Agricultural Revolution*.

Atwell (1658), Blith (1649), and Plattes (1639), all is tumult.[33] In the empiricism of the manuals of the eighteenth century, the emphasis is more on best practice within an established pattern of specialization. Laurence, for example, expressed impatience in 1727 with backward tenants, but urged caution on landlords in applying remedies.[34] Yarranton wrote in the midst of the period of greatest regional differentiation, and his works are bursting with infinite potential for change and improvement.[35] Half a century later, Defoe's descriptions may be overflowing with bustle, but not with volcanic upheaval (1727 and 1724–6). Stubborn Timothy Nourse, who had belligerent, ironic praise for the German custom of drinking from a cocked pistol, since the unsteady hand of the imbiber would help rid the world of drunkards,[36] sat in Herefordshire at the cusp of differentiation in 1701 railing against regional specialization, finding it a Continental failing; he disliked enclosure, too (except the enclosure of the wastes that had made cottagers unfit for honest employment), and he liked an abundance of poor, 'where they are kept in good order'.[37] On the last concern he echoed Reyce, who had found Suffolk sadly lacking in poor labourers desperate for employment.[38]

What had happened, that there was an agricultural drama to match the political convulsion of the seventeenth century, and that England, in consequence, became regionally differentiated in its marriage seasonality? What has been found is regional specialization of the rural economy, with many implications for productivity increase in agriculture, interregional migration, and the growth of rural industry, to be taken up in the next chapters.

The specialization occurred in the second half of the seventeenth century. How well does this placement synchronize with the judgements of this century? The findings do no more than accord with the timing suggested in many recent studies. Thirsk wrote of the farming systems of England becoming 'more sharply differentiated economically and socially' in the second half of the seventeenth century (although curiously, perhaps, she had earlier found farming specializations polarized by economic trends in the sixteenth cen-

---

[33] But cf. Worlidge, *Systema Agriculturae*. See Wrightson's discussion of the language of disorder in the seventeenth century in *English Society*, p. 149.

[34] Laurence, *Duty*; see also Lisle, *Observations*, Lawrence, *General Treatise* and *New Farmer's Calendar*, and Mortimer, *Whole Art*.

[35] Yarranton, *England's Improvement*; he provided an interestingly nearsighted survey of the regional specialization of his day, never looking north from Nottinghamshire and Lincolnshire on the east coast, nor from Herefordshire in the west, nor southwest from Dorset and Somerset.

[36] Nourse, *Campania Foelix*, p. 178.   [37] *Ibid.*, pp. 13ff., 26–7, 100.

[38] Reyce, *Suffolk*, p. 56.

tury).[39] Chambers and Mingay concurred, at least on the end-date of the process, detecting considerable specialization and commercial orientation in the early eighteenth century.[40] That England was still a country of autonomous regions in 1700 is not common currency today, although Westerfield had maintained that there was 'meager local specialization' for his period (1660–1760), John that autonomy persisted well into the eighteenth century, and Eversley that a national grain market awaited the Canal Age.[41]

Judgements for regional specialization predating the late seventeenth century fall into four groups. In some surveys, the change is trowelled neatly over the whole of the early modern period (see Chapter 1). The second set are limited to the area close to London, and there is no reason to doubt that they are correct, for that area, for the sixteenth and early seventeenth centuries (see below, Chapter 5).[42] A third set can be found in period-bound studies that end before the mid seventeenth century, whose authors may suspect that market integration and regional specialization imply progress, and borrow some for their own period. One gets this sense from Everitt's describing the specialization of market functions as having occurred 'by the end of the period [1640], or a little after', in the fourth volume of *The Agrarian History of England and Wales (1500–1640)*; Palliser occasionally succumbed in *The Age of Elizabeth*, but he agreed on one important aspect of the splitting into arable and pastoral specializations, that the sixteenth and early seventeenth centuries, with their increasing grain prices and population pressure on land, were not the best of times to contemplate increasing livestock holdings.[43] The works forming the fourth and final group were discussed in the last chapter. In them, the presence of marketed specialties of regions in the sixteenth century was called regional specialization.

It is useful, however, to retain a distinction between the existence of marketed specialties and regional specialization. The production of beef, or cheese, or wool, combined with subsistence crops of grain, was not the situation to which Atwell, teacher of mathematics at Cambridge, had reacted, when he asked where farmers would get their bread, if all turned their land to grass. He correctly grasped the

---

[39] Thirsk, 'Seventeenth-Century Agriculture', p. 148; Thirsk, 'Farming Regions', p. 3.
[40] Chambers and Mingay, *Agricultural Revolution*, p. 21.
[41] Westerfield, *Middlemen*, p. 130; John, 'Course of Agricultural Change', pp. 126–7; Eversley, 'Home Market', p. 211.
[42] Supple, *Commercial Crisis*, p. 3
[43] Everitt, 'Marketing', p. 490; Palliser, *The Age of Elizabeth*, p. 195, following Bridbury, 'Sixteenth-Century Farming', pp. 538–56.

implications of the changes in agricultural orientation that surrounded him in the seventeenth century, and answered his own question:

I do not say I would have every one that list should lay down for sward; but this I say, I would have all ground turn'd to the most advantage, first of the Common-wealth, then of the Owner.[44]

The next chapter will investigate the likely causes of the regional agricultural differentiation, and the nature of the advantages gained.

[44] Atwell, *Faithfull Surveyour*, p. 101.

5

Regional specialization, causes and consequences

An interpretive problem arises in the search for causes of the regional agricultural divergence. High autumn indices of marriages are ambivalent. They could have resulted from high employment in grain production for integrated markets and extralocal consumption, or from a lack of market integration between places, necessitating the subsistence production of grain. Parishes might have been producing grain, no matter what other additional employments were practised, because grain, the main foodstuff, was not being obtained from more distant suppliers. They would have been 'bound and localized' economies, with grain as the subsistence crop.[1] Low autumn seasonality, in contrast, is *prima facie* evidence for market orientation; it can only mean that the area is dependent on interregional trade for its supply of breadstuffs. The observed shift away from autumn seasonality in some regions, and its retention in others, is therefore subject to multiple constructions, not always mutually exclusive:

1. thoroughly integrated regions could have been readjusting their market-oriented specializations in response to changes in relative prices; or
2. regions could have been becoming better integrated into supraregional or international markets, dropping their dependence on local grain supplies; or
3. households in areas less suited to growing grain could have been becoming better integrated into market production, dropping the subsistence output of grain in favour of other products, Tawney's peasantry yielding to capitalist agriculture.[2]

[1] De Vries, *Dutch Rural Economy*, p. 1.
[2] Discussed in Palliser, *The Age of Elizabeth*, p. 178; see also Palliser 'Tawney's Century', pp. 339–53, and Clay, *Economic Expansion*, pp. 57–8.

If England's regions had been thoroughly integrated at the start of the marriage record, the shift to pastoral seasonality in some regions in the seventeenth century could have been a simple reaction to changing relative prices over that century. The premise of this first option, however, is not plausible for all of England, or even for most of it; it would constitute the most radical explanation of the three. But the English economy of the early sixteenth century was not composed of entirely self-contained, autonomous, and isolated regions either. This General View is blind before 1538, the beginning of official parochial marriage registration. So the first period of the series, the stub of a forty year period that nominally begins in 1521, but really in 1538, and then for only a minority of the 542 parishes, forms the intriguing corner around which I can not peer. Only seventy-nine non-market parishes are in observation (having a record of at least twenty-four marriages from 1538 to 1560) in that truncated period, 17.5 per cent of the non-market total. Tantalizingly, 11.3 per cent of those parishes are spring-marrying P-Types (see Table 3.3), and that percentage drops to 3.9 per cent in 1541–80, as if the short first period had captured a modest shift away from pastoral seasonality. This tentative finding, based on so few parishes for so few years (and on the unfounded assumption that the increasing of the effective sample size to 229 in the next period does not change the representativeness of the sample), is welcome, given what we know about marginal lands tumbling to grass after the great depopulation of the plague and the shift in relative prices away from grain in the later fourteenth and fifteenth centuries.[3] But that the whole of the English economy was commercially integrated in the reign of Henry VIII stretches credulity; more weight will be given to changing relative prices in connection with the other two constructions.

The third of the interpretations, the dropping of subsistence grain production in favour of marketed output, is the other extreme case. It presumes not widespread early market integration as did the first, but widespread subsistence production of grain for the household's own consumption in the sixteenth and early seventeenth centuries. In a model of household specialization proposed by Hymer and Resnick and later applied to early modern European development by De Vries, peasant householders are induced, by rising grain prices, to drop the production of non-agricultural subsistence goods for their own use and to throw their land and labour into the commercial production of

---

[3] Baker, 'Changes in the Later Middle Ages', pp. 186–247.

grain.[4] But the model, in this form, is poorly suited to explain the evidence provided by marriage seasons, because the later seventeenth century (the time of strong differentiation) was a time of falling relative prices of cereals, and what most strongly demands explanation is the selective regional dropping of grain production, not its reinforcement.

Two large aspects of the formulation could be usefully salvaged, however. Any change towards the greater commercial orientation of farmers in the sixteenth century, along the model's lines, might have left the farmers of the next century more attuned to react to the seventeenth-century's changes in relative prices.[5] And the offer of new goods, products of industry and of international and interregional trade in the seventeenth century, might then have further induced farmers to increase their production of marketable agricultural goods in order to purchase the new goods (Chapter 6 will press the marriage seasons into use to demonstrate industrial growth; see also Table 3.3 above). Farmers 'turning the ground to their most advantage' would concentrate on the production of those goods to which their land and other resources were best suited, and the falling cereal prices of the later seventeenth century would bias their choice away from grain. This is De Vries' 'capitalism creating its own demand', a demand, in this case, for money income to purchase the newly offered goods.[6] The later seventeenth century is as likely a time as any for the process to have occurred, and by inference it was there that De Vries put it.

But were the English farmers of the sixteenth century subsistence peasants, working mainly to produce food and other goods for their own consumption and to discharge rents and other obligations? Nourse smugly observed the comfortable self-sufficiency of English farms in 1700.[7] It is interesting in this respect that the advice to give up tillage that James Bankes gave to his son still urged him to keep enough tillage 'to serve your house'.[8] Ernle asserted the existence of a subsistence peasantry well into the eighteenth century,[9] but later interpretations have not been so extreme. Skipp located a watershed in the mid seventeenth century in his Midland parishes, discerning an increased export of agricultural goods from the Forest of Arden by the end of the century, and Joyce Appleby noted a profound shift in the language of production and trade in the seventeenth century, as if producers were newly, discontinuously, producing for strangers, for

[4] Hymer and Resnick, 'A Model of an Agrarian Economy', pp. 493–506; De Vries, *Dutch Rural Economy*, Chapter 1.
[5] Bridbury, 'Sixteenth-Century Farming', pp. 538–9.
[6] De Vries, *Economy of Europe*, Chapter 8; cf. Mokyr, 'Demand Vs. Supply', p. 985.
[7] Nourse, *Campania Foelix*, p. 14   [8] Thirsk, 'Farming Techniques', p. 198.
[9] Ernle, *English Farming*, p. 133.

an abstract market.[10] Hoskins and Thirsk found Midland farmers producing grain on a subsistence basis in the sixteenth and first half of the seventeenth centuries, Thirsk arguing that larger farmers had larger marketable surpluses.[11] Holderness located the ending of a subsistent peasantry in the seventeenth century, citing increasing urban demand as the cause.[12] It is more than a little perverse, in light of these interpretations, that it was the recent fifth volume of *The Agrarian History of England and Wales*, covering the later seventeenth and eighteenth centuries, that explicitly introduced 'subsistence corn' into its definition of four of its eighteen basic farming types, while the map of farming regions in the earlier fourth volume (1500–1640) made no explicit reference to the production of grain for local subsistence. The fourth volume, published in 1967, identified twelve basic farming types for 1500–1640;[13] the fifth volume, published in 1985, mapped at least thirty-one combinations of its eighteen basic types for 1640–1750.[14]

The possibility of widespread subsistence production of grain combined with the production of marketable specialties was discussed earlier. Chambers and Mingay declared the whole question of subsistence production a red herring, at least for their later period; so few acres were needed to feed a family, they argued, that most farmers were able to produce a considerable marketable surplus.[15] In any case, though, this bird's-eye view through the lens of marriage seasons cannot see into farmhouses and cottages, and cannot assess the intention of farmers. Those who mine the probate inventories that originate from within the farmhouses and cottages have enough trouble telling subsistence products and equipment from that devoted to market production. I cannot use marriage seasons to differentiate between movement from subsistence to market orientation by individuals, on the one hand, and the change from 'regional' subsistence to regional specialization, the last of the interpretations, on the other.

The simplest 'opening of trade' model, in which two regions with different resource endowments enter into trade, fits the available evidence of marriage seasonality neatly. With two autonomous regions (A and B) and one product (Figure 5.1), differences in factor

[10] Skipp, 'Economic and Social Change', p. 91; see also Skipp, 'Crisis and Development'; Appleby, *Economic Thought*.
[11] Hoskins, *Midland Peasant*, pp. 176–8; Thirsk, 'Agrarian History', p. 212. De Vries provided a related example in his *Economy of Europe* of the increase in the marketable output of small farms with subsistence constraints in the event of increased yield, p. 35.
[12] Holderness, *Pre-industrial England*, p. 70.   [13] Thirsk, 'Farming Regions', p. 4.
[14] *Ibid.*, pp. xx–xxi.   [15] Chambers and Mingay, *Agricultural Revolution*, p. 21.

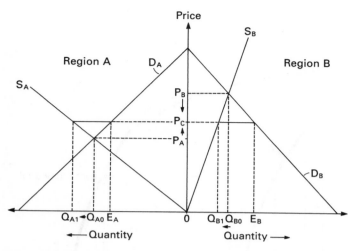

Figure 5.1 Opening of trade, with one product and two regions

endowments and other costs between the two regions create different prices for each commodity in each region (the figure has been drawn with identical demand curves in the two regions to simplify the demonstration). Excessive rainfall may depress average yields and increase the riskiness of arable production in a temperate country that is already rather wet, for example, while encouraging the growth of grass. Soil types and existing institutional arrangements may similarly give rise to differences in opportunity costs. The opening of trade between the regions causes the prices to converge (although only in a time-less, space-less world would they converge to a single price). Here, the focus is not on the hard-to-observe prices, the conventional vertical axis in textbook diagrams, but on the quantities produced in the two regions.[16]

As prices converge to P_c, the regional production diverges, with the locally excess supply of the relatively lower price region A (E_A to Q_{A1}) going to supply the new deficit (Q_{B1} to E_B) of the initially higher price region B. The agent operating the trade barrier would be transportation costs, or more generally, transactions costs, nature's great tariff. A growing body of evidence, flowing largely from one pen, has persuasively suggested the importance both of internal trade and of improvements in its means in the seventeenth century.[17] Bowden

[16] See the recent exercise in price studies and integration in Chartres, 'Marketing', pp. 459–65.
[17] Chartres, *Internal Trade*; Chartres, 'Road Carrying', pp. 73–94.

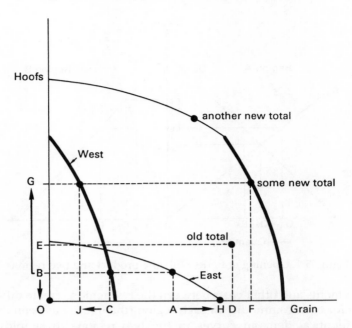

Figure 5.2 Opening of trade, with two products and two regions

argued, for the earlier period of the fourth volume of *The Agrarian History of England and Wales* (1500–1640), that transport difficulties meant no perfect conformance of production with the 'potentialities of the soil', and Chartres found that by 1700 'a complex and extensive home market was in existence'.[18] One might question the scale of these seventeenth-century improvements in road, river, and coastal transport compared with the drama of the canal and railway ages that followed, but it may still be that the less dramatic changes of the earlier period were sufficient to provoke far greater interregional trade, and trade's consequence and further encouragement, greater regional specialization.

A two-product two-region diagram, conceptually parallel to the crude Seasonal Types, further illustrates the potential for change, in abstract, as well as the possibility for refining the timing of change. Let us call the two regions East and West, and the two products Hoofs and Grain (Figure 5.2). The optimum production possibility combinations for the west are represented by the bold curve, illustrating high opportunity costs in the production of Grain, and those for the east by

[18] Bowden, 'Agricultural Prices', p. 611.

the thinner curve, showing high opportunity costs in the production of Hoofs. To simplify the figure, the regions have been given symmetrical production-possibility curves, and, at the unintegrated start, have been assumed to be producing identical outputs of Hoofs. Well outside these two is the optimum set of combinations with integration, the summed curves for the two regions. Let both regions begin, unintegrated, producing towards the grainy ends of their choices, as if the price of Grain were generally high relative to that of Hoofs, a reasonable presumption for the sixteenth and early seventeenth centuries. East combines OA of grain with OB hoofs, while the West produces the same amount of Hoofs and OC Grain. The total output, East plus West, would thus be OD Grain and OE Hoofs. Now let the regions be integrated, at some new total output, on the combined curve, such as OF Grain and OG Hoofs.

Two interesting points arise from the integration. First, the two regions experience a divergence in their Grain/Hoof mix. As illustrated, the East becomes entirely specialized, at OH Grain and no Hoofs, while the West becomes far more pastoral, at OG Hoofs and only OJ Grain (at 'another new total', a combination predicted by a lower Grain/Hoof price ratio, it is the West that becomes completely specialized, in Hoofs, while the East, as drawn, is still more grainy than it was at the unintegrated start). Secondly, productivity rises, caused by market integration alone; the output of Grain increases by DF, that of Hoofs by EG. Aggregate production thus grows, without new techniques, and without augmentation of the land, labour, or capital of the two regions.

The argument is not intended to rule out technological or organizational change in agriculture during the years of specialization; more precisely, the method is mute on this point. It is, as I have been the first to argue, a very crude method, far better at recognizing places dominated by grain production, rearing, and rural industry than at discerning degrees of alternation in husbandry or numbers of courses in rotation. Even dairying, with its annual demand for labour in milking and butter- and cheese-making, and seasonal demands both in calving and hay-making, has resisted identification. Turnips still have to be counted in inventories, not sought in little turnip-peaks in marriage seasonality.[19] And counting turnips and other goods in inventories is not without its problems, too, *vide* the recent debate over yields between Overton and Allen. Can both of these debaters keep the land under observation constant over time, between a Period 1 and

[19] Mark Overton, 'Estimating Crop Yields', pp. 363–78 and Allen, 'Inferring Yields', pp. 117–26.

Period 2, in their analysis? If not, and grain was no longer grown on the poorer land of the area in Period 2, grain yields may be observed increasing for no reason other than that only the yields on the better land are being measured in Period 2.

The organizational change of enclosure may have increased the flexibility of production choices, thus permitting greater differentiation in practice. The argument that the seventeenth century saw the greatest amount of land enclosed has recently been revived.[20] The relation of enclosure to changes in marriage seasonality, especially swings between autumn and spring seasonality, were discussed above in Chapter 4. Nothing was learned from the test about the primacy of causes, especially on the question of whether general movements in relative prices or the newly felt imperatives of comparative advantage were more important.

The findings are consistent, however, with a process of the adoption of better practice from an existing repertoire of techniques. Moreover, it is not far-fetched to think that the greater solidity of rural specializations in the eighteenth century, the consolidation of orientations suggested by Cramer's V in the last chapter, provided a stable ground for the successful dissemination of appropriate techniques. Increases in productivity in less developed regions are not limited to technological novelties.

Figure 5.2 abstracts from both time and space. It posits two regions, but costless exchange of goods between the regions. It posits two states, unintegrated and integrated, but instantaneous shifting between the states. But the figure implies increases in agricultural productivity through the sole agency of regional integration. The theoretical extent of the potential increase is limited by the real differences between opportunity costs in the two regions. In Figure 5.2 the increases in output were exaggerated for rhetorical effect (the total output of Hoofs was shown to double, along with a smaller increase in the output of Grain). The historical differences in opportunity costs, and the extent of increased physical productivity, can only be suggested by the divergence in marriage seasonality itself; aggregate direct measurements of agricultural output are limited by the patchiness of early modern sources. How much productivity increase? 'Some, associated entirely with integration', must be the less than satisfactory answer; Machlup found the direct measurement of integration in more recent times embarrassingly difficult, lying more in the domain of 'evaluative (normative)' than positive economics.[21]

---

[20] Wordie, 'Chronology'.
[21] Machlup, 'Conceptual and Causal Relationships', pp. 198 and 208.

The model, a simple application of comparative advantage, points to one reasonable aspect of early modern English economic development; the growth, especially during the seventeenth century, in the (hard-to-measure) volume of trade between regions, directed along the lines of (hard-to-measure) differences in opportunity costs in each region, leading to increases in (impossible-to-measure) total output, without the necessity of aggregate additions to land, labour, or capital, or of new techniques. If, in Figure 5.2, the integration and increase were shown to be instantaneous, at least this usefully suggests the once-and-for-all nature of productivity gains through this channel.

Nothing happens that fast in historical time, of course; England is not a two-region world, exchange was not costless; institutional changes such as enclosure may have altered regional opportunity costs by increasing the elasticity of substitution in production of arable and pastoral products, and shadings in soil type (see below), transportation costs, and other factors would have influenced the timing of integration of individual places. The process of differentiation shown by marriage seasonality, however, would suggest that these prizes had largely been won by the end of the seventeenth century, within fifty years of Atwell's call. While Coleman explained the stabilization of prices in the later seventeenth century with reference to new techniques, more intensive farming, and the extension of cultivated area, Bowden found that prices stabilized in the later seventeenth and early eighteenth centuries because, among other things, land was coming to be better utilized and costs of distribution were falling.[22]

The first and simpler implication of Figure 5.2 was increasing regional specialization, differentiation. Can real referrents of East and West, of Hoofs and Grain, and of the opening of trade be identified? Figures 5.3 and 5.4 should be interesting in this respect. They are a redrafting of Figures 4.10–4.12, the frequency distributions of ANG by region, with the addition of a new region, the southeast. The boundaries of the regions were shown on Figure 4.9; included in the southeast are the non-market, non-X-Type parishes of all of Kent and Middlesex, southern Essex and Hertfordshire, the eastern halves of Surrey and Sussex, and corners of Buckinghamshire and Berkshire. The first of the new figures superimposes the distributions for 1561–1640, and the second does the same for 1661–1740. In Figure 5.3, only the southeast, which encompasses London, stands out as different, different in being seasonally heterogeneous. The other three regions are nearly identical. Their parishes are largely bunched to the left, the high autumn, low spring, grain-harvesting end; all three, however,

[22] Coleman, *Economy of England*, p. 122; Bowden, 'Agricultural Prices', pp. 2–9.

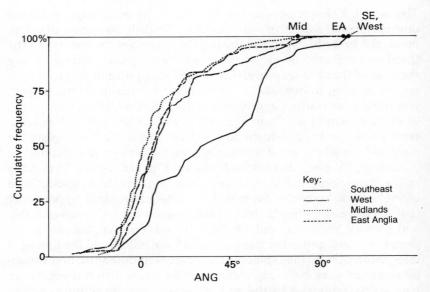

Figure 5.3 Cumulative frequency distribution of ANG, four regions, 1561–1640

have similar pastoral (high spring, low autumn) tails, almost as if the three regions were semi-autonomous, meeting their similar demand for grain, meat, and dairy products similarly internally (autumn seasonality would not preclude the production of marketed specialities in addition to grain for local consumption, though).

By the later seventeenth and early eighteenth centuries, however, the regions have become distinctive, East Anglia the virtual mirror image of the west (save for the one surviving low autumn outlier in the west), the Midlands heterogeneous, and the southeast even more formally so, bimodal (Figure 5.4). The divergence predicted by the model has occurred, and by implication the opening of far wider interregional trade has been located in the seventeenth century.

Why should such a change have occurred then? The improvement in internal trade described by Chartres is one candidate, although it was, as he argued, as much consequence as cause of increased interregional trade, and it was not concentrated in so short a span of time as the Canal Boom, for example, that so entranced Ernle. The period of most rapid improvement of trade suggested by Chartres was 1681–1715, in the midst of the differentiation, not preceding it; he found road carrying services to have increased by 36.5 per cent from

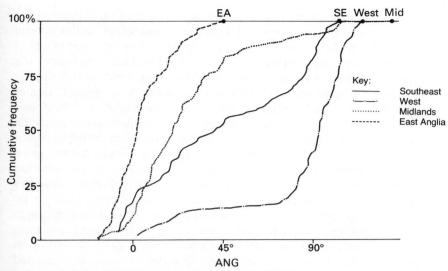

Figure 5.4 Cumulative frequency distribution of ANG, four regions, 1661–1740

1637 to 1681, and by 64.3 per cent from 1681 to 1715.[23] The reversal of price trends at mid century is a better candidate for the shot that set the avalanche of change in motion, with the prices of breadstuffs falling relative to those of all pastoral products (except wool) and inputs (hay and straw), analogous to a movement along the combined output curve of Figure 5.2. From 1640/79 to 1710/49, prices were volatile but largely trendless, Bowden found. The prices of wheat, rye, vegetables, wool, and industrial products declined; barley prices rose slightly, and the prices of livestock, hops, hay, and straw rose more markedly.[24] Farmers at the very least were encouraged by the ending of the inflation in the price of grain to rethink their strategies and choices.[25]

Why specialization occurred when it occurred is inherently difficult to answer; so much feedback exists in any explanation. Improvements in the productivity of labour in agriculture through specialization are both the effect and cause of increased real wages, and increases in real income cause shifts in the demand for agricultural products away from grain. Improvements in transportation and the institutions of trade both cause and are called forth by greater interregional trade. Urban growth was made easier by increases in agricultural productivity, and encouraged greater specialization and greater productivity. It is more than a little tempting to see changes in the distribution of income in the

[23] Chartres, 'Road Carrying', p. 78.   [24] Bowden, 'Agricultural Prices', 1985.
[25] Broad, 'Alternate Husbandry', pp. 82–3; Coleman, *Economy of England*, p. 122.

sixteenth century towards greater positive skewness, among other things, spurring the growth of London as organizer of the special trades the higher incomes of the relatively few supported. That growth in turn required the expansion of general trade to supply the ever-increasing urban population, yielding, first, time for learning by doing in the techniques of interregional commerce, second, higher rates of savings made available, at least, for investment, and third, low real costs of that highly labour intensive early modern activity, capital formation, the latter two spurring improvements in transportation. The final touch in the breaking of the pattern of ubiquitous grain production might then have been the combined effect of the cessation of aggregate population growth and of increasing real wages, whether caused by the slowdown in the growth of the labour force or by increased labour productivity. The disturbance of the Interregnum to the statistical series is particularly unfortunate with respect to isolating precise causes of change, that is, in nominating causes consistent in time with the changes in seasonality (if indeed the closely guarded tangle can ever be unravelled). This relates particularly to the relation of turning points in seasonality with turning points in real wage, population, and relative price series.

Why was the southeast added to Figures 5.3 and 5.4, if not to suggest another cause for the stronger integration of regions, the growth of London, strong integrator that it was.[26] Langton found regional differences to have been accentuated in the seventeenth century by growing trade among regions, and between all and London, by far the greatest spatially concentrated market in early modern England.[27] Supple saw London as the 'inevitable controller of much economic activity in other parts of the land' by the early seventeenth century, and evidence from the marriage record can be added to suggest two of the influences upon the location of specific agricultural activities.[28] The first influence is mean annual rainfall; the second is the distance, as the Euclidean crow flies, from the spire or tower of each parish church to the dome of St. Paul's. Rainfall was gauged from the modern Ordnance Survey Ten-Mile sheets, Yearly Averages, 1916–50 (London, 1967); there is no early modern substitute, but at least modern rain is less likely to have been influenced by past English agricultural practice than are modern soil types. In Figure 5.5, the mean combinations of rain and distance from London are plotted for each group of arable, pastoral, and non-seasonal Types for

---

[26] Chambers and Mingay, *Agricultural Revolution*, p. 32.
[27] Langton, 'Industrial Revolution', p. 149.
[28] Supple, *Commercial Crisis*, p. 4.

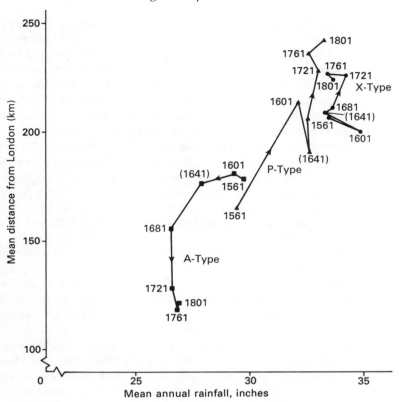

Figure 5.5 Rain and distance by Seasonal Type, 1541–80 to 1781–1820

each period, and the combinations connected to show change through time, as was done with the centroids of Figure 3.12. As was also done with Chapter 3's centroids, the heterogeneous H-Types have been parcelled into the A- and P-Types, according to whether the autumn or spring index was greater, and the observations have been weighted (see Chapter 3).

Fisher argued that it is one thing to speak of regional specialization in the language of economic geography, but that inherent tendencies towards specialization do not become actual without markets.[29] There is little difference in mean distance from London between the arable and pastoral types in the earliest period, nor is there a gap in the mean rainfall; the mean A-Type marker for 1541–80 actually sits in a slightly rainier position, slightly farther from London, than does the P-Type's.

[29] Fisher, 'Development', p. 57.

Over time, the means of the two Seasonal Types then move largely vertically; the arable type finds slightly drier parishes closer to London (and/or drops wetter, more distant parishes), while the pastoral type finds rainier parishes as it moves farther and farther from London. Except for the familiar period in parentheses (1621–60), the non-seasonal X-Type parishes are always the rainiest, on average, but from 1701–40 onwards they are not the most distant from London; that honour then falls to the pastoral, spring-marrying, P-Types.

There is every reason to suspect that the relation between the two 'independent' variables in Figure 5.5 is not orthogonal, as it was in Chapter 3's centroid map of eastness and northness; as it happens, London lies in the drier half of the country, so that the farther a parish lies from London, the higher the rainfall is likely to be (although anyone working in eastern England in the summers of 1987 and 1988 might have some reason to question the reliability of the maps of mean annual rainfall). What is interesting about Figure 5.5 is that while the whole set of observations, for all types, lies along the positive diagonal we would expect, the mean observations for any one type do so only to an attenuated extent, and in the case of the X-Type parishes, not at all. Autumn-marrying arable activities shun excessive rainfall, whatever the period; spring-marrying pastoral ones do not.[30]

England presents a splendid setting for an argument from the margin of cultivation around a fixed point, in this case, London, growing greatly both in absolute population and relatively to the national population; it reached a peak in terms of its share of the national population c. 1700, at 11 per cent.[31] Fisher wonderfully wrote of the tentacles, feeders, that London spread northward in the seventeenth century.[32] Conventionally, one explains why 'circles', zones, of agricultural practice exist with reference to returns to immobile factors, especially land, and to transportation costs; conventionally, one shows pastoral production (rearing) located farther from the central place than arable production with a diagram such as Figure 5.6.[33] Ignore, for the moment, the pastoral-after curve. Out to distance G_1, grain production reaps a greater return to land than rearing; from there to distance P_1, pastoral production reigns. Beyond P_1, no farming for the central place, London, earns positive rent; it is the margin of cultivation for all London-dominated production. The zone

---

[30] Overton, '1801 Crop Returns', p. 48. In (wet) Wales, wheat was grown mainly in areas with the least rainfall; oats, like barley, could tolerate more rain. Thomas, 'Climate and Cropping', p. 203.

[31] Corfield, 'Urban Development', p. 217; Wrigley, 'Urban Growth', pp. 157–93.

[32] Fisher, 'Development', p. 50.

[33] See, for examples, McCloskey, *Applied Theory*, pp. 427–32.

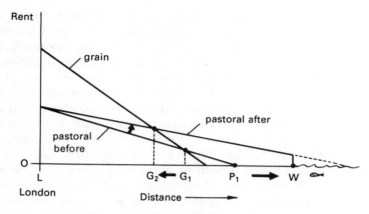

Figure 5.6 Margin of cultivation

P_1W in Figure 5.6 would be the 'empty land' in North American applications; such a conception is even less tenable applied to old settled England. Beyond P_1, English farmers would have produced with an eye on local or household self-sufficiency, especially in the most important foodstuff, grain. 'Margin of Cultivation' is not wholly apt here; beyond the margin, there is cultivation, but not for sale to the central market of the model. W represents the watery edges of Britain.

To simplify the diagram, only one change has been shown, a decrease in the transportation costs of pastoral products, with its new boundary between London-oriented grain and pastoral production shifted in to G_2 by the outward rotation of the pastoral rent curve, and its new boundary of pastoral production at P_2, that is, at W. In terms of the fossil record of marriage seasons, before the shift in transportation costs, zone LG_1 should register high autumn seasonality, but so should zone P_1W, because of its local self-sufficiency in grain (the local zone P_1W for sixteenth-century Kent, Sussex, and East Anglia, however, lies under the Channel and North Sea). Only the area they bracket, G_1P_1, should exhibit high spring/summer seasonality. The effect of improved transportation costs is to eliminate zone P_1W, the area of high harvest seasonality and local subsistence production, by driving it into the briny deep. LG_2 would become the area specializing in grain, and G_2W that specializing in pastoral products. Or the change could equally well be interpreted as driving the extramarginal zone into the Scottish highlands; rotate the diagram in real space, and P_1W becomes part of Scotland.

The changing margin of cultivation of Figure 5.6 focusses more on the locational influences on production rather than on total productivity, per se, and on a single centre of consumption, London, rather than on trade between agricultural regions. The slightly unconventional aspect of Figure 5.6, the zone outside London's reach, has a direct bearing, however, on the issue of productivity increase. The productivity enhancing arguments of the first model, that of comparative advantage, would also apply here, if the initially extramarginal regions produced, for their local subsistence, goods (such as grain) to which they happened to be less well suited than they were to the production of goods dictated by London's 'interest', when the margin shifted out to include them. Wrigley, following Adam Smith, pointed to the loss of productivity with small markets, where grain would be grown in areas better suited to grazing.[34] In the particular setting of England, expressing the argument purely in terms of distance from London has the advantage of nominating, as candidate for zone P_1W (places of local subsistence), all of upland Britain. The map of farming regions in the 5th volume of *The Agrarian History of England and Wales* (1640–1750) marks this area as 'subsistence corn with [various marketed specialties]';[35] the present findings suggest that such a characterization would have been far more appropriate in *The Agrarian History*'s 4th volume (1500–1640).

England is not a homogeneous plain, London does not lie at its centre, other central places existed (most notably, Amsterdam, lying outside the map-like diagram of Figure 5.6), London was not the only urban place in England (although after 1520 and until some time between 1750 and 1801 it was larger than the combined total of all other English towns with populations of more than 5000).[36] Exports of wheat and flour were negligible in the 1660s, and when they peaked in the 1750s they represented only c. 6 per cent of the country's output.[37] The southeast of Figure 5.3 contains London, and it is the most diverse in its marriage seasonality in 1561–1640. Blith depicted the ring of counties around London as feeding themselves and the growing metropolis in 1649.[38] Baker described the increasing local specialization near London in the sixteenth century, and Emery similarly found the farming of the southeast c. 1600 influenced by London's food market.[39] There is a fair amount of topographical diversity in the land to the south of London, with the flat lands of east Kent contrasting sharply with the Weald, and the growth of the London

---

[34] Wrigley, 'Parasite or Stimulus', p. 299.   [35] Thirsk, *Agrarian History*, vol. 5, p. xxi.
[36] Wrigley, 'Urban Growth', p. 159.
[37] Coleman, *Economy of England*, pp. 120–1.
[38] Blith wrote in 1649 of Hertfordshire, Essex, Kent, Surrey, Sussex, and the other counties near to London feeding themselves and London (*English Improver*, p. 40).
[39] Baker, *Changes*, p. 216; Emery, 'England circa 1600', pp. 271–2.

market in the sixteenth century had produced actual diversity in the exploitation of that well-placed land.[40] Holderness pointed to the increase in urban demand since 1600 as the force ending subsistence farming.[41]

It was the Midlands region that joined the southeast in expressing seasonal diversity in Figure 5.4, 1661–1740. The industrial growth of the Midlands in the later seventeenth century, to be discussed in the next chapter, had by the end of that century created a competing 'central place' to London in terms of the diagram of Figure 5.6, more spatially diffuse than London, but a growing market for food, nonetheless. The seasonal diversification of the Midlands in the later seventeenth and eighteenth centuries, which turned that area into a patchwork of Seasonal Types on Figure 1.1, had been strengthened by the growth of the London market for the region's cheese and cattle, by its exports of textiles and metalwares and their consequent linkage of higher regional demand for foodstuffs, as well as by shifts of relative prices operating over a region with diversity in soil types and drainage.[42]

'Distance', as the determinant of the return to land, is more realistically multivariate; only one of its components can be measured in miles (or kilometres). Grigg, in discussing twentieth-century rents, found many determinants. In general, rents were highest in market gardening, and declined through pig keeping, dairying, alluvial arable, heavy arable, mixed with dairy, poultry keeping, dairying and mixed (grass), light arable, general mixed, corn, sheep, and dairy, mixed livestock in lowlands, to their lowest with upland livestock keeping.[43] Varying physical attributes affect the return to land in particular activities. The nature of the soil and the drainage of that soil, for instance, somewhat constrained a farmer's choice of output. Table 5.1 illustrates both the possibility of a measurable impact of soil type on farming practices and the difficulties inherent in these measures. Seasonal Types are there contrasted with modern soil types, for the non-market parishes in the Cambridge Groups's 404-parish set, for 1661–1740. Of the fourteen basic soil types and three combinations of types into which the parishes fell, only eight of the soil types

---

40 Chalklin, *Seventeenth-Century Kent*; Short, 'The South-East', pp. 270–316; Richardson, 'Metropolitan Counties', pp. 239–69. Everitt, perhaps curiously, had found the south asleep relative to records of marketing ('Farm Labourers', p. 495). See also Fisher, 'Development', p. 56.
41 Holderness, *Pre-industrial England*, p. 70.
42 Mingay, 'The East Midlands', pp. 89–128, Hey, 'North-West Midlands', pp. 129–58, and Thirsk, 'South-West Midlands', pp. 159–96.
43 Grigg, 'An Index of Regional Change', p. 56.

Table 5.1. *Soil type and Seasonal Type, 1661–1740*
(non-market parishes only)[a]

| | Seasonal Types, percentages | | | |
Soil/drainage[b]	A-Type	P-Type	X-Type	n
gley/poor to very poor	70.3	20.3	9.4	64
mixed: brown forest and gley	52.6	42.1	5.3	19
grey-brown podzols/good to imperfect	47.6	33.3	19.1	21
calcareous/good to imperfect	46.4	35.7	17.9	28
brown forest/imperfect	41.2	33.3	25.5	51
brown forest/good	34.6	28.9	36.5	52
mixed: calcareous and gley	30.0	30.0	40.0	10
podzols/varied	23.1	23.1	53.9	13
these soil types	47.7	27.9	24.4	258
all soil types	45.9	28.8	25.3	281

[a] From the 404-parish Cambridge Group sample.
[b] All categories are lowland soil types.

contained at least ten of the sample's parishes, and it is those eight soil types that are included in the table (there are not enough parishes of light infertile soil in the sample, for example, to test for the seasonality of work involved with rabbits).[44] The soil types are listed in descending order by the proportion of parishes that were autumn-marrying A-Types in 1661–1740.

The most arable soil type is, at first sight surprisingly, the most poorly draining of the eight soil types; 70 per cent of these lowland gley parishes were autumn-marrying, and only 20 per cent pastoral spring-marrying, in the late seventeenth and early eighteenth centuries. But as Broad pointed out, turnips rotted and not all new grasses took well on the heavy clays of the south Midlands.[45] No other of these soil types associates so strongly with one of the Seasonal Types, and Cramer's V, a measure of association between these eight soil types and the three Seasonal Types, is only 0.262.

Table 5.2 shows change over time on these soil types, by noting the percentage of non-market parishes that were autumn-marrying A-Types and spring-marrying P-Types, by soil type, in each of the three long periods. The soil types are now ranked by their 1561–1640 A-Type proportions, and the ranking for each long period is shown in parentheses. The apparent agricultural orientation of labour working

[44] Sheail, 'Rabbits and Agriculture', pp. 343–55.
[45] Broad, 'Alternate Husbandry', p. 83.

Table 5.2. *Soil type and A- and P-Types, 1541–1640, 1661–1740, and 1741–1820*

(non-market parishes only)
percentages of soil type's parishes in each period
[period ranks in brackets]

Soil type[a]	A-Type			P-Type		
	1561–1640	1661–1740	1741–1820	1561–1640	1661–1740	1741–1820
gley	83 [1]	70 [1]	73 [1]	8 [6]	20 [8]	9 [8]
calcareous	82 [2]	46 [4]	36 [6]	4 [8]	36 [2]	21 [2]
mixed: bf/gley	67 [3]	53 [2]	58 [2]	17 [4]	42 [1]	16 [5]
podzols	62 [4]	23 [8]	46 [4]	8 [7]	23 [7]	15 [6]
bf/good	58 [5]	35 [6]	35 [7]	15 [5]	29 [5]	21 [3]
mixed: calc/gley	56 [6]	30 [7]	30 [8]	22 [3]	30 [4]	30 [1]
g-b podzols	42 [7]	48 [3]	52 [3]	32 [2]	33 [3]	19 [4]
bf/imperfect	41 [8]	41 [5]	39 [5]	35 [1]	26 [6]	14 [7]
these soil types	63.4	47.7	48.8	16.9	27.9	16.3
all soil types	62.2	45.9	47.3	18.2	28.8	16.4

[a] Ranked by A-Type percentages in 1561–1640. Abbreviations: bf=brown forest, calc=calcareous, g-b podzol=grey-brown podzol, good=good drainage, imperfect=imperfect drainage.

these soils was not constant over time; the well-drained calcareous parishes, for example, were the second most arable in the earliest period, but they work their way down the list to become third lowest in the proportion of A-Types in the last period, and concurrently rise from the lowest proportion of P-Types to the second highest. More rearrangement of ranks occurs between the first and the second long period than between the second and the third (the summed squares of differences in ranks drops from 48 to 22 for the A-Types, and from 76 to 32 for the P-Types), which is what we might expect from the other findings on the timing of agricultural change.

The reordering runs counter to any extreme hypothesis in which soil type alone determines agricultural orientation. In any case, twentieth-century measures of soil type and drainage cannot closely represent conditions in the sixteenth and seventeenth centuries, since past farming practice and draining influence present assessments of soil and drainage. The association between soil type and Seasonal Type grows no stronger over these three long periods (Cramer's V in fact drops from 0.268 in the first period to 0.234 in the third), but the massive nineteenth-century investments in draining, which might have been expected to open new possibilities, post-date the seasonality series.

The return to land might also be affected by what might be called the market awareness of farmers, institutional changes in markets for consumer goods and shifts in the demand for money income.[46] Any improvements to the return to land, whether through institutional means such as enclosure (if that was their effect), or changes in technique would have shifted the appropriate rent line out in Figure 5.6, tending towards the elimination of zone P_1W. Similarly, transportation costs were not wholly comprised by the costs of cartage, shipping, wharfage, and labour driving flocks of sheep and herds of cattle (and flocks of turkeys and gaggles of geese) to London, but also would also have included costs arising from the institutional means of finance and marketing.[47] These costs might reasonably have been expected to decline with the experience gained in provisioning the rapidly growing metropolis during Tawney's Century. It is most rewarding that the findings lend support to the concentration on the later seventeenth and early eighteenth centuries of Westerfield's classic of economic history, if not to his characterization of the whole period as one of 'meager local specialization'.[48]

Figure 5.6 is stark in its predictions of economic behaviour within its extramarginal and two intramarginal regions. Specialized grain production occupies the land closest to the central place, specialized hoofs production the outer intramarginal band, and subsistence production the extramarginal region. It is too simplified to allow a finer division of regions, assuming away, for instance, market gardening and milk production closest to the central place. It is based solely on the return to land; if labour were assumed to be Smithian in its mobility, the 'hardest of all baggage to transport', then a similar diagram including labour would place rural manufacturing in a band distant from the central place. Cloth and nails won't walk to London, as meat on the hoof will, but transport costs form a smaller part of their delivered price. Figure 5.6 further allows for no joint production of Hoofs and Grain, no alternate or convertible husbandry.

And the figure leaves stranded the possibility of a combination of local or subsistence production of grain with the production of hoofs (or nails, or cloth) for the distant central place. The profitability of

---

[46] De Vries, *Economy of Europe*, pp. 176–209; Thirsk, *Economic Policy*.
[47] After three month's journey from East Anglia, the geese won, by two days (Fussell and Goodman, 'Eighteenth Century Traffic', p. 235).
[48] Westerfield, *Middlemen*, p. 130.

commercial farming and rural manufacturing depended not only on revenues from the sale of hoofs or grain, or nails, or cloth, but also on the costs that households producing nothing but wool and mutton, or nails, or cloth incurred in obtaining costlier-to-transport breadstuffs. London was of course supplied with pastoral products and manufactured goods from farther afield than Kent and Hertfordshire in the sixteenth and earlier seventeenth centuries, but often by farmers and by–employed rural manufacturers who could not easily forgo the production of breadstuffs. High autumn marriage seasonality blanketed some regions in the sixteenth and early seventeenth centuries not because they were totally isolated and autonomous, but because grain markets were not adequate in supplying all regions.

The models of Figures 5.2 and 5.6 have distinct heuristic statuses. The changing 'margin of cultivation' helps explain the more diversified economy of London's neighbouring regions in the sixteenth and early seventeenth centuries; the 'opening of trade' points to the productivity increases available once regions less suited to the production of grain were encouraged to stop producing it (and many of these, to loop back to the other model, happened to lie farther from London). The models are wonderfully, horribly, abstract. Farmers are imagined to be constrained to make either/or choices about production, regions are assumed to be delineated by knife-edge boundaries, products and regions limited to one or two instances. The fossil record of marriage seasonality, however, is well suited to arguments made on that level, as it is to be fashioned into a diagnostic tool for local history, to throw major specializations and the timing of change into better focus. The evidence for the sixteenth and early seventeenth centuries suggests a predominant pattern of local or limited regional markets for the most important foodstuff, the most important item of national production and consumption, grain; the later disappearance of pronounced autumn seasonality over so wide a swath of the map mirrors, I have argued, the regional specialization of the rural economy and its necessary concomitant, the growth of far wider grain markets, supplying regions that had once been, but were no longer, dependent on local sources. The argument is hardly that, earlier, no interregional or international trade occurred in the products of rural England, but rather that no matter how much wool or butter, madder or woad, or how many woollens, nails, fish, cattle, or cheeses were produced in the sixteenth and early seventeenth centuries, no large area was so free from grain production as not to be dominated by its seasonality.

The arguments advanced to explain the strong differentiation of regions tend to collapse into one, in early modern England's case. When the divergence in marriage seasonality is observed, the movement towards spring seasonality in the soon-to-be-pastoral west is greater than the movement away from spring seasonality in the east (Figures 5.3 and 5.4). In the first model (the opening-of-trade), the explanation for the asymmetrical divergence flows from the initial production choices in both regions, to concentrate more on arable than pastoral production; when the west shifts away from grain to hoofs, the steep slope dictated by its opportunity costs produces a large increase in the output of hoofs, while in the east, the shift towards more grain leads to only a small decrease in its output of hoofs. The historical referrent of the initial positions might equally be the accidental coincidence of high grain prices in both regions, caused by generally high rates of population growth, or the necessity of autonomous regional production of grain, the main item of consumption (given income levels), or a large degree of subsistence production on the level of households, again with grain as the main staple of consumption; some combination of the latter two conditions are presumed to have characterized zone $P_1 W$ in the second, margin-of-cultivation, model.

Whatever the cause of generally high arable-indicating autumn indices before the middle of the seventeenth century, the evidence of marriage seasonality points to the relative disappearance of predominant household subsistence and autonomous local markets by the turn of the eighteenth century at the latest. To the extent that marriage seasonality might have been 'customary', a tacit rule guiding behaviour, a lag might be expected between changes in the pattern of work and changes in the pattern of marriages. But, as argued in earlier chapters, parallel sources as densely and precisely dated as marriage seasonality are not available against which to test for length of lags.

Support is also given to the old textbook chestnut on the advantages enjoyed by England, those advantages that made England first to industrialize. If the sketch of Figure 5.6 corresponds in some measure to reality, the evidence presented represents a sixteenth and early seventeenth century in which not all of England was integrated into a national market in grains and pastoral products, but one that was small enough to have been so integrated by the beginning of the eighteenth century, before the canal or turnpike manias. And the findings should be grist for the mill of champions of the seventeenth century as a key period of agrarian change, if not necessarily via innovations in crops and rotations.

The models thus account for the regional differentiation of marriage seasons. With the margin of cultivation (Figure 5.6), most regions should have exhibited high autumn seasonality before the shifting out of the margin, either because of their commercial production of grain for the central place (in zone LG_1) or because of extramarginal subsistence production of grain (in zone P_1W), sandwiching a third zone (G_1P_1) of commercial rearing. After the shift, only two regions of seasonality remain, commercial pastoral (G_2W) and commercial arable (LG_2) production. In the diagram illustrating the opening of trade (Figure 5.2), the two regions would have been producing both hoofs and grain before the integration, but after would have become differentiated in their work, and thus in their seasonality of marriage.

The observed changes in marriage seasonality also reflect what Atwell called for in the last chapter: England's ground was turned to most advantage, first of the Commonwealth, then of the farmer. Productivity increase is the second major consequence of the differentiation. Conditions conspired to produce this 'turning' in the later seventeenth century. But, even if there had been no implications touching on productivity increase, the observed differentiation implies disruption to local labour markets. Except for dairying (which in any case was as likely to have been A-Type as P-Type) most pastoral activities used less labour than the grain growing they displaced. Two responses might be predicted in regions undergoing the transition from arable A-Type to pastoral P-Type: either the outmigration of newly displaced workers, or an influx of labour-using rural manufacturing. It is to these implications I will return in Chapter 7, after considering the forces for change inherent in early modern manufacturing.

6

Rural manufacturing, location and labour

Early modern rural industry lacked locational stability. That may not be the most important thing to say about rural industry before the Industrial Revolution (one side of 'instability' is, of course, deindustrialization, with no few modern echoes in the transiently industrialized world), but it is well within the General View.[1] The evidence of earlier chapters may more have suggested exuberant industrial growth. Earsdon and Shepshed lost their agricultural seasonality in Figure 2.4; the relative number of X-Type, non-agricultural, parishes increased in Table 3.3. And the movement of the X-Type's centroid to the north and west (Figure 3.12) may have evoked visions of industry in the Midlands, the West Riding, and Lancashire. But the aggregate measures of those chapters masked spatial and temporal variation within the sample. Chapter 4, it will be remembered, showed that the pastoral centroid's western shift was in part caused by the withdrawal of vernal seasonality from the east, and the arable centroid's eastward drift by the near disappearance of autumnal seasonality in the west. The X-Type's centroid was drawn north and west in the seventeenth century not only by industrialization there, but also because deindustrialization in the south and east had cut the industrial centroid adrift from its southern anchor. In the next pages, further evidence for the instability of rural industrial location will be presented. The causes of the volatility will then be examined, first independently from the agrarian changes sketched in the last two chapters, as if their lessons had not been learned. The next chapter then reintegrates agricultural and industrial change, seeking the seasonal sources of newly industrial places.

Spatial volatility ruled England's rural industrial growth. Figures 6.1 and 6.2 are based on pairs of long periods centring on 1601, 1701, and

---

[1] Johnson, 'Proto-industrialization', p. 1.

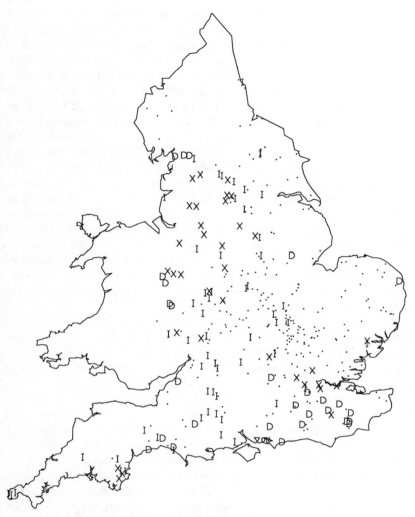

Figure 6.1 Rural industrialization and deindustrialization,
              1561–1640 to 1661–1740
         Key: X ever non-seasonal
               I   becoming non-seasonal
               D becoming seasonal
               .   ever seasonal

1781. Figure 6.1 contrasts seasonality in 1561–1640 with seasonality in 1661–1740, and Figure 6.2 seasonal typing in 1661–1740 with that of 1741–1820. The Seasonal Types of the earlier chapters have here been remixed, and the parishes divided into four new categories: consistently non-seasonal X-Types are ploted as 'X'; once seasonal parishes (A-, P-, and H-Types) that then lost their agricultural seasonality, the industrializing parishes, are plotted as 'I'; the deindustrializing parishes, X-Type in the earlier period but A-, P-, or H-Type in the latter, are plotted as 'D'; finally, the consistently seasonal agricultural parishes are shown with '·'. As with the maps of earlier chapters, parishes must have had at least twenty-four marriages recorded in each of the eighty year periods mapped, and must not have been market towns (see the companion maps in Chapter 4, Figures 4.4 and 4.5, sources of the A-Types and P-Types of 1661–1740 for Figure 6.1, and Figures 4.8 and 4.9 for Figure 6.2). The symbols 'X' and 'D' on Figure 6.1 would by themselves yield a map of rural industrial location in the sixteenth and early seventeenth centuries, and that map would reflect much of the pattern of rural industrial location in the later Middle Ages (except for the several methodological problems to be discussed below), following the late medieval excursion of industry into the countryside.

England north and west of a somewhat unconventional line drawn from Portsmouth to the eastern Wash contains all but three of the fifty-three 'I's of early modern rural industrialization. Little of that large area is missing the symbol; the southwest, the Midlands, and the West Riding all contain many parishes losing their agricultural seasonality. The twenty-nine putative rural deindustrializers are more spatially clustered; 'D' dominates the Weald, south of London, and clumps of 'D's appear in Dorset and eastern Devon, in Shropshire, and in the northwest. The Thames is bordered by the symbol 'X', signifying consistently low arable and pastoral seasonality (leaving the field clear for market gardening), and a large remainder of the thirty-one 'X's appear in Staffordshire, Cheshire, Derbyshire, and Lancashire. East Anglia almost lacks non-seasonal industrial typing in both the mapped periods. One Essex parish gained industrial typing ('I') while another maintained it ('X') in both periods; one Norfolk parish lost its industrial pattern ('D'). The other forty-three Cambridgeshire, Essex, Norfolk, and Suffolk parishes on the map remained agriculturally seasonal in both periods, as did all but one of the twenty-seven rural parishes of Bedfordshire (Chapter 4 told the companion story for East Anglia, of switching within the agricultural types).

I pause here to review the problems relating to this most indirect method of finding rural industrialization and deindustrialization, before moving into the later eighteenth and nineteenth centuries with Figure 6.2, and the new complications that that map will create. 'Cloud cover' was invoked in Chapter 2 to describe the obscured pattern of work in part of the northwest. It is appropriate to the mat of 'X's in parts of Staffordshire, Cheshire, and Derbyshire in Figure 6.1. Tendencies to marry in the winter, whatever the pattern of work, make it impossible to use combinations of the autumn and spring indices of marriages to differentiate between truly seasonal and truly non-seasonal work there.

That Figure 6.1 picks up the early decline of rural industry in the Weald, South Devon, and Shropshire is a gift; the non-seasonal X-Type was, at the outset of the study, a residual category, designed to differentiate true switchers between arable and pastoral seasonality from the losers of all agricultural seasonality. But where has the East Anglian textile industry gone, its woollens in the earlier of the two periods of Figure 6.1, its New Draperies in the latter? And where is the woollens industry of the West Country before the Civil War? Twenty-eight Wiltshire and Gloucestershire parishes are mapped onto Figure 6.1, and, while half of them show the 'I' sign of industrialization, that same symbol means that all fourteen typed as agricultural in 1561–1640. Only one of the twenty-eight typed as non-seasonal in the earlier period, and it is marked on the map with the 'D' of deindustrialization, having gained agricultural seasonality by 1661–1740. None of the twenty-eight typed as non-seasonal, industrial, in both periods (see Appendix for the country's parishes and their Early, Middle, and Late Seasonal Types). East Anglia and the West Country are well studied, and their manufacturing well described, but Figure 6.1 finds few parishes in which to locate the commercial crisis of the 1620s.[2] Where is the troubled woollens industry of East Anglia and the West Country hiding, in the earlier of the long periods (but see also Figure 3.10 above, the map of Relative Types, where the industry of East Anglia does peer through the haze of arable seasonality; using Relative Types, 'palpably plump' Lavenham, in Phythian-Adams' phrase, deindustrializes on cue)?[3]

When weaving was an occupation of men in towns, even if spinning for the town's weavers was a principal occupation of women in the surrounding countryside, the existence of the industry lies hidden

[2] Supple, *Commercial Crisis*, p. 5; Mann, *Cloth Industry*; Ponting, 'Wiltshire–Somerset Border', pp. 163–95.
[3] Phythian-Adams, 'Urban Decay', p. 159.

from my view. Defoe found the Norwich of the 1720s (towards the end of the second period of Figure 6.1) employing large portions of Cambridgeshire, Bedfordshire, and Hertfordshire in spinning for its weavers, the classic manifestation of this pattern.[4] Mann stressed spinning as an occupation of women over a very wide area of the West Country's otherwise principally agricultural districts.[5] But market towns have been dropped from the sample represented in Figures 6.1 and 6.2, because manufacturing in towns cannot be distinguished, via marriage seasons, from the non-seasonal pattern of marriages produced by a variety of commercial occupations.[6] And, as the second chapter found, women's work seems not to have strongly influenced the seasonality of marriage, especially where combined with men's work in agriculture. If the grooms of female spinners in the countryside were occupied in agriculture, as is likely, the seasonal pattern of marriages would have reflected the seasonality of their agricultural work. This means, moreover, that a movement of weaving from the towns out into the countryside would produce the apparent industrialization of the region in maps like Figure 6.1, without a net increase in manufacturing output or employment necessarily having occurred within the whole region, town plus countryside.

The Muster Roll for Gloucestershire in 1608 presents a convenient and rare chance to investigate the circumstances of the seasonal invisibility of the early seventeenth-century woollens industry. Table 6.1 ranks the seventeen Gloucestershire parishes in the 542-parish set by the percentage of males reported as employed in agriculture in the Muster Roll, and compares that ranking with that of the variable SEAS (the distance of each's parishes observations of (autumn index, spring index) from the random (100,100)) for 1581–1620 (see Chapter 3 for the derivation of SEAS and the Seasonal Types).[7] For three of the table's parishes, fewer than twenty-four marriages were recorded in 1581–1620, and accordingly SEAS for 1601–40 was used. The higher the SEAS index, the greater the likely impact of agriculture on the seasonality of work and weddings; in the definition of Seasonal Types in Chapter 3 (which underlies Figures 6.1 and 6.2), a SEAS index below 50 helped to identify the non-seasonal X-Types.

Only Westbury on Trym scores a SEAS index below 50. But this suburb of Bristol was not a textile-working parish; the seven italicized

---

[4] Defoe, *A Tour*, pp. 61–2.

[5] Mann, *Cloth Industry*, p. 125; Berg, *Age of Manufactures*, p. 121.

[6] Another reason for the non-seasonality of urban marriages was suggested in conversation with John Broad: inmigrants may have brought a mixture of contradictory traditions with them.

[7] Tawney and Tawney, 'Occupational Census', and John Smith, *Names and Surnames*.

Table 6.1. *Gloucestershire in 1608*
SEAS and the proportion of males in agriculture and textiles[a]

Parish	% in Agriculture	% in Textiles	SEAS 1581–1620	SEAS Rank
Clifford Chambers	91	—	115[b]	4.5
Bishop's Cleeve	82	—	120	2
Preston Upon Stour	82	—	90	8
Ampney Crucis	79	—	135	1
Kemerton	76	5	60	16
Dymock	75	3	67	14.5
Henbury	59	—	71	11.5
Westbury on Trym	67	8	30	17
Avening	58	26	96	6.5
Fairford	53	8	67[b]	14.5
Winchcombe	37	11	84	9
Cam	36	58	71	1.5
Eastington	28	52	115	4.5
Minchinhampton	26	49	96	6.5
North Nibley	23	61	72	10
Tetbury	20	31	68[b]	13
Wotton under Edge	9	45	119	3

[a] Source: see text. $\text{SEAS} = \sqrt{(\text{AUT}-100)^2 + (\text{SPR}-100)^2}$.
[b] SEAS, 1601–40.

parishes, which returned more than 20 per cent of their listed men as
employed in textile manufacturing, were, but they do not similarly
distinguish themselves by low agricultural seasonality of marriage.
The calculations of Spearman's r_s for correlation of ranks between the
SEAS index and the proportion listed in agriculture in each parish
yields a low value of 0.0772, from which we can infer an unacceptable
38 per cent chance of error in taking the two ranks to be related.
Avening might be excused for having a SEAS index as high as 96, because while 26 per cent of its men were listed with occupations in
textiles, 58 per cent were given agricultural ones. But Wotton under
Edge, with only 9 per cent returned in agriculture, recorded a still
greater SEAS index (119).

Chapter 4 showed Gloucestershire to have been autumn-marrying
in the sixteenth and early seventeenth centuries, and the Muster Roll
cannot reveal the number of textile workers who left their work for the
harvest, and then found that the high harvest wages conveniently
financed their wedding celebrations. There is also no way of knowing
the number of Gloucestershire's male textile workers who worked in

households also employed in agriculture, but who were listed for the muster as weavers, and not as yeomen, or husbandmen. Whether the indices of autumn and spring seasonality of marriages reliably find manufacturing within dual-employed households is a general problem. Where rural industry was truly slotted into seasonal gaps in the agricultural year, a pattern suggested by Mendels, we would expect marriages to have reflected the seasonality of the agricultural year as well.[8] The risks and costs of dropping work to marry would have been set by tyrant agriculture, not by greatly more flexible rural manufacturing.

How does the method fare in the next map, the comparison between seasonality in 1661–1740 and 1741–1820? The long span of the record, from the sixteenth into the nineteenth century, carries it into the urban growth of the classic Industrial Revolution, and produces in Figure 6.2 a new problem. The large region of earlier industrialization ('I'-Type on Figure 6.1, above) is now infected with a rash of 'D's, but the significance of that symbol has changed. The comparison of Figure 6.2 cannot differentiate between the death of industry in the south (*regional* deindustrialization) and the increasing spatial concentration of industry within the growing towns of the Midlands and north (showing in the mixture of 'X's and 'D's there); if the same process was occurring in Lancashire, it cannot be seen with marriage seasonality, because of what Chapter 2 called 'cloud cover'. Some of these new X-Type towns were 'new' in the sense of lacking market charters, towns that grew up around their industry. Because they were not market towns, they remain in the sample of plotted parishes, no matter how urban. Part of the dramatic movement of manufacturing from south to north described by Jones and others can be seen in Figure 6.2; the further north the eye moves up the map, the smaller the number of 'D's.[9] But to the extent that it was women's rural employment in industry, especially in spinning, that was devastated in the south by the first stages of northern mechanization, that rural work had in any case failed to influence the seasonality of marriage. Moreover, much of the shift had already occurred by 1740, and further spatial rearrangement of English industry remained to be done in the nineteenth century, beyond the range of this data.[10]

The impressionism of the maps can be neutralized by the more abstract statistics that gauge the constancy of seasonal typing over

[8] Mendels, 'Proto-Industrialization', p. 76, and Mendels, 'Seasons and Regions', p. 182.

[9] Jones, 'Constraints', pp. 423–30.

[10] Hudson, 'Proto-Industrialization', pp. 39–40; Wilson, 'Supremacy', p. 226.

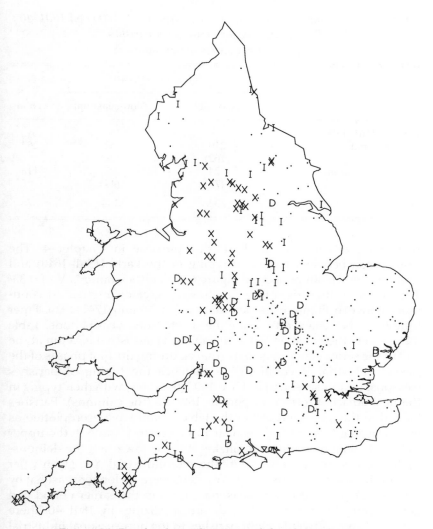

Figure 6.2 Rural industrialization and deindustrialization,
1661–1740 to 1741–1820
Key: X ever non-seasonal
     I becoming non-seasonal
     D becoming seasonal
     . ever seasonal

Table 6.2. *Seasonal and non-seasonal parishes, 1761–1800 and 1801–40*
Frequency table for non-market parishes
(expected frequencies in parentheses)

	Type in 1801–40		
	Seasonal	Non-seasonal	Total
Type in 1761–1800			
Seasonal	210	52	262
	(162)	(99)	
Non-seasonal	24	92	116
	(72)	(44)	
Total	234	144	378

time. Cramer's V was used for this purpose in Chapter 4. The comparison between industrial typing in the Early (1561–1640) and Middle (1661–1740) periods of Figure 6.1 yields a Cramer's V of 0.35. This measure then rises to 0.53, showing greater interperiod continuity between Figure 6.2's periods, 1661–1740 and 1741–1820. Finer tuning can be achieved by using the shorter forty year periods. Table 6.2 answers the question 'how unstable was industrial location at the end of the series of marriage data (that is, during the first phases of the classic Industrial Revolution)?' It matches the typing of parishes (seasonal or non-seasonal) in 1761–1800 (the rows) with their typing in the next adjacent forty year period, 1801–40 (the columns). Parishes lodged in the upper left cell of the table would have been plotted as ever-seasonal '·'s on maps similar to Figures 6.1 and 6.2; the upper right cell contains the industrializing 'I's, the lower left the deindustrializing 'D's, and the lower right the ever-industrial 'X's. Twenty per cent of the seasonal parishes of 1761–1800 were no longer seasonal by 1801–40; 21 per cent of non-seasonal places in the earlier period had gained agricultural seasonality, deindustrializing, by 1801–40; there was a net gain of twenty-eight parishes to the non-seasonal industrial camp between the two periods (parishes had to have recorded at least twenty-four marriages in each of the periods to register in the calculations, so the row and column totals differ from the totals that could be calculated from Table 3.3).

As in Chapter 4, the information contained in this and eleven other tables can be collapsed into single statistics for each comparison, and Cramer's V generated from the twelve possible comparisons of seasonal typing in adjacent periods. Cramer's V for the paired periods of

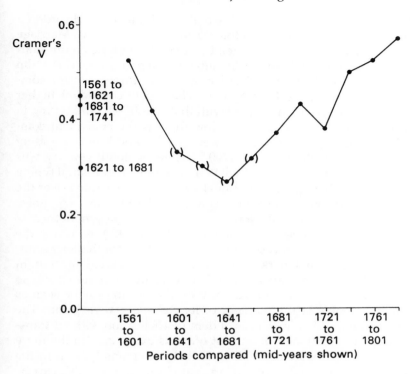

Figure 6.3 Cramer's V of interperiod seasonality, 1541–80 and 1581–1620 to 1741–80 and 1781–1820
(non-market parishes)

Table 6.2 is 0.57, and, as Figure 6.3 shows, that is the highest value that the statistic attains (cf. the similar exercise, Figure 4.1, which used the three main Seasonal Types, A, P, and X).

Lower values of Cramer's V would of course result from the imprecision of the mapping of work into marriage seasonality, and by slight movements of observations of autumn and spring seasonality over the knife-edge boundaries separating the seasonal from the non-seasonal places. The unmasking of rural industry, earlier hidden from view by extensive dual employment (with its attendant agri-culturally driven seasonality of marriage) could account for some of the instability of seasonal typing of parishes (and the appearance of 'I's and 'D's on Figures 6.1 and 6.2). The four comparisons involving the Interregnum are isolated in parentheses, and they are the four lowest values in the series.

But these low values are not wholly attributable to disordered records and the rush to marry before the introduction of Civil Marriage in late September, 1653 (in September 1653, three times more marriages were celebrated than in September of the preceding year).[11] On the vertical axis of Figure 6.3 are marked the three relevant comparisons that avoid the Interregnum. The nearly coincident higher values compare typing in 1541–80 with that in 1601–40, and typing in 1661–1700 with that in 1721–60. Below them is the equivalent comparison (skipping an intervening twenty-year period, here avoiding 1641–60) for 1601–40 and 1661–1700. The seventeenth century was unsettled, with or without the Civil War. Volatility in industrial typing increased, and then greater locational stability was regained over the eighteenth and early nineteenth centuries. Using the two types, seasonal and non-seasonal, Cramer's V traces a more symmetrical U than it did in the exercise with three types (Figure 4.1), reflecting the greater locational instability of rural manufacturing over this long span.

Volatility is not a hallmark of the theory of protoindustrialization. In its most criticized (and caricatured) abstract form, rural industry is so much a precursor of full industrialization that it can only be seen as generally unstable at the moment of its *Tod und Erklärung* into The Factory System. When instances of deindustrialization without transfiguration are mentioned, it is most often as exceptions to the more general rule, or in studies of failed industrial regions.[12] Even in the harsh criticism levelled at the theory's application to English experience, where much is made of the general failure of early modern industrial regions to become industrialized in the later eighteenth and nineteenth centuries, the focus is not on volatility *within* early modern manufacturing, on **de**industrialization before industrialization.[13] Locational instability, when discussed, is often explained with reference to the particularities of the unstable region or industry. Hammersley argued that the use of charcoal in iron-making inherently limited the expansion of that industry in the Weald;[14] Wilson stressed the entrepreneurial advantages the little clothiers of Yorkshire enjoyed over the large-scale clothiers of the West Country;[15] Peter and Margaret Spufford noted the transience of glass-making in Eccleshall, Staffordshire, as immigrant glass-makers from Lorraine moved to

[11] Wrigley and Schofield, *Population History of England*, p. 28, 28n.
[12] Mendels, 'Proto-Industrialization', p. 80; see discussions of Thompson, 'Variations', pp. 62–3, and of Kriedte, 'Proto-Industrialization', pp. 145–53.
[13] Coleman, 'Proto-Industrialisation', p. 443; Houston and Snell, 'Proto-Industrialization?', pp. 473–92; Hudson, 'Proto-Industrialization', p. 36.
[14] Hammersley, 'Charcoal Iron Industry', p. 612.
[15] Wilson, 'Supremacy', p. 237.

Staffordshire from the Weald, and then moved on to Newcastle on Tyne.[16] But the maps of Figures 6.1 and 6.2 are invitations to consider rural industrialization and deindustrialization in early modern England as aspects of a single process of linked change.

Why has volatility been so easily ignored? First, places that failed to remain industrial are hard to observe with methods more conventional and direct than mine. Rising industrial communities attracted more lasting attention to themselves than did the failing, as the latter slid back into agricultural oblivion. The example of the forgotten Hertfordshire textile industry, dying its strange death in the sixteenth century, cited by Thirsk in her oft-quoted article on rural industry, is salutary.[17]

Secondly, if the early modern deindustrialization of parishes or regions is viewed as a mere complication to the grand sweep of transformation, a back-eddy on the wave of change, it is unsurprisingly ignored. This is close to the charge levelled by Lees and Hohenberg against the protoindustrialists, in a related context. Following Braudel, they described the regular movement of manufacturing between town and country, country and town, from the thirteenth to nineteenth centuries.[18] But, sadly for this General View, industry in towns cannot be distinguished, by its unpeaked seasonality of marriage, from commercial activity, especially given the wide variety of trades and crafts of the larger town. If the volatility measure of Figure 6.3 and the maps of Figures 6.1 and 6.2 reflect this rural-urban ebb and flow, they can reflect only the rural half of the system.

A case can be made, however, for spatial volatility *within* early modern rural industry in England, without reference to the rural/urban nexus, to the introduction of new products, to technological change, or even to the agrarian changes of Chapters 4 and 5. I shall return in the next chapter to consider exogenous influences on rural industrialization and deindustrialization. But I shall first present the case for endogenous volatility, arguing for the inherent locational instability of early modern rural industry.

The placement of some of 1561–1640s non-agricultural markers on Figure 6.1 was determined by resource availability, such as the location of non-ubiquitous ore-bodies. But much early modern manufacturing was technically 'footloose', not restricted to particular places. Labour costs were far larger than material costs for most rural manufacturers.[19] Industry alit, and flourished, as Thirsk argued and many have followed, in areas of weak manorial control, partible

16 Spufford and Spufford, *Eccleshall*, pp. 27–8.   17 Thirsk, 'Industries', p. 87.
18 Hohenberg and Lees, *Making of Urban Europe*, pp. 113–16.
19 Coleman, *Industry*, p. 13.

inheritance, and pastoral farming.[20] The first condition permitted inmigration, the second the desire to supplement, through manufacturing, the earnings from subdivided holdings, and the third left more time in the day free, over more of the year, for industrial work. Continental theorists, especially, have stressed highland, poor land, locations, where rural industry was essential to the survival of the household.[21] Another influence on early modern industrial location has already been alluded to, in connection with the occluded vision of marriage seasons; spinning and other crafts employing women and children were often found in arable regions, especially where men were employed as day-labourers.[22]

Once industry had settled into its sixteenth-century locational pattern, why was there then volatility? Resource-exhaustion affected some places; but warring against the footloose wandering of industry should have been a variety of agglomeration effects, encouraging locational stability. Advantages accrued to larger industrial parishes or compact regions.[23] First, some manufacturing could be broken into separate steps, one step per specialized cottage, and the proximity of agglomerated producers to each other lowered the transportation costs of intermediate goods to the next producer along the chain. Mann, for instance, found agglomeration to be greater in the production of textiles, the more steps were involved in the process.[24] Secondly, agglomeration made communication among producers, about new products and markets, easier, and in general lowered marketing costs, by making the product simpler to marshal and vent. Thirdly, agglomeration encouraged the transmission of skills, and created deeper local pools of only frictionally unemployed labour, available for hiring; the four men Rowlands found employed in the typical metal-worker's workshop in the Black Country cannot all have been the sons of that typical metal-worker.[25] Finally, agglomeration improved the markets for second-hand equipment. Thus, anything that prevented the agglomeration of cottage industrialists limited the locality's chances of longer-term success.

[20] Thirsk, 'Industries', p. 86. Blanchard, though, argued that the tin-mining of Cornwall was slotted into the arable year, with miners going out to grub ore after spring ploughing and planting (and lambing) (Blanchard, 'The Miner', p. 100). But tin is a non-ubiquitous ore-body, its mining less prone to footloose locations.
[21] Braun, 'Early Industrialization', pp. 300–7.
[22] Gulluckson criticized Mendels, Jones, Braun, and others for ignoring rural industry, as she judged them as having done, when it was the work of women in the countryside (Gullickson, 'Agriculture', pp. 831–6).
[23] Richardson, *Regional Growth Theory*, pp. 182–7; Lloyd and Dicken, *Location in Space*, pp. 286–90.
[24] Mann, *The Cloth Industry*, p. 94.   [25] Rowlands, *Masters and Men*, pp. 39–40.

What, then, limited agglomeration, and what enhanced it? Greater efficiency in interregional trade, by lowering transactions and transportation costs separating producers from final consumers, should have increased the determining influence of factor costs and external economies in locational fortunes, removing nature's great tariff; better transportation, in encouraging shifts in agricultural orientation, also established new locational advantages. And since, in industry's early modern setting, growth in output largely proceeded from the replication of household work-units, anything that held back the natural increase of population and/or inmigration also impeded the creation of agglomeration effects. Cheaper labour attracted merchants, all else being equal, and a destabilizing force here was the tendency of wages to be higher in industrial than in other occupations. When more labour could be made to flood the parish or region, however, the tendency towards higher wages would be somewhat abated.[26] The determination of local population increase thus played a role in the early modern location of industry and in its agglomeration.

One could imagine two ideal forms of market-oriented rural industry, different in their agglomerative possibilities, and see part of the volatility as a result of the transition from one form to the other. First, consider the suggestions of Joan Thirsk in 'Industries in the Countryside' (picked up, sometimes carelessly and to the great confusion of their arguments, by others), in which textile manufacturing (to choose as Thirsk did the principal rural industry of early modern times) was slotted directly into a pastoral economy. The model she proposed was one in which the wife and children tended the farm animals while the husband worked, for example, as a weaver, because 'pastoral farming . . . required less labour than arable farming'.[27] I shall return to her explanation in the next chapter; it will be shown that it has greatest power when formerly arable places had only recently become pastoral, and found their local labour supply in sudden surplus, because most arable practices required more labour per acre than most pastoral. The argument for a pastoral setting is often tied to cases in which there were ample unstinted wastes and pastures, sufficient to attract inmigrants, who proceeded to put their own cattle, sheep, or cows on them.

The combination of pastoral with industrial work in 'Industries in the Countryside' was described as if the local economy consisted entirely of completed households, as if infants had passed to their middle teens in an instant, so that their and their mother's labour was available for the farm and/or industrial work. Now, when rural

26 Mann, *The Cloth Industry*, p. 105.   27 Thirsk, 'Industries', p. 73.

industry existed in just this dual-employed form, but with biologically reasonable spacing of births and spans of childhood development, it was burdened with two of the losing choices in the proposed list of agglomerative advantages: agglomeration would have been limited by the number of households that were caught in the deficit-labour phase of their development cycle, and skill and dexterity would have been limited by the length of time the industrial workers were unable to employ themselves in industry.

The possibility of enjoying other locational advantages would thus have been limited. The specialization of middlemen, for instance, would have been less likely, since the threshold of their interest would have been less easily reached. Thirsk, in a later article, found merchants dealing in both cheese and the stockings knit in the dual employed countryside.[28] There should, of course, have been a snappy market in second-hand looms, with households popping into and out of industrial work. In the surplus-labour phase of each household, however, the imputed cost of not working in farming, but in manufacturing, would have been low, thus keeping down local labour costs.

The combination of pastoral with industrial work certainly existed, as Thirsk demonstrated, and as the demonstration of Table 3.4, which contrasted Farming Types with Seasonal Types, and where a disproportionately large number of the wood pasture and open pasture parishes of 1581–1620 were shown to have been non-seasonal X-Types, reinforced. My earlier work on farm servants suggests a modification to the model. Much of northwestern European society had a solution to the development cycle of the nuclear family's labour force in agriculture, an off-the-rack institution that would have fit the dual-employed pastoral-industrial household remarkably well. The family could have hired in a farm servant or two, in the deficit-labour phase of the household. There were instances of this in the unusually detailed listings of eighteenth-century households in remote Westmorland, showing groupings of farm servants and crafts servants in the households of weavers. No pre-Census listing of parish population that I found while looking for farm servants was as detailed as that set.[29] These superb listings gave everyone's occupation, not just the occupation of the head of the household, and everyone's status in relation to the head. And there we find households that appear to have adopted the institution of farm service to the needs of the mixed pastoral–industrial household; the one I cited in

[28] Thirsk, 'Fantastical Folly', pp. 62–3.
[29] When I cited an example from it in *Servants in Husbandry*, it was disparaged as 'a single instance' of craftsmen hiring servants: Mendels, 'Farm Servants', pp. 1–2.

Servants in Husbandry was the household of Joseph Idle, weaver, and his wife, described as 'housekeeper'. The household contained no children to help with the sheep and cows, but instead, four servants: two women, the manager of the dairy and the spoolswinder, and two men, one described as husbandman and the other as shepherd. Whether the Idles had had no children, or whether the children had left the family, cannot be deduced from the listings, but their servants filled the roles allotted to children in Joan Thirsk's description.[30] Where rural industrialists had the luxury of their own holdings, or rights to ample pasture, the problem of cyclical deficit would thus be solved, for the servant-employer, without the loss of skill that time out for farming would have implied.

And there was a strong motive for youths to become farm servants in this setting, as well (besides the ordinary possibility of the servant-supplying households not being able better to employ their children, the desire of parents to get their children's feet under somebody else's table). The set-up costs of these tidy little combined operations, simply in terms of capital equipment, were not negligible; not only must a loom have been obtained, and habitation for the household and loom, but also the cattle, or sheep, or cows and dairy equipment, if dairying was the prevailing pastoral activity. For two related reasons, then, the age at marriage would have been propped up in dual employment; significant savings were necessary before entry into the 'occupation' of mixed pastoralist–industrialist, and live-in service was both a niche in which to delay marriage and an opportunity to accumulate savings.[31]

With the modification of this first ideal form, there will be better agglomeration effects, because more households in the region could participate in industry at any one time. Still, however, growth would have been limited by the high age at marriage. The main source of growth in the local labour force would have been inmigration, and that would have been limited by the availability of land in the locality, by the savings of inmigrants, and by information costs. The manufacturing labour would still not have been full-time, since farming servants required supervision, and middlemen may still have been encouraged not to be specialized by the local availability for trade in both pastoral and industrial products (although this is really a question of whether the quantity produced of each was sufficiently large to warrant specialization). The extent of this first form of rural industry limited

---

[30] Kussmaul, *Servants in Husbandry*, p. 14; the listing is of the parish of Murton in 1787, from the collection of the Cambridge Group for the History of Population and Social Structure.
[31] Guttman and Leboutte, 'Rethinking Proto-Industrialization', pp. 594–5.

the impact of industrialization on aggregate population growth, increasing the region's vulnerability to others better able to pursue agglomeration; its main demographic effect was to keep the age at marriage high. It should be noted, though, that there is debate over the general extent of dual employment in the sixteenth and early seventeenth centuries, especially in the southwest.[32]

The second ideal form should come as no surprise; it is rural industry without dual-employment. If the first ideal form was Thirsk-type rural industry, the second is, without doubt, Levine-type.[33] The whole return to the protoindustrialist of this second form was wages and profit, or wages alone, if the capital was owned by merchants. This is the simpler form; the density of rural industrialists in a place would have been limited only by space for the cottages and workshops of the family working units, encouraging the creation of the external economies of agglomeration. The west Midlands epitomized this new concentration, as it became, in Court's words,

more and more a strung-out web of iron-making villages, market towns next-door to collieries, heaths and wastes gradually and very slowly being covered by the cottages of nailers and other persons carrying out industrial occupations in rural surroundings.[34]

Set-up costs for rural manufacturers of this second form were lower than for the dual-employed of the first one, with no livestock and farming equipment to procure, and nothing beyond a cottage (and work-space, if needed) to rent. Rowlands has provided estimates of the value of tools and other equipment for metal-workers; she found that a nailer's tools were generally valued at only £1, and cited a 1676 Walsall rental for a nailer's cottage (£1 10s) and workshop (10s). Lorimers and scythesmiths, far less numerous than nailers, had equipment valued at £2 to £35.[35] Low set-up costs permitted earlier household formation and marriage, and this led to higher growth rates of the local population and thus of the potential local labour force (but see below, in Chapter 7, for the discussion of crisis mortality and rural industry).

The fundamental differences between the two ideal forms thus lie in (1) set-up costs, lower for the protoindustrialists of the second form; (2) the tendencies towards, and sources of, wage-depressing local population growth, natural increase plus inmigration in protoindustry but largely only modest inmigration in the case of dual employment;

[32] Bettey, 'Agriculture', pp. 298–9; Mann, *The Cloth Industry*, p. 102.
[33] Levine, *Family Formation*, passim; see also Armstrong, 'Origin of the Labour Force', pp. 40–2.
[34] Court, *The Rise*, p. 22.   [35] Rowlands, *Masters and Men*, pp. 27, 30 and 39.

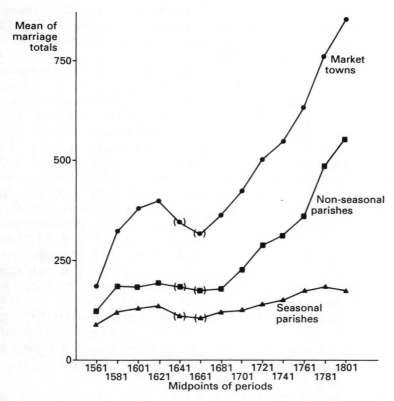

Figure 6.4 Mean totals of marriages by Seasonal Types, 1541–80 to 1781–1820

and (3) the degree of agglomeration effects, especially tendencies towards specialization among producers and distributors, greater in the second form than the first.

Support for the process of endogenous change within early modern rural industry comes from an investigation of the demographic implications of the two forms. In Figure 6.4, the 542 parishes have been divided into three sets (market towns, seasonal, and non-seasonal) in each of the overlapping forty year periods from 1541–80 to 1781–1820, and the mean number of marriages for the parishes in each set have been calculated. If parishes recorded no more than twenty-three marriages in the forty year period, no Seasonal Type was calculated, and so they were dropped from observation for that period. Therefore the means, especially of the smaller seasonal places, overstate the true means for agricultural parishes, because twenty-four is the smallest possible number of marriages in a parish in the period's working sample. Periods 1 and 15 have been dropped from the figure; Period 1 (1538–60) is only twenty-three years long, and there is a big dropout of parishes from the sample at 1812.

Market towns scored highest in mean totals of recorded marriages in every period. Of the remaining parishes, those with agricultural marriage seasonality (Types A, P, and H) consistently had the lowest mean totals. Sandwiched between the market towns and the agricultural parishes is the interesting sequence of mean totals for non-seasonal (X-Type) rural parishes. The curve tracks the curve for seasonal parishes until 1661–1700, always recording no more than half again as many marriages. From 1681–1720, though, the non-seasonal curve breaks free from the seasonal one, and floats up to join the market towns. The means are significantly different from each other throughout, at the 5 per cent level of error, using the Duncan-Waller K-ratio t-test. The biggest jump in the rural industrial curve is 1741–80 to 1761–1800, possibly influenced by Hardwicke's Marriage Act, implemented in 1754, which required the registration of marriages that before had gone unnoted in the Anglican registers. But the onset of the exuberant growth of these marriage totals predates Hardwicke, and is more than a little compatible with the argument about changing possibilities of agglomeration advanced above. The ascendant second, protoindustrial, form should have permitted more spatial agglomeration and promoted more rapid population growth within an industrial parish than did dual-employment.

Parishes falling within the two ideal forms of rural industrial organization have in common the production of goods for non-captive markets, and were thus open to competition from other parishes and other regions (and other products and techniques). Both were vulnerable to deindustrialization through endogenous processes, as well as through exogenous changes in these external conditions. Not every parish potentially suited to rural industry, through poor soil, poor location for agriculture, or surplus labour, for instance, became industrial at the same time. Information costs were not negligible, and the extent of the market for all industrial goods will have limited the possibility of rural industry's 'capture' of all suitable places. A lowering of these costs or a widening of the market may have created new competitors.

The second form, the parishes of rural proletarians, might always have been expected to win an open competition over time with the first form, the parish of pastoral-industrialists, with only local skills, raw material costs, or very low imputed returns to poorly located pastoral activities holding the first form in place. It is significant, in this respect, that all of the pastoral–industrial regions described by Joan Thirsk in 'Industries in the Countryside' were established industrial regions when the first Elizabeth became Queen; they were enjoying industrial specializations chased from towns by relatively high urban labour costs in previous centuries, and had tended to find pastoral locations partly because of the industrially crippling seasonality of arable work, compared to pastoral. Three of the four industrial regions Thirsk described deindustrialized well before the middle of the eighteenth century; these were not parishes of protoindustry, but more of Type One dual employment.

Some progress towards the comprehension of locational instability may have been gained in seeing it as self-driven. That model of endogenous volatility was not evolutionary. As others have shown, old rural industrial places do not necessarily become full industrial ones in the late eighteenth and nineteenth centuries; Form One pastoral–industrial places, with agricultural and industrial work combined in households, probably had less chance of becoming Form Two rural industrial places than did parishes within newly pastoral, lately arable, regions. Endogenous changes in rural industry were by no means the only things going on in the early modern English economy; as Chapters 4 and 5 demonstrated, the agrarian setting for industry did not remain constant from the sixteenth through the eighteenth centuries.

Rural industrial location in early modern England was found in this chapter to have been unstable, and the instability in part attributed to the nature of rural industry. The next chapter considers the impact upon industry of the restructuring of the agrarian economy in the later seventeenth and early eighteenth centuries, and the demographic implications of the spatial rearrangement.

7

Change, consolidation, and population

Thus the farming systems of England become more sharply differentiated economically and socially; and the stage was prepared for changes in the eighteenth century which wrought an agricultural revolution in arable regions and an industrial revolution in pastoral ones.

(Thirsk, 1970, p. 72).

Changes in regional agricultural orientation split apart the A-Type and P-Type centroids of marriage seasonality in Figure 3.12. Agricultural specialization would have disrupted locally sustained tendencies towards balance between local supplies of, and demand for, agricultural labour. Regions becoming more arable, like East Anglia, would have experienced labour shortages. Its rural industry declined, just as the cloth-making of Hertfordshire had declined as the county became more arable in the sixteenth century.[1] Regions turning from the production of grain to rearing, like the west, would have found themselves with labour surpluses, driving down local wages and attracting rural industry; John argued that while agricultural wages increased in the south and east after 1660, they were stationary in the west,[2] and Bowden found agricultural wages substantially higher in arable than in pastoral regions in 1640–1750.[3] Agricultural changes thus fed the fires of industrial volatility: there was a strong spatial association in the later seventeenth and early eighteenth centuries between **newly** pastoral (formerly arable) and **newly** industrial (also formerly arable) places, most notably in the Midlands and the West Country.

The new industrial regions were far less likely to have been characterized by mixed pastoral–industrial households, but rather by patchworks of industrial and pastoral parishes. They are mixed

[1] Thirsk, 'Industries', p. 87.   [2] John, 'The Course of Agricultural Change', p. 133.
[3] Bowden, 'Agricultural Prices', 1985, p. 18.

agricultural–industrial regions, only, and the newly industrial parishes often retained, as Shepshed displayed, remnants of the agricultural (there arable) seasonality of their past (also possibly reflecting the short-term harvest migration of Shepshed's stocking-knitters). These parishes became the Form Two protoindustrial places of the preceding chapter, often surrounded by more purely pastoral parishes.

Figures 7.1, 7.2, and 7.3 rework the maps of Chapter 6 in the light generated by the agricultural chapters, 4 and 5. They and their accompanying tables (7.1 and 7.2) touch on the question of the agricultural origins of rural industry, for the seasonal origins of the newly industrial parishes are there differentiated. Figure 7.1 compares the Seasonal Types of parishes in the Early (1561–1640) and Middle (1661–1740) periods (see above, Figure 3.8, for definitions of the Seasonal Types). The autumn-marrying arable parishes of 1561–1640 are designated by the letters 'A' and 'a'. Upper case 'A's show the newly non-seasonal (once arable) parishes of 1661–1740, and lower case 'a's newly spring-marrying pastoral parishes. Pastoral origins are indicated by the symbols 'P' and 's': 'P' marks a newly industrial, formerly pastoral parish, and 's' a newly arable place. Capital letters thus mark the industrializing parishes; I apologize for the symbolic inconsistency of using the pair 'A' and 'a' with 'P' and 's', but free-floating 'p's are difficult to distinguish from 'P's. Ever non-seasonal parishes are shown with dots. To simplify the map, ever-seasonal parishes of stable seasonality, those that were P-Type in both periods and those consistently A-Type, are not shown, nor are the deindustrializing gainers of autumn or spring marriages (see Figures 6.1 and 6.2 above for these).

Autumnal, harvest-driven, marriages had virtually disappeared from the west during the seventeenth century, and in Figure 7.1 can be found the seasonal fates of the region's parishes; some have become spring-marrying P-Type places (marked with 'a's), the rest non-seasonal X-Types, shown with 'A's. The same combination of 'A's and 'a's can be found in some concentration in the Midlands, a region that also retained many arable A-Type parishes (not shown on this map, but see below, Figure 7.2).

Regions losing harvest work, and with it, autumn marriages, almost certainly found themselves in pools of newly surplus labour. The pools might then have been drained by outmigration, or mopped up locally either by that most labour intensive of pastoral activities, dairying, or by even more labour intensive rural manufacturing. Hartlib recognized this, in arguing that enclosure for pasture need

Figure 7.1 Seasonal sources in 1561–1640 of rural industrial parishes of
1661–1740
Key: . non-seasonal, both periods
      A newly non-seasonal, from A-Type
      P newly non-seasonal, from P-Type
      a newly pastoral, from A-Type
      s newly arable, from P-Type

Table 7.1. *Agricultural origins of the new rural industry of 1661–1740*

	Seasonal Types, 1661–1740				
	(1) X	(2) A	(3) P	(4) n	(5) (%)
Seasonal Types 1561–1640					
A	46	171	45	262	(82.6%)
P	13	15	27	55	(17.4%)
n	59	186	72	317	
(%)	(18.6%)	(58.7%)	(22.7%)		(100.0%)

cause no depopulation as long as two conditions were met: first, there must be an outlet for the manufactures of the locality's workers newly surplus to the newly pastoral farming, and secondly, there must be a good supply of grain into the region, to feed it.[4] Hoskins found an eighteenth-century echo in the complaint in 1771 that Wigston Magna's enclosure meant that not enough grain was being produced for local consumption.[5] Interregional and international trade was increasingly meeting the first of the conditions, and the increases in the volume of interregional trade, suggested by the increase in Mindist in Figure 4.16 and by the productivity increase argued for in Chapter 5, the second.

The preponderance of 'A's over 'P's on Figure 7.1 shows the agricultural origins of the new rural industrial parishes of 1661–1740 to have been arable, not pastoral. Because this flies in the face of the conventional association of pastoral farming with nascent rural industry, closer investigation is warranted. Table 7.1 displays the agricultural origins (in 1561–1640) of the newly non-seasonal X-Types of 1661–1740 (col. 1). There were fifty-nine new rural industrial parishes in 1661–1740, and forty-six of them, 78 per cent, had been arable.

There were, of course, many more A-Type (262) than P-Type (55) parishes in 1561–1640 from which the new X-Types could be drawn.[6] Were the (relatively few) P-Type parishes of 1561–1640 more likely to turn industrially non-seasonal than were the A-Types? Yes, slightly; a higher proportion of 1561–1640s P-Types (23.6 per cent) became non-seasonal by 1661–1740 than did that earlier period's A-Types (17.6 per cent). But the difference in proportions is not statistically sig-

[4] Hartlib, *His Legacie*, p. 44.   [5] Hoskins, *The Midland Peasant*, p. 262.
[6] Cramer's V for the consistency of typing in this comparison is 0.346.

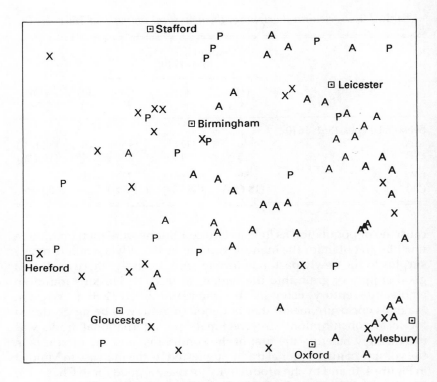

Figure 7.2 Seasonality in the Midlands, 1661–1740
Key:
A   A-Type
P   P-Type
X   X-Type

nificant, even at a 10 per cent level of error (Z=0.9804). And even if the pastoral parishes of 1561–1640 had been shown to have been more likely to industrialize than were that period's arable parishes, the origin of the great majority of newly industrial parishes was not pastoral.

Most of the new rural industry of the later seventeenth and early eighteenth centuries arose in parishes, and regions, that had recently been arable. The Midlands, for example, became a tricolour patchwork of industrial, arable, and pastoral local specializations, as the more detailed view of Figure 7.2 (and a colourful imagination) suggests. The map plots the Seasonal Types of parishes for 1661–1740, the period of rapid growth of the region's rural industry.

Table 7.2. *Agricultural origins of the new rural industry of 1741–1820*

| | Seasonal Types, 1741–1820 | | | | |
	(1) X	(2) A	(3) P	(4) n	(5) (%)
Seasonal Types 1661–1740					
A	24	172	5	201	(67.2%)
P	34	21	43	98	(32.8%)
n	58	193	48	299	
(%)	(19.4%)	(64.5%)	(16.1%)		(100.0%)

A similar map for 1561–1640 would have been monotonously covered with the 'A's of arable farming; only ten of the plotted parishes failed to record an autumn index of 150 then. The emergent pattern of specialization of the later seventeenth and early eighteenth centuries left many of the region's parishes remaining autumn-marrying, while others switched either to the spring marriages of the pastoral type ('P') or to industrial non-seasonality ('X'). Labour newly unemployed by farmers switching from arable to pastoral work did not have far to go to find industrial employment.

Table 7.2, companion for 1741–1820 of Table 7.1, returns to the national sample. Now there is more industrial recruitment directly from parishes dominated by pastoral seasonality in 1661–1740; the majority (58.6 per cent) of the new X-Types had been P-Types. And now the P-Type is shown to have been more likely than the A-Type to switch to non-seasonality, as well; 34.7 per cent of the Middle period's ninety-eight P-Types had become X-Types in 1741–1820, while only 11.9 per cent of the 201 A-Types had lost their agricultural seasonality. This time, the large difference in proportions is statistically significant, at the 1 per cent level of error. Cramer's V for the comparison is 0.527. The large minority (41.4 per cent) of new X-Types that had earlier looked arable characterizes the northern Midlands and the West Riding, especially (see Figure 7.3, where these parishes are plotted as 'A').

In the consolidating eighteenth century pools of rural unemployment were not being created by the abandonment of arable or of other labour-intensive agricultural practices, as had occurred in the preceding century. Far from it; more parishes exhibited arable seasonality in 1741–1820 than in 1661–1740, and 's's now outnumber the 'a's. New crop rotations, moreover, are reckoned to have increased the labour

Figure 7.3 Seasonal sources in 1661–1740 of rural industrial parishes of 1741–1820

Key: . non-seasonal, both periods
     A newly non-seasonal, from A-Type
     P newly non-seasonal, from P-Type
     a newly pastoral, from A-Type
     s newly arable, from P-Type

input per arable acre, making the now established arable regions even less attractive to rural industry, except where the wives and children of agricultural day-labourers found spinning, lace-making, and straw-plaiting more advantageous work than agricultural labour.[7] Some of the 'A's and 'P's on Figure 7.3 do not denote industrialization, but urban expansion (as near Bristol and in the ring around London); the lonely 'A' out on the peninsular East Riding is Winestead, still agricultural, but with its 'autumn', post-harvest marriages now pushed into December (and out of the range of the autumn index) by the mid century adoption of the new calendar (see above, Table 2.2). But the last expansion of the West Country's textile industry is caught by the scattering of 'P's there.[8]

One hardly needs a map of marriage seasons, 1741–1820, to know that industrialization was occurring in the north. The period includes the first phases of mechanization in textile manufacturing, and the application of water power and then coal-fired steam engines to larger versions of the machines. New influences, importantly energy costs, were now directing manufacturing location. The new non-seasonality of marriages in the northern Midlands and the West Riding no more than echoes the tales of northern grit and ingenuity in the classic Industrial Revolution (marriages in much of industrial Lancashire had already been non-seasonal in 1561–1640, for reasons not always associated with the low seasonality of the region's work and leisure). Recent studies have worked at discounting both the rapidity of industrialization in the late eighteenth and early nineteenth century and the sharpness of contrasts between south and north. Everitt found that 25 per cent of men in lowland England were given 'industrial' occupations in the 1861 census, while in the four most industrial counties (Lancashire, the West Riding, Warwickshire, and Notting-hamshire), only 43–46 per cent were; Berg challenged the older notion of a sharp discontinuity in Britain's manufacturing development, and several recent studies have similarly found less acceleration in industrial growth before the 1830s than had earlier been assumed.[9]

The continuation of non-agricultural seasonality in the West Country would lend some support to that interpretation. It cannot have been forgotten, though, that the seasonal typing of parishes

---

[7] Timmer, 'The Turnip, New Husbandry, and the English Agricultural Revolution', pp. 375–95; Jones, 'Constraints on Economic Growth'.

[8] Mann, *The Cloth Industry*, p. 52, 158–9.

[9] Everitt, 'Country, County and Town', p. 104 (Lee provided evidence running somewhat counter to this in 'Service Sector', pp. 139–55); Berg, *Age of Manufactures*, p. 20; Crafts, 'British Economic Growth', pp. 177–99; Harley, 'British Industrialization', pp. 267–89; Wrigley, *Continuity, Chance, and Change.*

forced them into the classes A-Type, P-Type, and X-Type, as if they had been all-arable, all-pastoral, or all-industrial, allowing nothing to be seen of the rural work of women in spinning, lace-making, or straw-plaiting, and likely often mistaking the part-time harvest labour of otherwise industrially employed workers for wholly agricultural, arable, employment. The only semblance of truth in exclusive interpretations of the Seasonal Types comes with the P-Type; a high spring/summer index of marriage seasonality was probably an accurate indicator of all-rearing.

Whatever the causes of the volatility of industrial locations, whatever the causes of the regional dropping of arable work in favour of pastoral, the changes had their impact on local populations. In the endogenous explanation of industrial instability, differences in the age at marriage and in rates of migration were predicted between the parishes of mixed pastoral–industrial households and the parishes of rural proletarians. The age at marriage would have been higher in the former, and rates of inmigration higher in the latter. Outmigration would have occurred from parishes switching from arable to pastoral orientation. The predictions were not contradicted by the differences in marriage totals over time in Figure 6.4 (above); the mean totals in the non-seasonal rural X-Types might have risen because the age at marriage was lower in the new-style X-Types or because more marriageable young adults had migrated to the protoindustrial places. In the more exogenous explanation of changes in industrial locations, the regional specialization in agriculture of Chapters 4 and 5 was seen to have disrupted local labour markets, chasing labour from agriculture where arable yielded to pastoral, and holding it more tightly to the land where the ploughman displaced the shepherd.

The local demographic impacts of the changes in economic orientation found through the changing seasonality of marriage can be demonstrated more directly, with a final reclassification of Seasonal Types into what are straightforwardly, if clumsily, called Switch Types. Each parish has two Switch Types, the first showing an alteration in seasonal typing between 1561–1640 and 1661–1740 (the Early/Middle Switch Type), and the second change between 1661–1740 and 1741–1820 (the Middle/Late Switch Type). Parishes that dropped autumn marriages and began to marry in the spring and early summer in 1661–1740, for instance, and so switched from A-Type to P-Type, are given an Early/Middle Switch Type of AP; the rarer pastoral to arable group is classified as PA. AX and PX signify industrializing parishes, parishes whose marriages lost their agricultural seasonality, and the deindustrializing parishes are classified either as XA or XP, depending on whether their seasonal fates were arable or pastoral. Parishes with consistently low autumn and low spring seasonality, which would have been classified as non-seasonal X-Type parishes in both the long periods being compared are given the Switch Type of XX. Similarly consistent A-Type and P-Type parishes are classed as AA and PP. The Early/Middle and Middle/Late Switch Types of each parish can be read from Table A.1 in the Appendix; merging the first with the second column of the table yields the Early/Middle, and the second with the third column the Middle/ Late Switch Types.

Figure 7.4 presents the parochial means of annual growth rates of totals of marriages by Switch Type over the 100 years separating 1561–1640 and 1661–1740 (to the left of the figure), and over the eighty years between 1661–1740 and 1741–1820. The mean growth rates for the Switch Types have been calculated over the parishes in each Switch Type that were not market towns; market towns form a separate tenth category. Brackets enclose the parochial means in each comparison that were not significantly different from each other, but which were significantly different from the non-overlapping group-ings of means (significant at the 5 per cent level of error, Waller-Duncan K-ratio t-tests between means). The number of parishes in each class is shown in parentheses. It should be recalled that the marriage totals on which the demonstration are based are truncated; if fewer than twenty-four marriages were recorded in the parish in either of the long periods being compared, no attempt was made to assign a Seasonal Type to the parish.

The Early/Middle growth rates are widely spaced. Industrial occu-pations allowed a greater density of population than did land-intensive agricultural ones, so it is not surprising to find that it was the newly industrial, formerly agricultural, parishes (AX and PX) that recorded the greatest increases in mean totals of marriages. The relatively few (13) industrializers that had before been the more land-intensively pastoral in their seasonality (PX) record a mean growth rate significantly higher than all others. The number of marriages in the newly arable, formerly pastoral, parishes also grew quickly, as might have been expected from the greater labour intensity of most arable than most pastoral farming; they grew at a faster rate even than the marriages in the consistently non-seasonal XX class. Dairying was also labour intensive, but dairying parishes were as likely to have married in the autumn as in the spring and early summer, as was demonstrated in earlier chapters. The brackets warn that the mean growth rate in the fifteen PA parishes is significantly

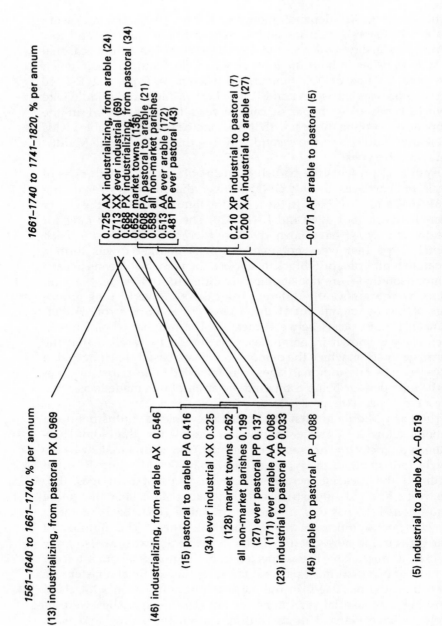

Figure 7.4 Mean annual growth rates of marriage totals by Switch Type

higher only than the mean rates in the two Switch Types losing marriages, the five deindustrializers to arable (XA) and the newly pastoral (formerly arable) group of forty-five AP parishes. The latter group's mean sits where all the sixteenth- and seventeenth-century's complainants against enclosure for pasture might have expected it, towards the bottom of the distribution. The totals of marriages in the consistent A-Types and P-Types grew at nearly the same low rate, significantly higher than only the deindustrializers to arable, but not significantly lower than the rates in the PA parishes, the consistent X-Types, or the market towns.

The mean annual growth rates in numbers of marriages between 1661–1740 and 1741–1820, to the right of Figure 7.4, differ in several respects from the first set. The rates are more tightly bunched, possibly reflecting the lowered reliability of Seasonal Typing in the last of the three periods, 1741–1820. Almost all the Middle/Late rates are greater than the comparable Early/Middle ones; seven of the ten right-hand means are 0.4 per cent per annum or more, while only two rates were so high in the earlier comparison. The mean growth rate for all the non-market parishes increased from 0.17 per cent per annum to 0.54 per cent. The AP, XA, and XP means are still the lowest, although the means of the deindustrializing parishes are not significantly lower than the means of the AA, PP, or PA places. The PA mean, along with those of the consistently non-seasonal X-Types and the two industrializing classes AX and PX, are the highest means of all the non-market classes, but they are not high enough to be significantly different from the means for the consistently arable (AA) and pastoral (PP) Switch Types.

Differences in growth rates of marriage totals in either of the comparisons can be partially understood with reference to migration. People left deindustrializing parishes and newly pastoral (formerly arable) ones, because fewer employment opportunities remained in each of the new types, compared to their former industrial or arable orientation, and they were drawn to the new jobs created in the industrializing and newly arable parishes. Inmigration brought more marriageable young adults together, increasing the local total of marriages, while outmigration left fewer behind to marry.

If all that had happened was a relocation of weddings that would otherwise have occurred, there would be no net impact on population size. But three more subtle consequences of migration could further have affected the number of marriages, and the size of the English population. First, migration was often sex-specific, creating imbalances in sex-ratios in both the regions gaining and the regions losing population, and presumably depressing marriage totals in general. Sex ratios, defined as the number of males per hundred females, in the enumerations made under the Marriage Duty Act of 1695, ranged from 80.2 to 92.5 in eight large towns, but the means of sex ratios in three groups of small villages ranged from 98.5 to 109.3.[10] Secondly, when the newly surplus labour left for towns, it moved into an unhealthier environment, with increased mortality eliminating potential marriage partners. Wrigley and Schofield explained the apparent deficit of urban baptisms relative to burials through a combination of adult inmigration to the towns and higher urban mortality, which acted as a drain on aggregate growth.[11] Wrigley further noted that urban inmigration helped check population growth.[12] Lastly, the pure movement of people from place to place brought more of them into contact with new microbes, also increasing mortality. Wrigley and Schofield explained the introduction and spread of new diseases in the seventeenth century in part as a function of the level and type of migratory movements.[13] Childhood mortality increased between 1550–99 and 1600–49 as the result of new infectious diseases that give no time for genetic or immunological adjustments of new generations.[14]

In *The Population History of England* Wrigley and Schofield produced authoritative aggregate estimates of national population, and a set of explanations of the long-term trends in population appropriate to that level of aggregation. What could have touched everyone in the population? Pandemics might have, but didn't; changing food prices and real wages did. The possibility of partitioning the 542-parish sample (dominated, it should be remembered, by the 404-parish set that underlay *The Population History of England*) by Switch Types opened a door to investigating the impact of **compositional** change on national population. The base periods Early, Middle, and Late are long enough for differences in nuptiality, fertility, and mortality unassociated with migration to have led to larger or smaller numbers of potential marriage partners in the next generation, but still within the period's eighty years. What if, for example, there had been no rural industrialization and deindustrialization, or no switching between arable and pastoral Seasonal Types? What difference might it have made to the size of the English population?

The method I use to address the question is simple to the point of

[10] Souden, 'Migrants and the Population Structure', p. 150.
[11] Wrigley and Schofield, *Population History of England*, p. 160.
[12] Wrigley, 'Parasite or Stimulus', pp. 304–5.
[13] Wrigley and Schofield, *Population History of England*, p. 416.
[14] Schofield and Wrigley, 'Infant and Child Mortality', pp. 61, 69.

artlessness. If there had been no switching between Seasonal Types, all of the A-Type parishes in 1561–1640 would still have been A-Types in 1661–1740, and the totals of marriages in all these AA, AX, and AP parishes (I posit for the purpose of the exercise) would have grown at 0.068 per cent per annum, the mean rate recorded by the AA parishes, that is, by the parishes that were indeed still autumn-marrying A-Types in 1661–1740 (see Table 7.3). The true AX rate was the much higher 0.546 per cent per annum, but had these parishes remained arable A-Types, their marriages, the exercise posits, would have grown at only 0.068 per cent per annum. The true AP rate was negative, a mean of −0.088 per cent per annum, as was expected from the lower labour intensity of pastoral work; the hypothesis of constancy of typing would see the marriages in these parishes also grow at 0.068 per cent per annum. Similarly the numbers of marriages in all of 1561–1640s P-Types (PP, PX, and PA) are assumed to have grown at the true PP rate of 0.137 per cent per annum, and totals in 1561–1640s X-Types (XX, XP, and XA) to have grown at the true XX rate of the brisk (for the time) annual rate of 0.325 per cent, instead of the low rate of 0.033 per cent for the deindustrializers to pastoral, or the negative rate recorded by the deindustrializers to arable, −0.519 per cent (see cols. c and d, Table 7.3). The growth rates used were those displayed on Figure 7.4, the mean growth rates in marriages of parishes in each of the Switch Types. Hypothetical totals and growth rates are indicated in boldface type. Summing the new hypothetical totals of marriages for 1661–1740 over the three posited unchanging Seasonal Types (and assuming no new effects on net emigration from England) yields a total of marriages in 1661–1740 for all the non-market parishes in the sample of 110,022, which can then be compared with the true total for 1661–1740, 115,264 (see Table 7.3, cols. h and i).

With no change between the Seasonal Types (row 1 of the summary section of the table), the number of marriages in the rural parishes in the sample would have been 4.5 per cent lower than the observed number in 1661–1740, that is, after the century that elapsed between the mid points of the Early and Middle periods. Repeating the exercise for the eighty years separating the Middle and Late totals (Table 7.4) results in a hypothetical no-switch total of the sample's marriages of 194,052 in 1741–1820, which is only 0.14 per cent lower than the observed total, a result that might have been anticipated from the bunching of the Middle to Late growth rates on Figure 7.4.

There are, therefore, compositional effects in the predicted directions. But the compositional effects are very weak. The difference between real and hypothetical annual growth rates attributable to

Table 7.3. *Real and hypothetical totals of marriages, 1661–1740*
non-market parishes only
(using mean growth rates by Switch Type)

Switch Type	number pars	(a) Total marriages 1561–1640	(b) Total marriages 1661–1740[1]	(c) Annual growth rate (%)[2]	(d) Hypo. growth (%)[3]	(e) Hypo. total 1661–1740[4]	(f) Diff. marrs (%)[5]	(g) Diff. growth[6]
XX	34	13 682	18 926	0.325	0.325	18 926	—	—
AX	46	9 996	17 231	0.546	0.068	10 699	37.9	0.478
PX	13	1 904	4 994	0.969	0.137	2 183	56.3	0.832
AA	171	38 573	41 286	0.068	0.068	41 286	—	—
AP	45	10 896	9 978	−0.088	0.068	11 662	−16.9	−0.156
PA	15	2 975	4 506	0.416	0.137	3 411	24.3	0.279
PP	27	9 306	10 671	0.137	0.137	10 671	—	—
XP	23	6 533	6 750	0.033	0.325	9 037	−33.9	−0.292
XA	5	1 550	921	−0.519	0.325	2 144	−132.8	−0.844
all	379	95 415	115 263	0.199				

3 hypotheses:	(h) Hypo. total marrs 1661–1740	(i) Real total 1661–1740	(j) Hypo. growth[7]	(k) Diff. marrs[8]	(l) Diff. growth[9]
(1) no switches	110 022	115 264	0.152	4.5	0.047
(2) no industrial change	109 430	115 264	0.147	5.1	0.052
(3) no intra-agri. change	115 852	115 264	0.204	−0.5	−0.005

[1] $b = a*(1+c/100)^{100}$
[2] Mean annual growth rate by Switch Type, 1561–1640 to 1661–1740.
[3] Assuming no change in Seasonal Type from 1561–1640 to 1661–1740.
[4] $e = a*(1+d/100)^{100}$
[5] $f = 100*[(b-e)/b]$
[6] $g = c-d$
[7] $j = 100*[(h/a)^{1/100}-1]$
[8] $k = 100*[(i-h)/i]$
[9] $l = 0.199-j$

Table 7.4. *Real and hypothetical totals of marriages, 1741–1820 non-market parishes only*
(mean growth rates by Switch Type)

Switch Type	number pars	(a) Total marriages 1661–1740	(b) Total marriages 1741–1820[1]	(c) Annual growth rate (%)[2]	(d) Hypo. growth (%)[3]	(e) Hypo. total 1741–1820[4]	(f) Diff. marrs (%)[5]	(g) Diff. growth[6]
XX	69	38 590	68 127	0.713	0.713	68 127	—	—
AX	24	7 834	13 963	0.725	0.513	11 797	15.5	0.212
PX	34	10 720	18 553	0.688	0.481	15 737	15.2	0.207
AA	172	38 099	57 371	0.513	0.513	57 371	—	—
AP	5	541	511	−0.071	0.513	815	−59.4	−0.584
PA	21	4 128	6 704	0.608	0.481	6 060	9.6	0.127
PP	43	12 961	19 026	0.481	0.481	19 026	—	—
XP	7	1 527	1 806	0.210	0.713	2 696	−49.3	−0.503
XA	27	7 038	8 258	0.200	0.713	12 425	−50.5	−0.513
all	402	121 438	194 319	0.589				

3 hypotheses:	(h) Hypo. total marrs 1741–1820	(i) Real total 1741–1820	(j) Hypo. growth[7]	(k) Diff. marrs[8]	(l) Diff. growth[9]
(1) no switches	194 052	194 319	0.588	0.14	0.001
(2) no industrial change	194 394	194 319	0.590	−0.04	−0.001
(3) no intra-agri. change	193 979	194 319	0.587	0.17	0.002

[1] $b = a * (1 + c/100)^{80}$

[2] Mean annual growth rate by Switch Type, 1661–1740 to 1741–1820.

[3] Assuming no change in Seasonal Type from 1661–1740 to 1741–1820.

[4] $e = a * (1 + d/100)^{80}$

[5] $f = 100 * [(b-e)/b]$

[6] $g = c - d$

[7] $j = 100 * [(h/a)^{1/80} - 1]$

[8] $k = 100 * [(i-h)/i]$

[9] $l = 0.589 - j$

compositional change is only 0.047 per cent per annum between 1561–1640 and 1661–1740; a derisory 0.001 per cent per annum separates the real and hypothetical growth rates in the second comparison.

Most of the small compositional effects were caused by net industrialization. If one assumes only no industrialization nor deindustrialization, with the hypothetical totals of marriages in the XA and XP parishes growing at the rate of the XX parishes, the totals in the AX and PX parishes at the AA and PP rates, respectively, while the others (AP and PA) grew at their recorded rates, the total of marriages for all rural parishes in 1661–1740 would have been only 5.1 per cent lower than the observed total at the close of that century of change, a difference in annual percentage growth rates of 0.052 per cent. The comparison for 1661–1740 and 1741–1820 yields a hypothetical total of marriages in 1741–1820 that is 0.04 per cent **higher** than the observed total, a difference in annual rates over the eighty years of −0.001 per cent.

Switches between arable and pastoral typing had an even smaller net effect. The number of marriages would have been, hypothetically, 0.17 per cent lower in 1741–1820 with no switches between agricultural types from the Middle to the Late period (Table 7.4, ròw 3 of the summary section). In the comparison of 1561–1640 with 1661–1740, no change in agriculture would instead have **increased** the total of marriages in 1661–1740, by 0.5 per cent. In that Early/Middle comparison, more arable parishes were switching to pastoral typing than pastoral parishes were to arable, and the mean growth rate for the consistently pastoral parishes was twice the rate, at 0.137 per cent per annum, of the consistently arable ones (0.068 per cent). The differences in growth rates attributable to agricultural switching, however, are only −0.005 per cent per annum for the Early to Middle comparison, and 0.002 per cent per annum for the Middle to Late one.

Wrigley and Schofield applied a model of aggregate homeostatic balance to English population history. National population growth depressed real wages, but lower real wages depressed nuptiality and checked the growth of the national population.[15] The crude test of compositional change of Tables 7.3 and 7.4 has uncovered a tiny measure of hodge-podge homeostasis, before the eighteenth century. Concurring seasonal changes (industrialization and deindustrialization, and the switches between arable and pastoral orientations) caused the growth in the numbers of weddings in some (largely the industrializing, partly the pastoral to arable) parishes to be cancelled

---

[15] Wrigley and Schofield, *Population History of England*, Chapter 11.

by the decline in the numbers in others, the deindustrializers and the parishes losing arable work to pastoral.

Contained within Figure 7.4 and Tables 7.3 and 7.4 was the increase in growth rates of the English population (or there, totals of marriages in the sample's parishes), from the first (Early/Middle) to the second (Middle/Late) comparison. The mean growth rate in Table 7.3 is 0.199 per cent per annum for the total of marriages in all the non-market parishes, but 0.589 per cent in Table 7.4 (1661–1740 to 1741–1820). Simple compositional effects of sufficient force to boost overall growth rates were not revealed by the exercises of Tables 7.3 and 7.4.

Might there still be a relation between the structural processes of industrialization and 'pastoralization' and aggregate population growth? The sharp increase in interregional trade implied by the last three chapters, an Early-to-Middle phenomenon, would by itself have been a vector of disease. I would by no means be the first to suggest that greater economic integration may have facilitated the spread of disease.[16] Slack associated extraordinary grain movements in times of sixteenth-century scarcity with the spread of epidemics, and Palliser noted the dissemination of influenza, the 'posting sweat', from town to town in that century.[17] In the longer run, increased exposure to many microbes (those causing, among other diseases, measles, small-pox, and whooping cough) conferred lifelong immunity to survivors, and the microbes themselves adapted, 'learning' to leave their hosts alive for the feeding of the next microbial generations.[18] Kunitz, however, argued that the decline in European mortality was not due to increased inherited resistance in humans, but to state intervention, and to density-dependent diseases (smallpox and measles) becoming endemic diseases of childhood instead of the epidemic killers of adults.[19] And not all diseases allow the accommodation; among diseases transferred directly among humans, tuberculosis and influenza were major early modern exceptions.[20] Mortality, Wrigley and Schofield noted, 'stabilized', with a declining incidence in large swings in mortality, but at a lower overall expectation of life, as if lethal epidemics had been transmuted by mutual accommodation of pathogens and hosts into unhealthy endemic coexistence.[21] As their count

[16] *Ibid.*, pp. 677, 416n.
[17] Slack, 'Mortality Crises', p. 23; Palliser, 'Dearth and Disease', p. 57. Chambers had held that pre-industrial mortality was autonomous; Taylor concurred, in 'Synergy among Mass Infections'.
[18] McNeill, *Plagues and Peoples*, p. 9.
[19] 'Speculations on the European Mortality Decline', *Economic History Review*, 2nd ser., vol. 36 (1983), pp. 349–64.
[20] McNeill, *Plagues and Peoples*, p. 13.
[21] Wrigley and Schofield, *Population History of England*, p. 316.

of crises shows, the division between high crisis and low crisis states comes fairly abruptly in the middle of the eighteenth century,[22] after the greatest quarter-century of crises in their series, 1726–50, which had four years in which mortality was at least 30 per cent higher than the twenty-five year average.[23] Flinn, however, reminded us that the stabilization of mortality was common to most of western Europe in the seventeenth and eighteenth centuries; he found administrative changes, and less war and civil unrest, to have been the causes.[24]

The method used in *The Population History of England* to chart the decline in crisis mortality can be applied to the Seasonal Types and Switch Types of the present study, to see if any distinctions emerge between Types. Wrigley and Schofield found that while remoteness from market towns reduced susceptibility to crisis mortality,[25] the farming types of Joan Thirsk, mapped from the fourth volume of *The Agrarian History of England and Wales* (1500–1640), did not explain variations in mortality. But as Chapters 3 to 5, above, showed, farming orientations were not stable over the long span of the Cambridge Group's English data. If some of the autumn-marrying, arable, parishes of the sixteenth century had married in the autumn because they were relatively isolated and largely self-sufficient, they might have suffered an increase in crisis mortality as they became exposed to more distant markets and their microbes in the Middle period.

Months of crisis mortality were identified relative to the trends in mortality experienced in each parish and expressed as a rates of crisis months per thousand months. I am grateful to the Cambridge Group, and especially to Robert Schofield, for the use of the data on crisis mortality. A crisis month met one of two conditions: either the total of burials in the month was more than 3.36 standard errors above the twenty year trend, or the month was part of a run of consecutive months in which the burial totals were at least 2.05 standard errors above the trend. In the case of runs of months, if one or two months fell below 2.05 standard errors above the trend, but were followed by at least one month of burials at least 2.05 standard errors above the trend, the bracketed months were still defined as crisis months.[26]

The first four rows of Table 7.5 show the mean crisis rates for 1561–1640 and 1661–1740 in the rural parishes that were A-Type, P-Type, and X-Type in the earlier of the two periods, and for the market towns. The sample of parishes employed here is the more

22 *Ibid.*, p. 322.   23 *Ibid.*, pp. 332–4.
24 Flinn, 'Stabilisation of Mortality', pp. 285–318.
25 Wrigley and Schofield, *Population History of England*, pp. 688–92.
26 *Ibid.*, Appendix 10 for the discussion of crisis index, especially pp. 645–50.

Table 7.5. *Mean crisis mortality rates in 1561–1640 and 1661–1740, by Seasonal Type in 1561–1640 and by Switch Type*

Seasonal Type in 1561–1640		Crisis rates[a]		% change
		1561–1640	1661–1740	
A-Type		4.43 C	4.39 B	−0.9%
P-Type		4.53 C	4.58 B	+1.1%
X-Type		6.53 B	5.22 B	−20.1%
market towns		9.84 A	8.33 A	−15.3%
Seasonal Type 1561–1640	Seasonal Type 1661–1740			
A	A	4.52 BCD	4.24 BCD	−6.2%
A	P	4.35 BCD	4.05 BCD	−6.9%
A	X	4.17 CD	5.35 BC	+28.3%
P	A	2.13 D	2.75 D	+29.1%
P	P	5.04 BCD	5.29 BCD	+5.0%
P	X	6.15 BC	4.95 BCD	−19.5%
X	A	4.00 CD	4.00 BCD	0.0%
X	P	5.10 BCD	3.81 CD	−25.3%
X	X	7.87 AB	6.41 AB	−18.6%

[a] See text for definition of crisis rates.

restricted aggregate set that underlay *The Population History of England*. With the Switch Types, the crisis months counted were for the second of the two long periods considered in each Switch Type, 1661–1740 for the Early to Middle Switch-Types, and 1741–1820 for the Middle to Late. The crisis rates in the table are different from those reported in Wrigley and Schofield for two reasons: market towns are not included here, or rather are separately reported, and parochial means are employed. The crisis rates in the earlier period's A-Types did not increase in the period of specialization; they instead declined slightly, by 0.9 per cent. The crisis rates in the earlier P-Types bucked the trend and increased, although only from 4.53 to 4.58 per thousand. The letters A to D show the groupings of means that were not significantly different from each other in each column (Waller-Duncan *t*-test, 5 per cent level of error). Small numbers in some of the Switch Types reduce the chance of finding their crisis mortality significantly higher or lower than others. I was concerned, in matching crisis mortality with the Seasonal Types, that migration would have removed burials, as it were, from the outmigrant deindustrializing parishes into the inmigrant industrializing ones, creating too large a base against which to measure crises in the industrializing parishes and too small a base in the deindustrializing ones. But, since crises were defined by Wrigley and Schofield relative to the twenty years preceding the crisis, and the mid-points within the two Switch Types span 100 and 80 years, respectively, the problem is not as serious as it might have been.

Of the rural parishes, the X-Type seems most prone to crises, but, as Wrigley and Schofield showed in their use of the crisis rates, true mortality crises in larger places are easier to identify than are those in smaller parishes, where the measurements of excess mortality could too easily have been spurious.[27] The Standard Errors used to define the crisis months vary with N, the number of underlying events. This affects the interpretation of the meaning of the crisis rates in both the X-Type parishes and the market towns, which easily scored the highest crisis rates. With the rural Switch Types of the bottom part of the table, it is the parishes remaining industrial (XX), and those becoming industrial (AX and PX), that rank highest in 1661–1740, with only one agricultural interloper, the consistently pastoral (PP) Switch Type.

The association of crisis mortality with industrial typing may be an artefact of the method, but it is also consistent with the inmigration of microbes along with some of the inmigrant labour, or via contact with traded goods; it may also reflect the greater density of settlement in industrial places, with the greater opportunities for the transmission of pathogens from person to person, or person to flea to person. Market towns consistently suffered months of crisis mortality at higher rates than even the X-Type parishes, although once again this might only reflect the easy identification of crises in still larger places. The market towns' rates are significantly higher than the rates for the three non-market types in every period. The slightly higher pastoral crisis rates may be tantalizingly suggestive of Philpot's argument concerning human mortality from animal-borne diseases such as bovine tuberculosis, brucellosis, and anthrax, but only tantalizingly, since the pastoral means are never significantly higher than the arable.[28] And there should have been at least one mortality-reducing impact of increased pastoral specialization, because while the mosquito bearer of malaria will happily sup on cattle, the malarial plasmodium does not thrive in cattle blood. The increased cattle-keeping that was part of Chapter 4's shift to pastoral seasonality

[27] *Ibid.* Appendix 10.   [28] Philpot, 'Enclosure and Population Growth', pp. 29–46.

should therefore have weakened the chain of transmission from human to mosquito to human.[29]

There is no support here for the tentative hypothesis ventured several pages ago, that increased specialization and interregional trade may have increased crisis mortality in arable places, some of which may have been isolated and self-sufficient in the first long period. The crisis rate for the arable A-Type parishes is always the lowest of the three. What emerges instead is the possibility of greater crisis mortality in non-agricultural rural places. In the comparison of growth rates of marriage totals (Figure 7.4) and in the counterfactual exercises (Tables 7.3 and 7.4), the consistently non-seasonal XX parishes enjoyed the highest growth rates in marriage totals. Inmigration to these rural industrial places, and the lower ages at marriage and higher marital fertility often associated with rural industry may all have contributed to that difference. But Table 7.5 should remind us that the rural industrial demographic constellation may also have included higher rates of crisis mortality, tempering any positive compositional impact of rural industrialization on aggregate population growth.[30] The contradictory demographic effects evoke Wrigley's writing on towns. He argued that towns helped check population growth but did so at the expense of producing a less efficient age structure in the population; the young and productive moved, and exposed themselves to new density-dependent diseases.[31]

The tentative finding of high crisis mortality in the rural industrial parishes also has a bearing on arguments concerning the recruitment of labour into the factories and mills of the later eighteenth and nineteenth centuries and on the Standard of Living Debate. If labour was being bid out of a Sweet Auburn of agriculture into the new industrial towns, the SATMILLS of Williamson's demonstration, we might expect to have to take the greater unhealthiness of towns (compared to the healthier agricultural countryside) into account in assessing the meaning of higher industrial wages.[32] But if urban labour was instead being bid out of rural industry, as in Mokyr's model of 'Growing-Up', the compensation for the town's higher mortality would not have had to have been as great, since the

---

[29] Beaver found milk a wonderful vector for other diseases, so much so that the expectation of life with a milkless diet was greater than with a diet including raw milk. 'Population, Infant Mortality, and Milk', p. 246; McNeill, *Plagues and Peoples*, pp. 247–8.

[30] Cf. Levine, *Family Formation*, on Shepshed.

[31] Wrigley, 'Parasite or Stimulus', p. 306.

[32] Williamson, 'Was It Worth It?', pp. 221–45. Williamson used infant mortality, not crisis mortality, to demonstrate the differences in living standards between town and country.

protoindustrial parishes look almost as crisis-ridden as the towns, and
that would have left even more of the wage differential as a net benefit
to the urban workers.[33]

Increased interregional trade in agricultural products should have
increased the general reliability of food supply, riots prompted by the
movement of grain in times of shortage notwithstanding. And grain
riots were not common occurrences in the England of the late seventeenth and early eighteenth centuries, as they had been in the
sixteenth century.[34] As I argued in Chapter 5, regional specialization
implied increases in agricultural productivity. Whether an increasingly reliable food supply lowered mortality in the later seventeenth
and early eighteenth centuries is another matter. Widespread deaths
from starvation were strikingly not a characteristic of England in that
period, although they had been earlier, and continued to be, for
example, in remoter parts of France.[35] Did an improved food supply
reduce mortality in the later seventeenth and early eighteenth century
in England? Debate on the importance of nutrition in early modern
demographic history merited a special issue of a recent *Journal of
Interdisciplinary History*.[36] Its contributors were divided on both the
general strength of the links between hunger and disease and the
specific application of the links to early modern England. Some of the
major microbial killers of the period were nutritionally indiscriminant
in their lethal impact (smallpox and Plague, among them); others,
such as typhus and influenza, had only an equivocal link to nutrition.[37] McKeown continued his campaign for mortality as the major
determinant of English population levels, arguing that slow growth
before the eighteenth century could be attributed to lack of food, and
its consequence, lowered resistance to disease.[38] Schofield countered,
sustaining the position taken in *The Population History of England*,

[33] Mokyr, 'Growing-Up', pp. 371–96.
[34] Walter and Wrightson, 'Dearth and the Social Order', pp. 22–42.
[35] Appleby, 'Grain Prices', pp. 865–87; Wrigley and Schofield, *Population History of England*, p. 341.
[36] *Journal of Interdisciplinary History*, vol. 14, no. 2 (Autumn 1983).
[37] Diseases with definite links to nutrition include measles, diarrhoea, tuberculosis and other respiratory infections, pertussis, intestinal parasites, cholera, leprosy, and herpes; those with more equivocal links are typhus, diphtheria, staphylococcus and streptococcus infections, influenza, syphilis, and systemic worm infections; small-pox, malaria, plague, typhoid, tetanus, yellow fever, encephalitis, and poliomyelitis show a minimal link to hunger ('Summary Report', *Journal of Interdisciplinary History*, vol. 14 (1983), p. 505). Cf. Ann G. Carmichael, who argued that the immune system fails only with extreme starvation, not with malnutrition, and that healthy hosts are better sites for pathogens, continuing the spread of diseases ('Infection, Hidden Hunger, and History', *Journal of Interdisciplinary History*, vol. 14 (1983), p. 250).
[38] McKeown, 'Food, Infection, and Population', p. 227.

arguing that there is little evidence that mortality varied with standard of living in England's early modern record.[39] Gooder's argument, that mortality was increased by hunger in the Midlands' mortality crisis in the 1720s, could be the exception proving that rule.[40]

In *The Population History of England*, Wrigley and Schofield held that the stabilization of mortality in the later seventeenth and eighteenth centuries (illustrated here in Table 7.5, above), the reduction in crises, was due in part to improved agricultural production, better storage and distribution (lessening the variability of supply), and the operation of the Poor Law, leading to a more equitable distribution of food.[41] Marriage seasons can reveal nothing of the Poor Law, or of storage, but wider spatial distribution was implied by the regionally selective abandonment of harvest-driven seasonality. The greater assurance of London's grain supply, as Outhwaite observed, allowed state controls on the export of grain to wither away from the 1630s to the 1670s.[42] The size of the English population had ceased rising, to be sure, but more importantly, London was by the end of the seventeenth century orchestrating the trade of a far wider area of England in ensuring its own supply. And that had, by itself, permitted the more efficient use of land.

This and the preceding chapters used Seasonal Types to map changes in agriculture and changes in industry, and to suggest the spatial interrelatedness of the transformation. The relation between regional differentiation and industrial growth of this chapter's epigraph was substantiated, if for the seventeenth- and eighteenth-centuries' industry instead of the nineteenth's. Different lights were shone on the marriage data, yielding different reflections of variation over space, within agriculture in Chapters 4 and 5, mostly within manufacturing in this and the last one. The final chapter will leave the spatial aspects of early modern economic change behind, and concentrate instead on time.

[39] Schofield, 'The Impact', p. 277; Wrigley and Schofield, *Population History of England*, p. 415.
[40] Gooder, 'Population Crisis', p. 10.
[41] Wrigley and Schofield, *Population History of England*, pp. 318–19.
[42] Outhwaite, 'Dearth and Government Invervention', pp. 389–406.

8

What the view saw

The demographic record, therefore, points to an increasing integration of market networks over the seventeenth and early eighteenth centuries.[1]

When Roger Schofield wrote these words, he referred not to the marriage registers that form a part of the English demographic record, but those registers have led to the finding of market integration by the start of the eighteenth century. I finish by taking a longer view, investigating the economic implications of the upheaval already sketched. What was gained through the regional specialization that the economy underwent in the later seventeenth century established a stable ground of sorts for the consolidation of gains in the eighteenth century, and for the more widespread introduction of the new techniques that would further enhance productivity.

The later seventeenth century saw the spatial rearrangement of economic activity over the English countryside, its regional integration. Productivity increased in agriculture, as Chapter 5 argued, with, in its simplified formulation, more hoofs and more grain produced from the given amount of land. And since the size of the English population had ceased rising at mid century, while the non-agricultural population was increasing (if not seamlessly, with some towns contracting as London grew, and some areas deindustrializing as others turned to manufacturing), increase in the productivity of agricultural labour was implied as well. The simple model of Figure 5.2, the Opening of Trade, implied increases in total factor productivity. Nothing was implied by the seasonality data, one way or the other, about new techniques. Productivity was rising, possibly simply because land could now be turned to its best use.

As broad a brush as this obscures variations in welfare during the

---

[1] Schofield, 'Impact', p. 289.

170

transition. Established farming practices would have been disrupted, and not every farmer will have hit upon the best techniques in the new circumstances. Workers accustomed to and trained in particular occupations would have had to leave their home parishes to find work in which their skills could be used, or risk unemployment if they failed to move. On a slightly higher level of abstraction, the integration of the trade of regions, simplified into the model of two regions in Figure 5.2 above, only implies with certainty an increase in the total output (of Hoofs and Grain in that figure) of the integrated economy, and does not speak to the question of the regional distribution of the gains from trade, let alone to the distribution of the benefits and costs of the integration between the regions and within each region. Harold Brookfield, in commenting on Bertil Ohlin's contribution to *The International Allocation of Economic Activity*, reminded us that any trading partner may be made worse off by economic integration, or may lose the opportunity to have become even better off under another arrangement.[2]

The combination of general increases in English agricultural productivity with stable numbers of people in the later seventeenth and early eighteenth century put downward pressure on agricultural prices, squeezing returns to farming. This was not the best of times, Little argued, to expect farmers and landlords to have been able to finance experimentation, and considerable new capital must have had to have been created simply to procure the integration itself.[3] The increase in Mindist (the mean distance from consumers of grain to the nearest producers, Figure 4.16, above) in the second half of the seventeenth century could not have occurred without a larger volume of bulky grain having been transported over longer distances.[4] To some extent, sufficient investment was not forthcoming, as evidenced by complaints over the deteriorating state of roads in the Midlands, which was growing into a diffuse market centre competing with London.[5] Credit shortages were noted in the eighteenth-century countryside, plausible evidence of an increase in the demand for funds to finance the increase in trade.[6] The regional specialization is itself evidence for increased investment in transportation, creating both fixed capital and variable capital to finance the time taken to move goods from producers to now more distant consumers.

[2] Ohlin, Hesselborn, and Wijkman, *International Allocation*, pp. 70–9.
[3] Little, *Deceleration*, pp. 28–32.
[4] On road and river improvements, see Willan, *River Navigation*; Willan, *Inland Trade*; Chartres, *Internal Trade*.
[5] Court, *The Rise*, p. 15.
[6] Cf. Holderness, 'Credit in English Rural Society', pp. 97–109.

Within agriculture, the shifts within arable and pastoral farming could partially have been financed out of current revenues; instead of putting aside a portion of the current crop for next year's seed, the whole crop might have been sold, and animal stocks built up, or new and different seeds purchased.[7] The composition of a farmer's capital stock would have changed, without there necessarily having been a large increase in the farmer's net investment. But when the early modern shift from A-Type to P-Type was accompanied by enclosure, as in parts of the Midlands, net investment was needed, to enclose the land with hedges and fences. Nothing in the method of charting the variations in marriage seasons over time, though, implied an instantaneous change; the shortest period over which shifts from arable to pastoral orientations could be observed was twenty years, with the overlapping forty-year estimates generated in Chapter 3. And to the extent that the integration had made farming more profitable, despite the change in relative prices, new investment could have been financed out of profits. The easing of population pressure released farmers from the desire to produce ever more grain, whatever the land and labour mix of the locality, but instead allowed every (different) region to operate out on the fatter parts of their production-possibility curves. A stable ground, from the later seventeenth to the middle of the eighteenth century, had moreover been established within which new techniques, especially those sailing over the North Sea from the Netherlands, could be applied. A better chance to finance new investments came, very possibly, after the mid eighteenth century, when agricultural prices began increasing again.

There had been a secular boom in prices in the century before the regional specialization of the later seventeenth century, but its outcome had been different. The result instead had been involution, an increase in the production of grain at the expense of other products, involving the application of more labour to the land.[8] The land/labour ratio was still higher in the early seventeenth century than it had been since before the fourteenth-century's Plague, leaving room to intensify farming.[9] In some parts of England, more and more labour was being applied to given acres; in others, forests were being cleared and pastures and wastes ploughed. The latter case is not necessarily

---

[7] Forty-four of the sample's parishes changed from A-Type to P-Type between 1561–1640 and 1661–1740; fifteen changed from P-Type to A-Type.

[8] The classic on involution is Geertz, *Agricultural Involution*. For discussion within the English context, see Bridbury, 'Sixteenth-Century Farming', pp. 538–56. See Thirsk, 'Farming Techniques', for the great labour requirements in manuring in the sixteenth and early seventeenth centuries, p. 167.

[9] Palliser, 'Tawney's Century', p. 342.

involution, but represented, at best, extensive growth, with the real possibility of declining productivity as less and less appropriate land was brought into cultivation. Much was land, after all, that had been abandoned in the fourteenth and fifteenth centuries, and was land, if we are to give any credit to late medieval decision-makers for knowing which acres most advantageously to desert, that was less suited to the ploughmen who had abandoned it.[10]

The marriage series that revealed the timing of regional specialization begins too late to watch the whole process of the erosion of agricultural productivity. No other early modern source for economic history may have such wide coverage, such a long run, but there is still the only tantalizingly larger proportion of pastoral P-Types in the first period, 11.3 per cent in 1538–60 compared to only 3.9 per cent in the next period, 1541–80 (see above, Table 3.3). The accident of timing that led to the start of national marriage registration caught the process of involution, the turning of most land to the production of grain under the great incentive of increasing grain prices, in its midst. Population had begun rising in the later fifteenth century. Grain prices had responded to the increase in demand (and to the contraction in marketed supply, as more grain would have been eaten up by the larger farming population instead of getting to market). And then the rise in the price of grain, coupled to the price–inelasticity of demand for that basic foodstuff, lessened the expenditure on other goods such as pastoral products, as the income effect kicked in.

The involution continued in the sixteenth and early seventeenth centuries, within the view of the marriage seasons. It is probable that regional differences narrowed, as Yelling argued, under the incentive felt in most regions to grow more grain.[11] Mindist, the simple measure of spatial differentiation between arable and non-arable parishes of Chapter 4, did not rise until the second half of the seventeenth century. There was famine at times in the north, and general dearths through the first half of the seventeenth century.[12] Fisher pointed to the anomalous legislation of the 1560s, seemingly reacting to population decline and labour shortages (the Statute of Artificers with its wage limits), explaining it with reference to unusually high mortality from influenza; another Act of 1563, the one directed at the

---

[10] Bridbury, 'Sixteenth-Century Farming'. See also the discussion in R. B. Outhwaite, 'Progress and Backwardness', pp. 1–18.

[11] Palliser, *The Age of Elizabeth*, p. 200.

[12] Everitt, 'Marketing', p. 575. Everitt found 1608, 1621–3, 1630–7, and 1645–51 all to have been periods of dearth in the first half of the seventeenth century.

maintenance of tillage, was more in line with the longer-term process of population growth and involution.[13]

As Palliser reminded us, there is much debate on the relationship between population growth and the economy in this period (1982). One effect of the long secular rise in grain prices may well have been the greater commercialization of agriculture; rising prices were the key De Vries isolated in the early modern transformation from subsistence to commercial orientations.[14] Land and labour became too valuable as factors in grain production to waste them on the production of other goods, when these other goods might as easily be purchased with the increased revenue from the sale of more grain at the higher prices.

Population had reached its fifteenth- to seventeenth-century maximum in the 1650s, its growth decelerating strongly in the decades leading to mid-century; the level of population then declined in half of the next ten quinquennia, the peak of 1656 not being matched again until c. 1720.[15] Real wages bottomed out in the first quarter of the seventeenth century; 1621 was the turning point in the modified series of Wrigley and Schofield.[16] The improvement in real wages must have played a role in the timing of the seventeenth-century's regional specialization; the higher income elasticity of demand for pastoral and industrial products than for grain produced greater advantages for the producers of meat and metal-wares, and marginal producers of grain dropped out.

There ensued no catastrophic drop in population, though, as had occurred to end the long secular rise in the medieval population, and the result was not the widespread abandonment of land nor retreat into dual employment. The lessons of commercialization were not erased by the reversal of relative prices. Farmers were encouraged to seek the most profitable use of land in the new context. In some areas, there was a reversion from convertible husbandry to permanent grass.[17] Further west, less advanced arable rotations were given up in favour of pasture. In the east, farmers intensified their production of field crops, finding new ways to adjust to the changed terms of trade, by exploiting new markets (Dutch brewers) and new products (fodder crops), or employing new techniques.

London had already housed 7.7 per cent of the English population when aggregate population growth ceased in the 1650s; over the next half-century, that proportion increased to 11.5 per cent, and could not

13 Fisher, 'Influenza and Inflation', pp. 120–9.
14 De Vries, *Dutch Rural Economy*, pp. 7–10.
15 Wrigley and Schofield, *Population History of England*, pp. 408, 528–9.
16 *Ibid.*, p. 431.
17 Broad, 'Alternate Husbandry'.

have failed to further the demands placed on the countryside, to feed and clothe it.[18] London's role was never stronger than at the beginning of the eighteenth century, in terms of the size of its market relative to the rest of England, encouraging regional specialization to serve it. The later seventeenth and early eighteenth century is as good a time as any for the completion of the transition from bound and localized to economically integrated regions. That the dating of the specialization post-dates 1661 is partly an artefact of the method; 1661–1700 is the first reliable period after 1601–40 to view the regional orientations of agriculture because of the disruption to record-keeping in the Interregnum. But the timing confirms the judgement of Charles Wilson that the Restoration marked a turning point in England's economic development.[19]

A peculiarity of the method of charting economic change with marriage seasons helps strengthen this conclusion. The later seventeenth and early eighteenth century is the latest possible dating for the regional differentiation. The possibility of lags between the economic change and the social response of changed seasons of marriage would have made it possible for the timing of weddings to have remained stuck in newly inappropriate seasons, with only the tendency for the young, the marrying, to respond to changed circumstances before their elders operating against the lag. This glue of tradition might then have weakened with time. The true regional differentiation in economic orientations will not, moreover, have happened much earlier than the later seventeenth century, since the sixteenth and early seventeenth century had given most farmers such strong incentives to produce grain.

The integration gave farmers in all regions the opportunity to concentrate on the output to which their land was best suited, whether by soil type, elevation, drainage, or rainfall, and sagging grain prices provided the goad. Agricultural output could increase, without the necessity of technological change, without additions to land and labour, as was seen in the model of integration sketched earlier as Figure 5.2. The late seventeenth and early eighteenth centuries reaped a bonanza of productivity increase, at least in part through the agency of regional integration. Once farmers had become accustomed to the new orientations, a ground had been prepared for experimentation to find the best techniques to further augment profitability.

Any estimation of the timing of the Agricultural Revolution, if it is

[18] Corfield, 'Urban Development', p. 217; Wrigley, *People, Cities, and Wealth*, p. 162.
[19] Charles Wilson, *England's Apprenticeship*.

understood narrowly with reference to new crops and new techniques, and inferred from price trends or from numbers fed, is bound
to be complicated by the nearly coincident spatial integration.[20] As
illustrated in Figure 8.1 below, a modified recapitulation of Figure 5.2,
the integration appears as a unique chance to increase the output of
both Hoofs and of Grain, 'simply' by adjusting the production of the
East and the West. Once again in Figure 8.1, AB and CD are the
production-possibility curves (of Hoofs and Grain) for the East and the
West. When trade opens, the combined output of Hoofs and Grain
increases from a combination like point L, with G_1 Grain and H_1 Hoofs,
to a point like M, yielding more Grain (G_2) and more Hoofs (H_2). Adam
Smith did not model the eighteenth-century English economy in this
fashion, but when he stressed the importance of the extent of the
market in promoting the wealth of nations, simple gains from trade
were among the effects he described.[21]

With respect to the diagrams of Figures 5.2 and 8.1, once the new
production-possibility curve, EF in Figure 8.1, had been created, no
further productivity increase could be anticipated from integration
alone. The diagrams show the change to be instantaneous, as if trade
had been impossible at point L, and costless at point M. But, if new
techniques were simultaneously being adopted, the whole curve
enveloping the possible production choices could then shift outwards,
illustrated in Figure 8.1 as a shift out from the curve EF to JK. If M had
represented the pre-improvement (post-integration) total of Hoofs and
Grain produced in the two regions, any set of choices of output on the
new envelope JK between points Z_1 and Z_2 would yield more Hoofs
and the same amount of Grain, or more Grain and the same amount of
Hoofs, or more of both products.

If the eventual combination was in fact represented by point W, how
much of the increase in England's output of hoofs and grain, from H_1
and G_1, could we attribute to technological change, and how much to
integration, from the trails left in relative prices and from inferences of
output from population growth alone? It is difficult to see how the
knot could be unravelled, especially since the economy did not hold
still for our measurements. The size of the English population
increased again in the eighteenth century, more rapidly towards its

---

[20] Mark Overton has provided a concise survey of the conflicting timings and definitions recorded for the Agricultural Revolution, ranging from Kerridge's emphasis
on the sixteenth and seventeenth centuries to Chamber and Mingay's placement after
1750, in 'Agricultural Revolution?', pp. 121–2.

[21] Fisher, 'Development', p. 46. Fisher described the transition from the medieval to the
modern economic system as a function of capital accumulation, improved techniques, and an increased size of the market.

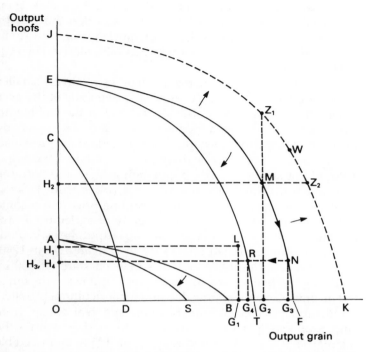

Figure 8.1 Technological change, wheat mining and changed relative prices

conclusion, and the proportion of the population employed outside agriculture increased as well. The proportion of English city dwellers was estimated by Wrigley to have been 17.0 per cent of the English population at the start of the century, and 27.5 per cent one hundred years later.[22] As well, that declining proportion of the rural English men and women was now also being employed in agriculture to a diminishing extent. I have only the cheap and nasty numbers of X-Type, non-seasonal, non-agricultural rural parishes to offer in support of that judgement, but the proportion of X-Types in the non-market sample increased over time, (see Table 3.3, above), and the biggest increase in that proportion (if we discount the small-numbered Period 1, 1538–60) came between Period 10 (1701–40) and Period 11 (1721–60). Hardwicke's Marriage Act comes too late in Period 11 to much affect the seasonality of that Period's marriages. The overlap of Periods 10 and 11 allows us a narrow range of inferences on

[22] Wrigley, *People*, p. 162.

the period of fastest growth in the proportion of industrial X-Type parishes in the sixty years between 1701 and 1760; either the growth was quick from 1721–40 to 1741–60, and even quicker from 1701–20 to 1721–40, or growth was at its strongest between 1721–40 and 1741–60, and slow beforehand.

It may very well have been asking too much of the relatively smaller agricultural population to meet the ever greater demands of the ever larger non-agricultural numbers in the second half of the eighteenth century; the relative prices of agricultural products responded by rising. This is not equivalent to saying that agricultural progress had decelerated. As great as the productivity increase might have been, though, it could not keep pace with population growth and with the increasingly non-agricultural labour force, and prices rose. Jackson argued, however, using estimates of the prevailing price and income elasticities for agricultural products, for a failure of agricultural progress in the later eighteenth century. Aggregate output, he estimated, increased from an indexed 100 in 1660 to 158 in 1740 and 172 in 1790, but per capita consumption fell to near its indexed start in 1660 by 1790, after having reached a value of 144 in 1740.[23] But using the range of price and income elasticities of the demand for agricultural products he suggested, and price data from Bowden and real wages from Wrigley and Schofield, per capita consumption in 1561, within the view of the marriage seasons, would range from 125 to an incredible 288, and aggregate output from 73 to 162, just a little lower than the estimated output for 1790 (again setting aggregate output and per capita output to 100 in 1660).[24]

The simple diagram of Figure 8.1 is more complicated than it needed to be, had demonstrating the gains from regional integration and technological change been its only objects. It can also be used to show that the increases in output attained through the opening of trade, represented here by the shift out from L to M, can be lost, given extreme enough relative prices. In the late eighteenth century, grain prices rose sharply, marginal land was ploughed once again, and there is a possibility that some farmers on intramarginal land, avid for short-term gain, turned to 'wheat mining', the dropping of productivity-maintaining rotations in order instead to maximize a few years' output of wheat. Thompson suggested that on lighter lands that had before the late eighteenth century supported pastoral farming, farmers turned to wheat production in response to high grain prices;

[23] Jackson, 'Growth and Deceleration', p. 345.
[24] Bowden, 'Agricultural Prices', 1967; Wrigley and Schofield, *Population History of England*, pp. 642–4.

Hueckel disputed this, arguing that the relative prices of grain and pastoral products did not move strongly in favour of grain, only that grain prices were more volatile in the short run.[25] On Figure 8.1, the possibility of a shift towards grain production and wheat mining are represented by:

(a) the combined output of Hoofs and Grain sliding down from M to N, to one of the two steep portions of the production-possibility envelope, where not that much more Grain was produced (G_2 to G_3) for all the effort that high grain prices had encouraged farmers to put into it, and for all the Hoofs foregone (H_2 to H_3), because of the change in relative prices, and

(b) the possibility of a shrinkage of the whole envelope from EF to ET, if wheat mining (here shown only in the East, with that region's production-possibility curve rotating in from AB to AS) was protracted enough to strip the land of its nutrients.

In the diagram, the first of these changes sees a large decrease in the output of Hoofs, from H_2 to H_3; the second sees a decline in the output of Grain, from G_3 to G_4. The seasonality of marriage obligingly reflected the choices induced by the new price ratios of the later eighteenth and early nineteenth centuries. ANG, the ratio of spring/ summer to autumn marriages, declined (see Figures 3.5 and 3.6 above); autumn-marrying arable A-Types, which had been less than 70 per cent of the combined number of A- and P-Types in 1701–40, were not less than 80 per cent of the combined number from 1761–1800 to 1801–40 (see Table 3.3). Most of the (very arable) Bedfordshire parishes drop out of the sample after 1812, so do not make any contribution to post-Napoleonic seasonality.

The Napoleonic Wars ended, and relative prices moved to fatter parts of the production-possibility envelope. The nineteenth century brought much agricultural improvement, through the drainage of heavy clay soils, the introduction of new fertilizers, and other means. The repeal of the Corn Laws in 1846 removed the floor that had been built under the price of wheat in 1815; imports of cheap grain from outside Europe increased, and then wheat prices collapsed in the 1870s. England became more pastoral than it had been in modern times. The seasonality of marriage had identified a period of maximal pastoral orientation within the range of its data, when in the late seventeenth and early eighteenth centuries 42.3 per cent of seasonal non-market parishes had registered as spring-marrying P-Types, but that had still left 57.7 per cent as autumn-marrying A-Types (see Table

[25] Thompson, *English Landed Society*, pp. 216–17; Hueckel, 'Relative Prices', pp. 401–2.

3.3, above). The era of High Farming and of adjustments to more thorough international integration of trade, though, are beyond the General View of the marriage seasons.

Conditions parallel to those that led farmers to forsake other crops and instead produce grain on nearly any land in the very late eighteenth century have been recapitulated in the later twentieth. Farmers have responded to the incentives offered by the Common Agricultural Policy of the E.C., and have ploughed up land that had not produced arable crops for any extended period since the early seventeenth century, creating the fenceless, hedgeless 'prairies' that so offend the eye longing for The Historic Landscape. The commentator cited in the first chapter, observing that God had made Leicestershire for grass, not cereal grains, was more concerned with the deteriorating environment of the foxes he hunted than with economic optimality. But the grain-growing prairies may also be suboptimal, on the level of physical productivity, if more pastoral products could be produced without much sacrifice in the quantity of arable ones. It is suboptimal, on another level, for Europe to be producing grain at all. But I'm not going to advance that argument with much force now, especially as I write this last chapter among daily reports of the growing drought in the great grain producing prairies, the new dust bowl, of North America.

This work has offered a series of views of the rural economy of early modern England, never from close enough to see clearly the adjustments that must have had to have been made to market integration, to deindustrialization and industrialization, and to reliance on distant suppliers of breadstuffs, by the people of that age. I have felt, at times, as if I had been processing the images sent not by the high-flying bird conjured up in the first chapter, but by the satellites whose transmitted images are far more computer-assisted than mine have been.

This is not a rewriting of England's economic history, using all available sources. The timing of regional specialization in the rural economy has been identified, and the relation between the integration of England's agricultural regions and its rural industry and population explored. The distance the study has taken to the ordinary world of early modern experience has its echoes in the simultaneously entrancing and disturbing Landsat images of known corners of our own world. Much detail has been obscured, but change has been seen, whole.

Appendix

Parishes: representation and Seasonal Types, by county

The substance of the appendix is the Table A.1, a list of the parishes in the sample. A county's non-market parishes are listed first; the county's market towns, according to Adams' *Index Villaris* of 1700, follow, in italics. The table touches on the representativeness of the 542 parish sample, showing the number of the sample's parishes in each county and the proportion of the county's total that the sample represents.

The table then displays the Seasonal Types calculated for each parish, according to the rules of Chapter 3, in the Early (1561–1640), Middle (1661–1704), and Late (1741–1820) periods. A ' · ' in the place of a Seasonal Type indicates that fewer than twenty-four marriages were recorded over the eighty year period. The geobox (rectilinear divisions of England's area) into which each parish fell is also given.

In the final column of the main list the contributions of others to the 542 parish sample are noted. 'PHE' indicates that the parish was one of the 404 parishes used by Wrigley and Schofield in the *Population History of England*. For these parishes, the map coordinates and farming type of each parish, and their status as market towns was also provided by the Cambridge Group. Of the other 138 parishes, the gifts of marriage data from John Broad and Susan Wright are indicated by 'BW', and those from Glynis Reynolds by '+'. The rest of the marriage dates were drawn from printed registers, from the aggregative listings in the collection of the Cambridge Group, and from original registers and typescript transcripts in the county record offices of Norfolk, Northamptonshire, Staffordshire (and from Stafford's William Salt Library), and Warwickshire.

The list begins with Bedfordshire and its mass of A-Type, autumn-

181

marrying, parishes. Two lonely X-Types appear in the ninety-three calculations for the county; twenty-nine of the thirty-one parishes were A-Type in all three periods. To help in the reading of the list, a table (A.2) has been included at its end. There were twenty-seven possible combinations of the three main Seasonal Types over the three long periods, and the numbers and proportions of occurrences of these combinations is displayed there. This may provide some context to the main list, to know whether a combination of Early-Middle-Late Seasonal Types of a particular parish or group of parishes was common (as was Bedfordshire's standard of A-A-A) or rare (P-A-X).

Table A.1. *Seasonal Type by parish*[a]

| | Seasonal Type[b] | | | | |
	1561–1640 (Early)	1661–1740 (Middle)	1741–1820 (Late)	Geobox	Gifts[c]
Bedfordshire (31 parishes, 25.0 per cent of county's total)					
Blunham	A	A	A	22	PHE
Bolnhurst	A	A	A	22	PHE
Chalgrave	A	A	A	22	PHE
Clophill	A	A	A	22	PHE
Cranfield	A	A	A	21	PHE
Felmersham	A	A	A	22	PHE
Flitwick	A	A	A	22	PHE
Harlington	A	A	A	22	PHE
Kempston	A	A	A	22	PHE
Maulden	A	A	A	22	PHE
Millbrook	A	A	A	22	PHE
Milton Earnest	A	X	A	22	PHE
Northill	A	A	A	22	PHE
Pavenham	A	A	A	21	PHE
Pulloxhill	A	A	A	22	PHE
Riseley	A	A	A	22	PHE
Sandy	A	A	A	22	PHE
Souldrop	A	A	A	21	PHE
Southill	A	A	A	22	PHE
Stevington	A	A	A	22	PHE
Studham	A	A	A	22	PHE
Sutton	A	A	A	22	BW
Thurleigh	A	A	A	22	PHE
Tingrith	A	A	A	22	PHE
Totternhoe	A	A	A	21	BW
Wilden	A	A	A	22	BW
Wootton	A	A	A	22	PHE
Ampthill	A	A	A	22	PHE

Campton with Shefford	A	A	A	22	PHE
Toddington	A	A	A	22	PHE
Woburn	A	A	X	21	PHE

Berkshire (3 parishes, 1.9 percent of county's total)

Harwell	A	A	A	11	PHE
Sonning	A	A	A	11	PHE
Winkfield	P	A	X	11	PHE

Buckinghamshire (17 parishes, 8.3 per cent of county's total)

Aston Abbots	A	A	A	21	BW
Bierton	A	X	A	21	BW
Chicheley	A	A	A	21	BW
Harwell	A	A	A	11	BW
Hedgerley	A	P	X	11	BW
Hulcott	A	A	A	21	BW
Little Marlow	A	A	A	11	BW
Medmenham	X	A	A	11	BW
Shalstone	A	P	A	21	BW
Stoke Poges	A	A	A	11	BW
Stone	A	A	A	21	BW
Upton Chalvey	X	X	X	21	BW
Walton	.	X	A	21	BW
Wing	A	A	A	21	PHE
Worminghall	A	A	A	21	BW
Aylesbury	A	A	A	21	PHE
Princes Risborough	A	A	A	21	PHE

Cambridgeshire (10 parishes, 5.8 per cent of county's total)

Fowlmere	A	A	A	22	PHE
Haddenham	A	A	A	22	PHE
Melbourn	A	A	A	22	PHE
Orwell	A	A	A	22	PHE
Sawston	A	A	A	22	PHE
Waterbeach	.	A	A	22	PHE
Willingham	A	A	A	22	PHE
Linton	A	A	A	22	PHE
March	A	X	A	22	R
Wisbech St. Peter	A	X	X	22	R

Cheshire (7 parishes, 5.7 per cent of county's total)

Bunbury	X	X	X	30	PHE
Gawsworth	X	X	X	30	PHE
Wilmslow	X	X	X	30	PHE
Chester Holy Trinity	X	X	X	30	PHE
Frodsham	X	X	X	30	PHE
Nantwich	X	X	X	30	PHE
Sandbach	X	X	X	30	PHE

Cornwall (5 parishes, 2.5 per cent of county's total)

Gulvall	A	A	X	10	
Lezant	A	X	P	10	
Madron	A	X	X	10	

Sancreed	A	X	X	10	
St Just-in-Penrith	A	X	X	10	

Cumberland (5 parishes, 3.7 per cent of county's total)

Bridekirk	P	P	X	50	PHE
Crosthwaite	P	P	P	50	PHE
Dalston	A	P	X	50	PHE
Greystoke	P	P	P	50	PHE
Wigton	X	P	X	50	PHE

Derbyshire (3 parishes, 1.7 per cent of county's total)

Norton	X	X	X	31	
Dronfield*	X	X	X	31	PHE
Wirksworth*	X	X	X	31	PHE

Devonshire (15 parishes, 3.2 per cent of county's total)

Berry Pomeroy	A	X	X	10	PHE
Blackawton	X	X	X	10	PHE
Branscombe	X	P	X	10	PHE
Chardstock	A	X	X	10	PHE
Hemyock	A	X	P	10	PHE
Islington	A	X	X	10	PHE
Offwell	P	P	P	10	PHE
Paignton	A	X	X	10	PHE
Staverton	X	X	X	10	PHE
Stoke Gabriel	X	X	X	10	PHE
Widecombe in the Moor	P	P	X	10	PHE
Colyton	X	P	X	10	PHE
Hartland	A	X	P	10	PHE
Modbury	X	X	X	10	PHE
Topsham	A	X	X	10	PHE

Dorset (8 parishes, 3.1 per cent of county's total)

Askerswell	X	P	X	10	
Charminster	A	P	P	10	
East Stour	X	P	X	10	
Rampisham	A	P	.	10	
Swanage	A	P	X	10	PHE
Swyre	P	X	P	10	
Symondsbury	A	P	X	10	PHE
Thorncombe	X	P	X	10	PHE

Durham (3 parishes, 3.0 per cent of county's total)

Middleton St. George	A	P	P	51	PHE
Whitburn	A	P	P	51	PHE
Darlington	X	P	P	51	PHE

Essex (17 parishes, 4.2 per cent of county's total)

Ardleigh	P	X	A	22	PHE
Bradwell juxta Mare	A	A	A	22	PHE
Dedham	X	X	A	22	PHE
Dengie	A	A	A	22	PHE

Great Baddow	A	A	A	22	PHE
Great Burstead	A	A	A	12	PHE
Great Sampford	A	A	A	22	PHE
Great Yeldham	A	A	X	22	PHE
Hadleigh	A	A	A	12	PHE
Little Sampford	P	A	A	22	PHE
Stanford Rivers	A	A	A	22	PHE
Stow Maries	A	A	P	12	PHE
White Notley	A	A	A	22	PHE
Wickford	A	A	A	12	PHE
Maldon All Saints and St Peters	X	X	X	22	PHE
Romford	X	A	A	22	PHE
Thaxted	A	A	A	22	PHE

Gloucestershire (21 parishes, 6.3 per cent of county's total)

Ampney Crucis	A	X	A	21	
Aston Subedge	A	P	A	21	
Avening	A	X	X	10	PHE
Bishops Cleve	A	A	A	20	PHE
Cam	A	P	X	10	PHE
Clifford Chambers	A	A	A	21	
Dymock	A	X	X	20	PHE
Eastington	A	P	X	20	PHE
Elkstone	P	X	A	20	
Henbury	P	P	P	10	
Horsley	.	X	X	10	PHE
Kemerton	A	X	A	20	
North Nibley	A	P	X	10	PHE
Preston Upon Stour	A	A	A	21	
Westbury on Trym	X	P	X	10	PHE
Fairford	A	A	A	21	PHE
Minchinhampton	A	X	X	20	PHE
Stroud	A	X	X	20	PHE
Tetbury	A	X	X	10	PHE
Winchcombe	A	X	A	21	PHE
Wotton under Edge	A	X	X	10	PHE

Hampshire (10 parishes, 3.3 per cent of county's total)

Aldershot	A	X	A	11	PHE
Boldre	A	X	X	11	PHE
Ellingham	A	X	A	11	PHE
Fordingbridge	.	A	X	11	PHE
Headley	A	A	A	11	PHE
Meonstoke	P	A	A	11	PHE
Selborne	A	A	A	11	PHE
Odiham	A	A	A	11	PHE
Ringwood	A	X	X	11	PHE
Romsey	X	X	X	11	PHE

Herefordshire (6 parishes, 2.7 per cent of county's total)

Eaton Bishop	A	X	P	20	PHE
Lugwardine	X	X	P	20	PHE

Yarkhill	A	P	X	20	PHE
Bromyard	X	X	X	20	PHE
Ledbury	A	X	X	20	PHE
Wigmore	P	P	P	20	PHE

Hertfordshire (26 parishes, 19.8 per cent of county's total)

Aldenham	A	A	A	12	PHE
Anstey	A	A	A	22	BW
Ayot St Lawrence	A	A	P	22	BW
Barley	A	A	A	22	PHE
Benington	A	A	A	22	BW
Buckland	.	A	A	22	BW
Digswell	P	A	A	22	BW
Graveley	A	A	A	22	BW
Harpenden	A	A	A	22	BW
Hinxworth	A	A	A	22	BW
Hunsdon	A	A	A	22	PHE
Kelshall	A	A	A	22	BW
Kings Langley	A	A	A	22	BW
Pirton	A	A	A	22	BW
Stapleford	A	A	A	22	BW
Therfield	A	A	A	22	BW
Thorley	A	A	A	22	BW
Totteridge	A	A	X	12	BW
Walkern	A	A	A	22	BW
Baldock	A	A	A	22	BW
Berkhampstead St Mary	.	A	A	21	PHE
Berkhampstead St Peter	A	A	A	21	PHE
Hemel Hempstead	A	A	A	22	PHE
Hitchin	A	A	A	22	PHE
Rickmansworth	.	A	A	21	PHE
Watford	X	A	A	21	PHE

Huntingdonshire (1 parish, 1.0 per cent of county's total)

Great Stukeley	A	A	A	22	PHE

Kent (29 parishes, 7.3 per cent of county's total)

Benenden	P	P	P	12	PHE
Biddenden	X	P	A	12	PHE
Chiselhurst	X	X	X	12	PHE
Eastry	A	A	A	12	PHE
Eltham	X	X	X	12	PHE
Herne	A	A	A	12	PHE
Milton next Gravesend	X	X	X	12	PHE
Newenden	X	P	A	12	PHE
Reculver	A	A	A	12	PHE
Sandhurst	X	P	P	12	PHE
Speldhurst	X	P	A	12	PHE
St Nicholas at Wade	.	A	A	12	PHE
Staplehurst	A	A	A	12	PHE
Sundridge	X	A	A	12	PHE

Wickhambreux	A	A	A	12	PHE
Yalding	X	A	A	12	PHE
Ashford	X	A	X	12	PHE
Bromley	X	X	X	12	PHE
Cranbrook	X	X	P	12	PHE
Goudhurst	X	P	A	12	PHE
Gravesend	.	X	X	12	PHE
Hythe	X	A	X	12	PHE
Lenham	A	A	A	12	PHE
Sevenoaks	X	X	X	12	PHE
Sittingbourne	X	A	A	12	PHE
Tenterden	X	P	P	12	PHE
Tonbridge*	X	A	A	12	PHE
Westerham	X	X	A	12	PHE
Wye	A	A	A	12	PHE

Lancashire (10 parishes, 5.3 per cent of county's total)

Deane	X	X	X	40	PHE
North Meols	P	X	X	40	PHE
Radcliffe	X	X	X	40	PHE
Torver	A	P	P	40	PHE
Tunstall	X	P	X	40	PHE
Warton	X	P	X	40	PHE
Ashton under Lyne	X	X	X	30	PHE
Chorley	X	X	X	40	PHE
Hawkshead	A	P	P	40	PHE
Rochdale	X	X	X	40	PHE

Leicestershire (25 parishes, 10.0 per cent of county's total)

Ashfordby	A	A	X	31	PHE
Bottesford	A	P	X	31	PHE
Breedon on the Hill	A	A	A	31	PHE
Coleorton	A	A	X	31	PHE
Desford	A	X	X	31	PHE
Enderby	P	A	X	21	PHE
Great Bowden	A	A	A	21	PHE
Husbands Bosworth	A	A	A	21	PHE
Kibworth Beauchamp	A	A	A	21	PHE
Kirby Muxloe	.	X	A	31	PHE
Kirkby Mallory	A	X	A	31	PHE
Long Clawson	A	A	A	31	PHE
Medbourn	A	A	A	21	PHE
Prestwold	A	P	A	31	PHE
Saddington	A	P	A	21	PHE
Shepshed	A	A	X	31	PHE
Wigston Magna	A	A	A	21	PHE
Wymondham	A	P	P	31	PHE
Ashby de la Zouche	A	X	X	31	PHE
Castle Donnington	A	X	A	31	PHE
Hinckley	A	X	X	21	PHE
Loughborough	A	A	X	31	PHE

Market Bosworth	A	A	X	31	PHE
Market Harborough	X	X	A	21	PHE
Melton Mowbray	A	X	X	31	PHE

Lincolnshire (13 parishes, 2.1 per cent of county's total)
Holland

Wrangle	P	P	P	32	PHE
Wyberton	P	P	P	32	PHE

Kesteven

Leasingham	A	P	P	32	PHE
Quarrington and Old Sleaford	X	P	P	32	PHE
Ropsley	A	P	P	31	PHE
Grantham	A	X	X	31	PHE

Lindsey

Clee	P	P	P	42	PHE
Frodingham	A	P	P	41	PHE
Haxey	A	A	X	31	PHE
Irby on Humber	A	P	P	42	PHE
Scartho	P	P	P	42	PHE
Gainsborough	A	P	X	31	PHE
Great Grimsby	P	P	P	42	PHE

Middlesex (2 parishes, 1.1 per cent of county's total)

Edmonton	X	X	X	12	PHE
Northolt	X	X	X	12	PHE

Norfolk (29 parishes, 4.2 per cent of county's total)

Banham	A	A	A	22	PHE
Blickling	A	A	A	32	
Docking	P	A	A	32	PHE
Feltwell	A	A	A	22	
Foulden	A	A	A	22	
Frettenham	A	A	A	32	
Halvergate	P	A	A	32	
Kenninghall	A	A	A	22	PHE
North Elmham	A	A	A	32	PHE
Runham	X	A	A	32	
Scottow	P	A	A	32	
Sculthorpe	P	A	A	32	PHE
Sedgeford	P	A	A	32	PHE
Shipdham	A	A	A	32	PHE
Trunch	A	A	A	32	
Wells	A	A	A	32	PHE
Cawston	A	A	A	32	
Diss	A	A	A	22	
East Dereham	.	A	A	32	
Fakenham	.	A	A	32	
North Walsham	X	X	A	32	
Norwich St Benedict	X	X	X	32	PHE
Norwich St Giles	X	X	X	32	PHE

Norwich St James with Pockthorpe	X	X	X	32	PHE
Norwich St Margaret	X	X	X	32	PHE
Norwich St Martin	.	X	X	32	
Norwich St Saviour	X	X	X	32	PHE
Swaffham	A	A	A	32	PHE
Wymondham	A	A	A	32	PHE

Northamptonshire (31 parishes, 10.6 per cent of county's total)

Castor	A	A	A	22	
Chipping Warden	A	A	A	21	
Courteenhall	A	A	A	21	BW
Earl's Barton	A	A	A	21	BW
East Farndon	A	A	A	21	
Etton	A	A	A	32	
Floore	.	A	A	21	
Fotheringay	A	A	A	22	
Glinton	A	A	A	32	
Lamport	A	A	A	21	BW
Little Billing	.	P	X	21	
Little Bowden	.	A	A	21	BW
Loddington	A	A	A	21	
Marholm	A	P	A	32	
Naseby	A	A	A	21	BW
Newbottle	A	X	A	21	
Newton Bromswold	A	A	A	21	BW
Orlingbury	A	A	A	21	
Raundes	A	A	X	21	BW
Roade	A	A	A	21	BW
Stanwick	A	A	A	21	
Stoke Bruern	A	A	A	21	
Sywell	A	X	A	21	BW
Tansor	.	X	A	22	BW
Titchmarsh	A	A	A	22	BW
Twywell	A	X	A	21	
Winwick	A	A	A	21	
Yardley Hastings	A	X	A	21	
Aynho	A	A	A	21	PHE
Northampton All Saints	A	X	X	21	BW
Rockingham	A	A	X	21	

Northumberland (5 parishes, 5.4 per cent of county's total)

Earsdon	P	P	X	51	PHE
Felton	.	P	P	51	PHE
Tynemouth	A	X	X	51	PHE
Woodhorn	P	P	P	51	PHE
Berwick upon Tweed	X	X	X	50	PHE

Nottinghamshire (9 parishes, 4.2 per cent of county's total)

Arnold	A	A	X	31	PHE
Burton Joyce	A	X	A	31	PHE
Cropwell Bishop	A	P	X	31	PHE
Darlton	A	A	P	31	PHE

Edwinstowe*	P	X	X	31	PHE
Fledborough	A	A	X	31	PHE
Gedling	A	A	X	31	PHE
Warsop	X	X	X	31	PHE
Blyth	A	A	X	31	PHE

Oxfordshire (5 parishes, 2.2 per cent of county's total)

Chinnor	P	A	A	21	PHE
Standlake	A	X	A	21	PHE
Wootton	A	A	A	21	PHE
Banbury	A	X	A	21	PHE
Chipping Norton	A	A	A	21	PHE

Rutland (1 parish, 2.0 per cent of county's total)

Oakham	A	A	A	31	PHE

Shropshire (17 parishes, 7.4 per cent of county's total)

Alberbury	X	P	P	30	PHE
Albrighton	X	X	X	30	PHE
Baschurch*	X	X	P	30	PHE
Bitterley	.	P	P	20	PHE
Bromfield	X	P	P	20	PHE
Ercall Magna*	X	X	X	30	PHE
Onibury	X	P	P	20	PHE
Pontesbury	X	P	P	30	PHE
Stanton Lacy	P	P	P	20	PHE
Westbury*	.	P	P	30	PHE
Ludlow St Lawrence	X	X	X	20	PHE
Oswestry	X	X	P	30	PHE
Shrewsbury St Alkmund	X	X	X	30	PHE
Shrewsbury St Chad	X	X	X	30	PHE
Shrewsbury St Julian	A	X	X	30	PHE
Shrewsbury St Mary	X	X	X	30	PHE
*Wem**	X	X	X	30	PHE

Somerset (10 parishes, 2.1 per cent of county's total)

Congresbury	A	P	P	10	PHE
Milborne Port	A	P	X	10	PHE
North Cadbury	A	P	X	10	PHE
Pitminster	A	P	P	10	PHE
Wedmore	A	P	P	10	PHE
Bridgewater	A	X	X	10	PHE
Bruton	A	X	X	10	PHE
Crewkerne	A	X	X	10	PHE
Martock	A	X	X	10	PHE
North Petherton	A	X	X	10	PHE

Staffordshire (19 parishes, 10.7 per cent of county's total)

Aldridge	.	X	X	31	
Alrewas	A	P	X	31	
Alstonefield	X	X	X	31	PHE
Audley*	A	X	X	30	PHE

Barton under Needwood	A	P	X	31	PHE
Burslem	.	X	X	30	PHE
Darlaston	X	X	X	20	
Elastone	P	X	X	31	PHE
Hanbury	X	X	X	31	
Rowley Regis	A	X	X	20	
Sedgley*	A	X	X	20	PHE
Stowe by Chartley	P	P	X	31	PHE
Tatenhill	P	P	A	31	PHE
Tipton	A	P	X	20	
Wednesbury	A	X	X	21	
Brewood	X	X	X	30	
Eccleshall	X	X	X	30	PHE
Rocester	P	P	X	31	PHE
*Stone**	X	X	X	30	PHE
Suffolk (29 parishes, 5.8 per cent of county's total)					
Cavendish	A	P	A	22	PHE
East Bergholt	.	A	A	22	PHE
Fressingfield	A	A	A	22	PHE
Laxfield	A	A	A	22	PHE
Marlesford	.	A	A	22	PHE
Peasenhall	A	A	A	22	PHE
Rattlesden	A	A	A	22	PHE
Sibton	A	A	A	22	PHE
Stradbroke	A	A	A	22	PHE
Wickhambrook	A	A	A	22	PHE
Wortham	A	A	A	22	PHE
Yoxford	A	A	A	22	PHE
Eye	A	A	A	22	PHE
Framlingham	A	A	A	22	PHE
Hadleigh	X	X	A	22	PHE
Horringer	A	A	A	22	PHE
Ipswich St Clement	X	X	X	22	PHE
Ipswich St Lawrence	X	X	X	22	PHE
Ipswich St Mary Elms	X	A	X	22	PHE
Ipswich St Mary Stoke	X	X	A	22	PHE
Ipswich St Matthew	X	X	X	22	PHE
Ipswich St Nicholas	X	X	X	22	PHE
Ipswich St Peter	.	A	X	22	PHE
Ipswich St Stephen	X	X	X	22	PHE
Lavenham	X	A	A	22	PHE
Mendelsham	A	A	A	22	PHE
Mildenhall	P	A	A	22	PHE
Saxmundham	A	A	A	22	PHE
Woodbridge	X	A	A	22	PHE
Surrey (13 parishes, 9.1 per cent of county's total)					
Abinger	P	A	A	12	PHE
Beddington	P	P	X	12	PHE
Carshalton	X	P	X	12	PHE

Cobham	A	A	A	12	PHE
Cranley	P	P	P	12	PHE
Gatton	P	A	P	12	PHE
Limpsfield	P	P	A	12	PHE
Nutfield	A	P	X	12	PHE
Putney	X	X	X	12	PHE
Walton on the Hill	.	X	A	12	PHE
Wimbledon	P	X	X	12	PHE
Wotton	X	P	A	12	PHE
Reigate	X	X	X	12	PHE

Sussex (15 parishes, 5.1 per cent of county's total)

Ardingley	P	P	P	12	PHE
Bolney	P	P	P	12	PHE
Brede	A	P	P	12	PHE
Cowfold	X	P	P	12	PHE
Felpham	X	P	X	11	PHE
Frant	X	X	X	12	PHE
Harting	X	A	X	11	PHE
Hurstpierpoint	P	P	P	12	PHE
Northiam	X	P	P	12	PHE
Pevensey	P	P	A	12	PHE
Salehurst	P	P	X	12	PHE
Woodmancote	P	P	A	12	PHE
Worth	X	P	A	12	PHE
East Grinstead	P	P	X	12	PHE
Hailsham	X	P	X	12	PHE

Warwickshire (24 parishes, 11.5 per cent of county's total)

Budbrooke	A	A	A	21	PHE
Butler's Marston	A	A	A	21	
Chilvers Coton	.	A	X	21	PHE
Curdworth	.	X	A	21	PHE
Dunchurch	A	P	A	21	PHE
Edgbaston	.	X	X	21	PHE
Elmdon	A	P	P	21	
Harbury	A	A	A	21	PHE
Kingsbury	A	A	A	21	PHE
Knowle	.	X	A	21	
Ladbroke	A	A	A	21	
Monks Kirby	.	A	A	21	PHE
Napton	A	A	A	21	PHE
Polesworth	A	A	A	31	PHE
Rowington	A	A	A	21	PHE
Sheldon	X	X	X	21	
Studley	.	A	.	21	
Tanworth	A	A	A	21	PHE
Tredington	A	A	A	21	PHE
Wormleighton	.	A	A	21	
Alcester	A	A	A	21	PHE
Kenilworth	P	A	A	21	PHE

*Mancetter**	A	X	X	21	PHE
Solihull	A	P	A	21	

Westmorland (no parishes in sample)

Wiltshire (14 parishes, 4.5 per cent of county's total)

Beechingstoke	A	X	X	11	
Bishops Canning	A	X	A	11	PHE
Britford	A	X	A	11	
Bromham	A	X	X	10	PHE
East Knoyle	A	X	X	10	
Eisey	A	X	A	11	
Idmiston	A	A	A	11	
Latton	A	P	A	11	
Luckington	A	A	P	10	
Lydiard Millicent	A	P	A	11	
Milston	A	A	.	11	
Stockton	A	X	X	10	
Wishford Magna	A	X	X	11	PHE
Woodborough	A	P	A	11	

Worcestershire (12 parishes, 6.1 per cent of county's total)

Alstone	A	A	A	20	
Bushley	X	X	A	20	
Churchill in Oswaldslow	A	A	A	20	
Eastham	A	P	P	20	
Elmbridge	A	X	P	20	
Hanley William	P	.	P	20	
Kings Norton	P	P	A	21	PHE
Kingston	A	A	A	20	
Offenham	A	P	A	20	
Over Areley	P	X	X	20	
Rous Lench	A	A	A	21	
Worcester St Helen	X	X	X	20	PHE

Yorkshire

  East Riding (8 parishes, 3.5 per cent of East Riding's total)

Brandsburton	A	A	A	42	
Bubwith	A	A	A	41	PHE
Etton	A	A	A	41	PHE
Hunmanby	A	A	A	42	PHE
Settrington	A	A	A	41	
Winestead	A	A	X	42	
Wintringham	A	A	A	41	
Bridlington	A	A	X	42	PHE

  North Riding (8 parishes, 3.6 per cent of North Riding's total)

Easingwold*	P	A	X	41	PHE
Gilling	A	X	X	41	PHE
Kirkdale	A	A	A	41	PHE
Marske in Cleveland	A	A	X	51	PHE
Oswaldkirk	A	X	X	41	PHE

Sessay	A	A	A	41	PHE
Stainton in Cleveland	A	P	P	51	PHE
Yarm	.	A	X	51	PHE

West Riding (26 parishes, 9.4 per cent of West Riding's total)

Addingham	P	X	X	41	PHE
Adel	P	X	X	41	PHE
Almondbury*	X	X	X	41	PHE
Bolton Percy	A	A	A	41	PHE
Brodsworth	A	A	X	41	PHE
Burnsall	P	P	X	41	PHE
Carlton juxta Snaith	A	X	A	41	PHE
Clapham	P	X	X	40	PHE
Conisborough	A	A	X	31	PHE
Darfield	P	X	X	41	PHE
Dewsbury	X	X	X	41	PHE
Emley	P	A	X	41	PHE
Farnham	A	A	X	41	PHE
Gisburne*	X	X	X	40	PHE
Guiseley*	X	X	X	41	PHE
Hartshead	X	X	X	41	PHE
Horbury	P	X	X	41	PHE
Ilkley	A	X	X	41	PHE
Kippax	A	X	X	41	PHE
Ledsham	A	A	A	41	PHE
Thornhill with Flockton*	A	P	X	41	PHE
Thornton in Lonsdale	X	P	P	40	PHE
Waddington	X	X	X	40	PHE
Wath upon Dearne*	A	A	X	41	PHE
Otley	X	X	X	41	PHE
Skipton	X	X	X	40	PHE

total 542 parishes, 5.34 per cent of England's 10,141

[a] An asterisk next to the parish name indicates that the data was drawn from registers of a chapelry, or chapelries, in the parish. The number of parishes in each county was taken from Wrigley and Schofield, 1981, Table 2.4, p. 41.

[b] For the definitions of Seasonal Types, see above, Figure 3.8.

[c] Key: PHE=from 404 parish set of Wrigley and Schofield, *Population History of England*; BW=gift of John Broad and Susan Wright; R=gift of Glynis Reynolds.

Table A.2. *Parish numbers, by combination of Seasonal Types,*
early-middle-late
(column percentages in parentheses)[a]

		Non-market		Market		All	
consistently arable	A-A-A	149	(39.5)	28	(21.9)	177	(35.0)
consistently pastoral	P-P-P	15	(4.0)	2	(1.6)	17	(3.4)
never seasonal	X-X-X[b]	30	(8.0)	38	(29.7)	68	(13.5)
early changers	A-X-X[c]	25	(6.6)	20	(15.6)	45	(8.9)
	P-X-X	10	(2.7)	0		10	(2.0)
	X-A-A[d]	4	(1.1)	6	(4.7)	10	(2.0)
	P-A-A	10	(2.7)	2	(1.6)	12	(2.4)
	A-P-P[e]	16	(4.2)	1	(0.8)	17	(3.4)
	X-P-P	9	(2.4)	2	(1.6)	11	(2.2)
late changers	A-A-X[f]	17	(4.5)	6	(4.7)	23	(4.6)
	A-A-P	4	(1.1)	0		4	(0.8)
	P-P-A	5	(1.3)	0		5	(1.0)
	P-P-X	7	(1.9)	2	(1.6)	9	(1.8)
	X-X-A[g]	2	(0.5)	5	(3.9)	7	(1.4)
	X-X-P	2	(0.5)	2	(1.6)	4	(0.8)
reverters	A-P-A	11	(2.9)	1	(0.8)	12	(2.6)
	A-X-A	17	(4.5)	4	(3.1)	21	(4.2)
	P-A-P[h]	1	(0.3)	0		1	(0.2)
	P-X-P	1	(0.3)	0		1	(0.2)
	X-A-X	1	(0.3)	3	(2.3)	4	(0.8)
	X-P-X	9	(2.4)	3	(2.3)	12	(2.4)
the permutations	A-P-X	17	(4.5)	1	(0.8)	18	(3.6)
	A-X-P	4	(1.1)	1	(0.8)	5	(1.0)
	P-A-X	4	(1.1)	0		4	(0.8)
	P-X-A	2	(0.5)	0		2	(0.4)
	X-A-P	0	·	0		0	
	X-P-A	5	(1.3)	1	(0.8)	6	(1.2)
missing Seasonal Types[i]		29		8		37	
total		406		136		542	
total non-missing		377		128		505	

[a] Percentages of the combinations with no missing Seasonal Types, Early, Middle, or Late.
[b] This combination characterizes non-agricultural, industrial and commercial, places in much of England, but is the dominant pattern in parts of the northwest, regardless of economic orientation.
[c] With P-X-X, A-X-A, A-X-P, P-X-P, and P-X-A, the early industrializers.
[d] With X-P-P, X-A-P, and X-P-A, the early deindustrializers.
[e] With A-X-X, above, the common combinations in the West.
[f] With P-P-X, A-P-X, and P-A-X, the late industrializers.

Notes to Table A.2 (*cont.*)

[g] To the extent that the earlier X-typing did indicate an industrial orientation, this and the X-X-P combinations are the late deindustrializers.

[h] This was bound to be an uncommon pattern: most parishes were A-Type in the first and last of the three periods, and it was more likely that a parish would have been a P-Type in the middle period (cf. the A-P-A combination, above).

[i] Fewer than 24 marriages recorded the period.

Bibliography

Abrams, P. and E. A. Wrigley, eds. *Towns in Societies: Essays in Economic History and Historical Sociology.* Cambridge University Press, 1978.

Adams, J. *Index Villaris.* London, 1700.

Alcock, N. W. *Warwickshire Grazier and London Skinner, 1532–1555: The Account Book of Peter Temple and Thomas Heritage.* London, British Academy, Records of Social and Economic History, n.s., vol. 4, 1981.

Allen, Robert C. 'Inferring Yields from Probate Inventories', *Journal of Economic History,* vol. 48, 1988, pp. 117–26.

Appleby, A. B. 'Grain Prices and Subsistence Crises in England and France, 1590–1740', *Journal of Economic History,* vol. 39, 1979, pp. 865–87.

Appleby, Joyce Oldham. *Economic Thought in Seventeenth-Century England.* Princeton University Press, 1978.

Armstrong, W. A. 'Origin of the Labour Force in England', *Third International Conference of Economic History,* Section VII, ed. D. E. C. Eversley. Munich, 1965, pp. 39–47.

Atwell, George. *The Faithfull Surveyour* [Cambridge]. 1658.

Baker, Alan R. H. 'Changes in the Later Middle Ages', in *A New Historical Geography of England before 1600,* ed. H. C. Darby. Cambridge University Press, 1976, pp. 186–247.

Bayson, Reid A. and Christine Padoch. 'On the Climates of History', *Journal of Interdisciplinary History,* vol. 10, 1980, pp. 583–98.

Beaver, M.W. 'Population, Infant Mortality, and Milk', *Population Studies,* vol. 27, 1973, pp. 243–74.

Berg, Maxine. *The Age of Manufactures, 1700–1820.* London, Fontana, 1985.

Best, Henry. *Rural Economy in Yorkshire in 1641, being the Farming and Account Books of Henry Best of Elmswell in the East Riding of the County of York,* ed. C. B. Robinson. Surtees Society, vol. 33, 1857.

Bettey, John. 'Agriculture and Rural Society in Dorset, 1570–1670'. Unpublished Ph.D. thesis, Bristol, 1976.

Blalock, H. M. *Social Statistics.* New York, McGraw-Hill, 1960.

Blanchard, Ian. 'The Miner and the Agricultural Community in Late Medieval England', *Agricultural History Review,* vol. 20, 1972, pp. 93–106.

Blayo, Yves et Louis Henry. 'Données Démographique sur la Bretagne et l'Anjou de 1740 à 1829', *Annales Démographie Historique,* 1967, pp. 91–171.

197

Blith, Walter. *The English Improver*. London, 1649.

Bowden, Peter J. 'Agricultural Prices, Farm Profits, and Rents', in *The Agrarian History of England and Wales*, vol. 4, *1500–1640*, ed. Joan Thirsk. Cambridge University Press, 1967, pp. 593–695.

'Agricultural Prices, Farm Profits, and Rents', in *The Agrarian History of England and Wales*, vol. 5, *1640–1750*, ed. Joan Thirsk. Cambridge University Press, part 1, 1985, pp. 1–118.

Brassley, Paul. 'Northumberland and Durham', in *The Agrarian History of England and Wales*, vol. 5, *1640–1750*, ed. Joan Thirsk. Cambridge University Press, part 1, 1985, pp. 30–58.

Braun, Rudolf. 'Early Industrialization and Demographic Change in the Canton of Zurich', in *Historical Studies in Changing Fertility*, ed. Charles Tilly. Princeton University Press, 1978, pp. 289–334.

Breton, Nicholas. *The Twelve Moneths*. 1626. New York, Clarke and Way, 1951.

Bridbury, A. R. 'Sixteenth-Century Farming', *Economic History Review*, 2nd series, vol. 27, 1974, pp. 538–56.

[Bridge, J.] A book of fairs [n.d., n.p.].

Broad, John. 'Alternate Husbandry and Permanent Pasture in the Midlands, 1650–1800', *Agricultural History Review*, vol. 28, 1980, pp. 77–89.

Carmichael, Ann G. 'Infection, Hidden Hunger, and History', *Journal of Interdisciplinary History*, vol. 14, 1983, pp. 249–64.

Chalklin, C. W. *Seventeenth Century Kent: A Social and Economic History*. London, Longmans, 1965.

Chambers, J. D. 'Enclosure and Labour Supply in the Industrial Revolution', *Economic History Review*, 2nd ser., vol. 5, 1952–3, pp. 319–43.

Chambers, J. D. and G. E. Mingay. *The Agricultural Revolution, 1750–1880*. London, Basford, 1966.

Charlesworth, John, ed. *The Registers of the Chapel of Horbury in the Parish of Wakefield in the County of York, 1598–1812*, Yorkshire Parish Registers Society, vol. 3, 1900.

Chartres, J. A. *Internal Trade in England, 1500–1700*. London, Macmillan, 1977a.

'Road Carrying in England in the Seventeenth Century, Myth and Reality', *Economic History Review*, 2nd ser., vol. 30, 1977b, pp. 73–94.

'The Marketing of Agricultural Produce', in *The Agrarian History of England and Wales*, vol. 5, *1640–1750*, ed. Joan Thirsk. Cambridge University Press, part 2, 1985, pp. 406–502.

Cheshire Record Office. Settlement Examinations. Handforth (P/10/14), Lymm (P119/25), Tattenhall (P5/23), and Wilmslow (P123 Acc 2472/C 3ff).

Clay, Christopher. *Economic Expansion and Social Change: England 1500–1700*, 2 vols. Cambridge University Press, 1984.

Coleman, D. C. *Industry in Tudor and Stuart England*. London, Macmillan, 1975.

The Economy of England, 1450–1750. London, Oxford University Press, 1977.

'Proto-Industrialisation: A Concept Too Many', *Economic History Review*, 2nd ser., vol. 36, 1983, pp. 435–48.

Corfield, Penelope. 'Urban Development in England and Wales in the Sixteenth and Seventeenth Centuries', in *Trade, Government and Economy in Pre-Industrial England*, eds. D. C. Coleman and A. H. John. London, Weidenfeld and Nicolson, 1976, pp. 214–47.

Court, W. H. B. *The Rise of the Midland Industries, 1600–1838*. London, Oxford University Press, 1953.

Crafts, N. F. R. 'Income Elasticity of Demand and the Release of Labour by Agriculture during the British Industrial Revolution', *Journal of European Economic History*, vol. 9, 1980, pp. 153–68, rpt. in *The Economics of the Industrial Revolution*, ed. Joel Mokyr. London, Allen and Unwin, 1985, pp. 151–63.

'British Economic Growth, 1700–1831', *Economic History Review*, 2nd ser., vol. 36, 1983, pp. 177–99.

Croix, Alain. 'La Démographie du Pays Nantais au XVIe Siècle', *Annales de Démographie Historique*, 1967, pp. 63–90.

De Vries, Jan. *The Dutch Rural Economy in the Golden Age, 1500–1700*. New Haven, Yale University Press, 1974.

The Economy of Europe in an Age of Crisis. Cambridge University Press, 1976.

'Measuring the Impact of Climate on History: The Search for Appropriate Methodologies', *Journal of Interdisciplinary History*, vol. 10, 1980, pp. 599–630.

Defoe, Daniel. *A Tour Through the Whole Island of Great Britain*. 2 vols., 1724–6. London, Dent, 1962.

The Compleat English Tradesman, 2 vols., London, 1727.

Duckham, A. N. *Agricultural Synthesis: the Farming Year*. London, Chatto and Windus, 1963.

Dupaquier, Michel. 'Le Mouvement Saisonnier des Mariages en France (1856–1968)', *Annales de Démographie Historique*, 1977, pp. 131–49.

Dupree, Marguerite Wright. 'Family Structure in the Staffordshire Potteries, 1840–1880'. D.Phil. thesis, Oxford, 1981.

Edwards, W. J. 'Marriage Seasonality 1761–1810: An Assessment of Patterns in Seventeen Shropshire Parishes', *Local Population Studies*, 1977, pp. 23–7.

Elliot, Vivien. 'Marriage Licenses and the Local Historian', *The Local Historian*, vol. 10, 1973, pp. 282–90.

Emery, F. V. 'England circa 1600', in *A New Historical Geography of England Before 1600*, ed. H. C. Darby. Cambridge University Press, 1976, pp. 248–301.

Ernle (Lord). *English Farming Past and Present*, 5th edn, ed. Sir A. D. Hall. London, Longmans, 1936.

Everitt, Alan. 'Farm Labourers', in *The Agrarian History of England and Wales*, vol. 4, *1500–1640*, ed. Joan Thirsk. Cambridge University Press, 1967a, pp. 396–465.

'The Marketing of Agricultural Produce', in *The Agrarian History of England and Wales*, vol. 4, *1500–1640*, ed. Joan Thirsk. Cambridge University Press, 1967b, pp. 466–592.

'Country, County, and Town: Patterns of Regional Evolution in England', *Transactions of the Royal Historical Society*, 5th ser., vol. 27, 1979, pp. 79–108.

Eversley, D. E. C. 'The Home Market and Economic Growth in England, 1750–1780', in *Land, Labour, and Population in the Industrial Revolution*, eds. E. L. Jones and G. E. Mingay. London, Arnold, 1967, pp. 206–59.

Finberg, H. P. R. *Gloucestershire: An Illustrated Essay on the History of a Landscape*. London, Hodder and Stoughton, 1955.

200   *Bibliography*

Finch, Mary E. *The Wealth of Five Northamptonshire Families, 1540–1640*, Northamptonshire Record Society, vol. 19, 1956.
Fisher, F. J. 'The Development of the London Food Market, 1540–1640', *Economic History Review*, vol. 5, 1935, pp. 46–64.
'Influenza and Inflation in Tudor England', *Economic History Review*, 2nd ser., vol. 18, 1965, pp. 120–9.
Flinn, M. W. 'The Stabilisation of Mortality in Pre-industrial Western Europe', *Journal of European Economic History*, vol. 3, 1974, pp. 285–318.
Frost, Pauline. 'Yeoman and Metal Smiths: Livestock in the Dual Economy of South Staffordshire, 1560–1720', *Agricultural History Review*, vol. 29, 1981, pp. 29–41.
Fussell, G. E. F. *The English Dairy Farmer, 1500–1900*. London, Cass, 1966.
The Old English Farming Books from Fitzherbert to Tull, 1523–1730. London, Crosby Lockwood, 1947.
Fussell, G. E., ed. *Robert Loder's Farm Accounts, 1610–1620*, Camden Society, 3rd ser., vol. 53, 1936.
Fussell, G. E. and Constance Goodman. 'Eighteenth Century Traffic in Livestock', *Economic History*, vol. 3, 1936, pp. 214–36.
Geertz, Clifford. *Agricultural Involution: The Process of Ecological Change in Indonesia*. Berkeley, University of California Press, 1963.
Gillis, John R. 'Peasant, Plebian, and Proletarian Marriage in Britain, 1600–1900', in *Proletarianization and Family History*, ed. D. Levine. Orlando, 1984, pp. 129–62.
For Better, For Worse: British Marriages, 1600 to the Present. New York and Oxford, Oxford University Press, 1985.
Gonner, E. C. K. *Common Land and Inclosure*, 1912. 2nd edn. London, Cass, 1966.
Gooder, A. 'The Population Crisis of 1727–30 in Warwickshire', *Midland History*, vol. 1, 1972, pp. 1–22.
Googe, Barnaby (Conradus Heresbach). *Foure Bookes of Husbandry*, 1577. Amsterdam, Da Capo Press, 1971.
Great Britain, Parliamentary Papers. *Abstract of Answers and Returns to the 1821 Census*, 1822.
Greenslade, M. W. and L. Margaret Midgley. 'Brewood', in *Victoria County History of Staffordshire*, vol. 5, ed. L. Margaret Midgley. London, Oxford University Press, 1959, pp. 18–48.
Grigg, D. B. 'An Index of Regional Change in English Farming', *Transactions of the Institute of British Geographers*, vol. 36, 1965, pp. 55–67.
'The Changing Agricultural Geography of England: A Commentary on the Sources Available for the Reconstruction of the Agricultural Geography of England, 1770–1850', *Transactions of the Institute of British Geographers*, no. 41, 1967a, pp. 73–96.
'Regions, Models and Classes', in *Models in Geography*, eds. Richard J. Chorley and Peter Haggett. London, Methuen, 1967b, pp. 461–509.
Gullickson, Gay. 'Agricultural and Cottage Industry: Redefining the Causes of Proto-Industrialization', *Journal of Economic History*, vol. 43, 1983, pp. 831–50.
Guttman, Myron P. and René Leboutte. 'Rethinking Proto-Industrialization and the Family', *Journal of Interdisciplinary History*, vol. 14, 1984, pp. 587–607.

Hammersley, G. H. 'The Charcoal Iron Industry and Its Fuel', *Economic History Review*, 2nd ser., vol. 26, 1973, pp. 593–613.

Harley, C. Knick. 'British Industrialization before 1841: Evidence of Slower Growth During the Industrial Revolution', *Journal of Economic History*, vol. 42, 1982, pp. 267–89.

Harris, Marvin. *Good to Eat: Riddles of Food and Culture*. New York, Simon and Schuster, 1985.

Hartlib, Samuel. *His Legacie*. London, 1655.

Havinden, M. A. 'Agricultural Progress in Open-Field Oxfordshire', *Agricultural History Review*, vol. 9, 1961, pp. 74–82.

Hey, David. *The Rural Metalworkers of the Sheffield Region: A Study of Rural Industry before the Industrial Revolution*, Leicester University, Department of English Local History, *Occasional Papers*, 2nd series, no. 5, 1972.

'The North-West Midlands: Derbyshire, Staffordshire, Cheshire, and Shropshire', in *The Agrarian History of England and Wales*, vol. 5, *1640–1750*, ed. Joan Thirsk. Cambridge University Press, 1985, pp. 129–58.

Hicks, J. D., ed. *The Parish Register of Brandsburton, 1558–1837*, Leeds, Yorkshire Archaeological Society, Parish Register Section, vol. 142, 1979.

Hobsbawm, E. J. 'Introduction: Inventing Traditions', in *The Invention of Tradition*, eds. Hobsbawm and Ranger. Cambridge University Press, pp. 1–14, 1983.

Hobsbawm, Eric and Terence Ranger, eds. *The Invention of Tradition*. Cambridge University Press, 1983.

Hohenberg, Paul M. and Lynn Hollen Lees. *The Making of Urban Europe, 1000–1950*. Cambridge Mass., Harvard University Press, 1985.

Holderness, B. A. 'Credit in English Rural Society before the Nineteenth Century, with Special Reference to the Period 1650–1720', *Agricultural History Review*, vol. 24, 1976a, pp. 97–109.

Pre-industrial England: Economy and Society, 1500–1700. London, Dent, 1976b.

'East Anglia and the Fens: Norfolk, Suffolk, Cambridgeshire, Ely, Huntingdonshire, Essex, and the Lincolnshire Fens', in *The Agrarian History of England and Wales*, vol. 5, *1640–1750*, ed. Joan Thirsk. Cambridge University Press, 1985, pp. 197–238.

Hole, Christina. *Traditions and Customs of Cheshire*, 1937. Wakefield, S.R. Publishers, 1970.

Hoskins, W. *The Midland Peasant: The Social and Economic History of a Leicestershire Village*. London, Macmillan, 1957.

Devon [1954], new edn. Newton Abbott, D & C, 1972.

Houlbrooke, Ralph A. *The English Family, 1450–1700*. London, Longman, 1984.

Houston, Rab and K. D. M. Snell. 'Proto-industrialization? Cottage Industry, Social Change, and the Industrial Revolution', *Historical Journal*, vol. 27, 1984, pp. 473–92.

Hudson, Pat. 'Proto-industrialization: The Case of the West Riding Wool Textile Industry in the Eighteenth and Early Nineteenth Centuries', *History Workshop*, no. 12, 1981, pp. 34–61.

Hueckel, Glenn. 'Relative Prices and Supply Response in English Agriculture during the Napoleonic Wars', *Economic History Review*, 2nd ser., vol. 29, 1976, pp. 401–2.

Hymer, Stephen and Stephen Resnick. 'A Model of an Agrarian Economy with Nonagricultural Activities', *American Economic Review*, vol. 59, 1969, pp. 493–506.

Ingram, Martin. 'Spousals Litigation in the English Ecclesiastical Courts, c. 1350–c.1640', in *Marriage and Society: Studies in the Social History of Marriage*, ed. R. B. Outhwaite. London, Europa, 1981, pp. 35–57.

Innis, Harold A. *The Cod Fisheries: The History of an International Economy*. Toronto University Press, 1954.

Ippolito, Richard A. 'The Effect of the "Agricultural Depression" on Industrial Demand in England', *Economica*, n.s. vol. 42, 1975, pp. 298–312.

Jackson, R. J. 'Growth and Deceleration in English Agriculture, 1660–1790', *Economic History Review*, 2nd ser. vol. 38, 1985, pp. 333–51.

John, A. H. 'The Course of Agricultural Change, 1660–1760', in *Studies in the Industrial Revolution Presented to T. S. Ashton*, ed. L. S. Presnell. London, Athlone, 1960, pp. 125–55.

Johnson, Arthur H. *The Disappearance of the Small Landholder*. Oxford, Clarendon, 1909.

Johnson, Christopher H. 'Proto-industrialization and De-industrialization in Languedoc: Lodève and its Region, 1700–1870', Section A-2, 8th International Economic History Congress, Bad Hamburg, 1981.

Jones, E. L. *Seasons and Prices: The Role of the Weather in English Agricultural History*. London, Allen and Unwin, 1964.

    'Agriculture and Economic Growth in England, 1660–1750: Agricultural Change', *Journal of Economic History*, vol. 25, 1965a, pp. 1–18.

    'The Constraints on Economic Growth in Southern England, 1650–1850', in *3rd International Conference of Economic History*, Munich, 1965b, pp. 423–30.

Jones, E. L., ed. *Agriculture and Economic Growth in England, 1650–1815*. London, Methuen, 1967.

Jones, E. L. and G. E. Mingay, eds. *Land, Labour, and Population in the Industrial Revolution*. London, Edward Arnold, 1967.

Kerridge, Eric. *The Agricultural Revolution*. London, Allen and Unwin, 1967.

Kriedte, Peter. 'The Origins, the Agrarian Context, and the Conditions in the World Market', in *Industrialization Before Industrialization: Rural Industry in the Genesis of Capitalism*, eds. Peter Kriedte, Hans Medick, and Jurgen Schlumbohm. Cambridge University Press, 1981a, pp. 12–37.

    'Proto-industrialization between Industrialization and De-Industrialization', in *Industrialization Before Industrialization: Rural Industry in the Genesis of Capitalism*, eds. Peter Kriedte, Hans Medick, and Jurgen Schlumbohm. Cambridge University Press, 1981b, pp. 135–60.

Kunitz, Stephen J. 'Speculations on the European Mortality Decline', *Economic History Review*, 2nd ser., vol. 36, 1983, pp. 349–64.

Kussmaul, Ann. *Servants in Husbandry in Early Modern England*. Cambridge University Press, 1981.

    'Agrarian Change in Seventeenth Century England: The Economic Historian as Paleontologist', *Journal of Economic History*, vol. 45, 1985a, pp. 1–30.

    'A Note on Industrialisation, De-industrialisation and Marriage Seasons in Early-Modern England', *Working Papers from the Warwick Workshop on Proto-Industrial Communities*, University of Warwick, 1985b.

    'Time and Space, Hoofs and Grain: The Seasonality of Marriage in England', *Journal of Interdisciplinary History*, vol. 15 (1985), pp. 755–79; rpt. in *Popu-*

lation and Economy: Population and History from the Traditional to the Modern World, eds. R. I. Rotberg and T. K. Rabb. Cambridge University Press, 1986, pp. 195–219.

'Statute Sessions and Hiring at Fairs', unpublished paper.

Kussmaul, Ann, ed. *The Autobiography of Joseph Mayett of Quainton (1783–1839)*, Buckinghamshire Record Society, no. 23, 1986.

Langton, John. 'The Industrial Revolution and the Regional Geography of England', *Transactions of the Institute of British Geographers*, n.s., vol. 9, 1984, pp. 145–67.

Laurence, Edward. *The Duty of a Steward to his Lord*. London, 1727.

Lawrence, John. *New Farmer's Calendar or Monthly Remembrancer*, 3rd edn. London, 1801.

A General Treatise on Cattle, the Ox, the Sheep, and the Swine, 2nd edn. London, 1808.

Lebrun, François. *La vie conjugale sous l'ancien régime*. Paris, Armand Colin, 1975.

Lee, C. H. 'The Service Sector, Regional Specialization, and Economic Growth in the Victorian Economy', *Journal of Historical Geography*, vol. 10, 1984, pp. 139–55.

Levine, David. *Family Formation in an Age of Nascent Capitalism*. New York, Academic Press, 1977.

Lisle, Edward. *Observations in Husbandry*. Dublin, 1957.

Little, Anthony J. *Deceleration in the Eighteenth Century British Economy*. London, Croom Helm, 1976.

Lloyd, Peter E. and Peter Dicken. *Location in Space: A Theoretical Approach to Economic Geography*, 2nd edn. New York, Harper and Row, 1977.

Mabey, Richard, ed. *Second Nature*. London, Jonathan Cape, 1984.

Macfarlane, Alan. *Marriage and Love in England: Modes of Reproduction 1300–1840*. Oxford, Basil Blackwell, 1986.

Machlup, Fritz. 'Conceptual and Causal Relationships in the Theory of Economic Integration in the 20th Century', in *The International Allocation of Economic Activity*, ed. Bertil Ohlin *et al.* London, Macmillan, 1977, pp. 196–215.

Mann, Julia de Lacy. *The Cloth Industry in the West of England from 1640 to 1880*. Oxford, Clarendon, 1971.

Mascall, Leonard. *The Government of Cattell*. London, 1627.

Mayo, H. R., ed. *The Registers of Over Areley, 1564–1812*, Worcestershire Parish Registers Society, vol. 5, 1916.

McCloskey, D. N. 'The Enclosure of Open Fields: Preface to a Study of its Impact on the Efficiency of English Agriculture in the Eighteenth Century', *Journal of Economic History*, vol. 32, 1972, pp. 15–35.

'English Open Fields as Behavior Towards Risk', *Research in Economic History*, vol. 1, 1976, pp. 124–70.

The Applied Theory of Price. New York, Macmillan, 1982.

McKeown, Thomas. 'Food, Infection, and Population', *Journal of Interdisciplinary History*, vol. 14, pp. 227–47, 1983.

McNeill, William H. *Plagues and People*. Oxford, Blackwell, 1977.

Mendels, Franklin F. 'Seasons and Regions in Agriculture and Industry during the Process of Industrialization', in *Region und Industrialisierung*, ed. S. Pollard. Gottingen, Vandenhoeck und Ruprecht, pp. 177–95, 1980.

'Proto-industrialization: Theory and Reality', in *'A' Themes* of *General Report of the 8th International Economic History Conference*, Akadémiai Kiadó, Budapest, pp. 69–105, 1982.

'Farm Servants, Family Formation, and the Rural Economy in Flanders (c. 1800) and France (c. 1860)', Tocqueville Society Conference on Work and the Family in Europe and the United States, La Saline Royale (Arc-et-Senans), 1983.

Miller, Norman J., ed. *Yorkshire Parish Register Society*, vol. 4, 1900.

Mills, Dennis R., ed. *English Rural Communities: The Impact of a Specialized Economy*. London, Macmillan, 1973.

Mingay, G. E. *Enclosure and the Small Farmer in the Age of the Industrial Revolution*. London, Macmillan, 1968.

'The East Midlands: Northamptonshire, Leicestershire, Rutland, Nottinghamshire, and Lincolnshire (Excluding the Fenland)', *The Agrarian History of England and Wales*, vol. 5, *1640–1750*, ed. Joan Thirsk. Cambridge University Press, 1985, pp. 89–128.

Mokyr, Joel. 'Growing-Up and the Industrial Revolution in Europe', *Explorations in Economic History*, vol. 13, pp. 371–96, 1976.

'Demand vs. Supply in the Industrial Revolution', *Journal of Economic History*, vol. 37, 1977, pp. 981–1008; rpt. in *The Economics of the Industrial Revolution*, ed. *idem*. London, Allen and Unwin, 1985, pp. 97–118.

Mokyr, Joel, ed. *The Economics of the Industrial Revolution*. London, Allen and Unwin, 1985.

More, Thomas. *Utopia, 1516*, ed. E. Surtz. New Haven, Yale University Press, 1964.

Mortimer, John. *The Whole Art of Husbandry, or The Way of Managing and Improving of Land*. London, 1707.

Neeson, J. M. 'Common Right and Enclosure in Eighteenth Century Northamptonshire'. Ph.D. thesis, University of Warwick, 1977.

Norden, John. *The Surveiors Dialogue*. London, 1618.

Northamptonshire Record Office. Courteenhall enclosure agreement, 1650 (86P/32, 33).

Nourse, Timothy. *Campania Foelix, or a Discourse of the Benefits and Improvements of Husbandry*. London, 1700.

Ogden, Philip. 'Patterns of Marriage Seasonality in Rural France, 1860–1970', *Local Population Studies*, vol. 10, 1973.

Ohlin, Bertil, Hesselborn, Per-Ove, and Per Magnus Wijkman. *The International Allocation of Economic Activity*. London, Macmillan, 1977.

Outhwaite, R. B. 'Age at Marriage in England from the Late Seventeenth to the Nineteenth Century', *Transactions of the Royal Historical Society*, 5th ser., vol. 23, pp. 55–70, 1973.

'Dearth and Government Intervention in English Grain Markets, 1590–1700', *Economic History Review*, 2nd ser., vol. 33, pp. 389–406, 1981.

'Progress and Backwardness in English Agriculture, 1500–1650', *Economic History Review*, 2nd ser., vol. 39, pp. 1–18, 1986.

Outhwaite, R. B., ed. *Marriage and Society: Studies in the Social History of Marriage*. London, Europa, 1981.

Overton, Mark. 'The 1801 Crop Returns for Cornwall', in *Husbandry and Marketing in the Southwest, 1500–1800*, ed. Michael Havinden. Exeter Papers in Economic History, University of Exeter, pp. 39–62, 1973.

'Estimating Crop Yields from Probate Inventories: An Example from East Anglia', *Journal of Economic History*, vol. 39, 1979, pp. 363–78.

'Agricultural Change in Norfolk and Suffolk, 1580–1740', unpublished dissertation, Cambridge, 1980.

'Agricultural Revolution? Development of the Agrarian Economy in Early Modern England', in *Explorations in Historical Geography*, eds. A. R. H. Baker and D. J. Gregory. Cambridge University Press, 1984, pp. 118–39.

'The Diffusion of Agricultural Innovations in Early Modern England: Turnips and Clover in Norfolk and Suffolk, 1580–1740', *Transactions of the Institute of British Geographers*, n.s., vol. 10, pp. 205–21, 1985.

Palliser, David. 'Dearth and Disease in Staffordshire, 1540–1670', in *Rural Change and Urban Growth*, eds. C. W. Chalklin and M. A. Havinden. London, Longman, pp. 54–75, 1974.

'Tawney's Century: Brave New World or Malthusian Trap', *Economic History Review*, 2nd ser., vol. 35, pp. 339–53, 1982.

The Age of Elizabeth: England under the Later Tudors, 1547–1603. London, Longmans, 1983.

Parliamentary Papers, Great Britain, *Abstract of Answers and Returns to the 1821 Census*, 1822, p. 254.

Perrenoud, Alfred. 'Calendrier du Mariage et Coutume Populaire: le Creux de Mai en Suisse-Romande', *Population*, vol. 38, 1983, pp. 925–40.

Phillimore, W. P. W. ed. *Gloucestershire Parish Registers: Marriages*, vol. 16, 1912, pp. 1–71.

Phillimore, W. P. W. and Edmund Nevill, eds. *Dorset Parish Registers: Marriages*, vol. 6. London, Phillimore and Co., 1912, pp. 105–20.

Philpot, G. 'Enclosure and Population Growth in Eighteenth Century England', *Explorations in Economic History*, vol. 12, 1975, pp. 29–46.

Phythian-Adams, Charles. 'Urban Decay in Late Medieval England', in *Towns and Societies*, eds. Abrams and Wrigley, 1978, pp. 159–85.

Plattes, Gabriel. *A Discovery of Infinite Treasure Hidden Since the World's Beginning*, 1639. Amsterdam, 1974.

Ponting, K. G. 'The Wiltshire–Somerset Border Woollens Industry', in *Textile History and Economic History: Essays in Honour of Miss Julia de Lacy Mann*, eds. N. B. Harte and K. G. Ponting. Manchester University Press, 1973, pp. 163–95.

Presnell, L. S., ed. *Studies in the Industrial Revolution Presented to T. S. Ashton*. London, Athlone, 1960.

Reyce, Robert. *Suffolk in the XVIIth Century: the Breviary of Suffolk by Robert Reyce*. London, 1902.

Richardson, Harry W. *Regional Growth Theory*. London, Macmillan, 1973.

Richardson, R. C. 'Metropolitan Counties: Bedfordshire, Hertfordshire, and Middlesex', in *The Agrarian History of England and Wales*, vol. 5, *1640–1750*, ed. Joan Thirsk. Cambridge University Press, 1985, pp. 239–69.

Rickman, John. 'Preliminary Observations', 1821 Census, 1822.

Roper, J. S. *Sedgley Probate Inventories, 1614–1787*, typescript transcription, William Salt Library, Stafford [n.d.].

Rowlands, Marie B. *Masters and Men in the Midlands Metalware Trades before the Industrial Revolution*. Manchester University Press, 1975.

Schlumbohm, Jurgen. 'Seasonal Fluctuations and Social Division of Labour: Rural Linen Production in the Osnabruck and Bielefeld Regions and the

Urban Woollen Industry in the Niederlausitz c. 1770–c. 1850', in *Manufacture in the Town and Country before the Factory*, eds. Maxine Berg, Pat Hudson, and Michael Sonenscher. Cambridge University Press, 1983, pp. 92–123.

Schofield, Roger, 'The Impact of Scarcity and Plenty on Population Change in England, 1541–1841', *Journal of Interdisciplinary History*, vol. 14, 1983, pp. 265–91.

Schofield, Roger and E. A. Wrigley. 'Infant and Child Mortality in England in the Late Tudor and Early Stuart Period', in *Health, Medicine, and Mortality in the Sixteenth Century*, ed. Charles Webster. Cambridge University Press, 1979, pp. 61–95.

Sheail, John. 'Rabbits and Agriculture in Post-Medieval England', *Journal of Historical Geography*, vol. 4, 1978, pp. 343–55.

Short, Brian M. 'The South-East: Kent, Surrey, and Sussex', in *The Agrarian History of England and Wales*, vol. 5, *1640–1750*, ed. Joan Thirsk. Cambridge University Press, 1985, pp. 270–316.

Skipp, V. H. T. 'Economic and Social Change in the Forest of Arden, 1530–1649', in *Land, Church, and People: Essays Presented to Professor H. P. R. Finberg*, ed. Joan Thirsk. Supplement to the *Agricultural History Review*, vol. 18, 1970, pp. 84–111.

  Crisis and Development: An Ecological Case Study of the Forest of Arden, 1570–1674. Cambridge University Press, 1978.

Slack, Paul. 'Mortality Crises and Epidemic Disease in England, 1485–1610', in *Health, Medicine, and Mortality in the Sixteenth Century*, ed. Charles Webster. Cambridge University Press, 1979, pp. 9–59.

Slater, Gilbert. *The English Peasantry and the Enclosure of Common Fields*. London, Constable, 1907.

Smith, A. W. Letter in *Local Population Studies*, vol. 2, 1969, p. 67.

Smith, John. *The Names and Surnames of all the Able and Sufficient Men in Body Fit for His Majesty's Service in the Wars, within the County of Gloucester*. London, Southern, 1902.

Souden, David. 'Migrants and the Population Structure of later Seventeenth-Century Provincial Cities and Market Towns', in *The Transformation of English Provincial Towns, 1600–1800*, ed. Peter Clark. London, Hutchinson, 1984.

Speake, Robert, ed. *Audley: An 'Out of the Way, Quiet Place'*. Department of Adult Education, Keele [n.d.].

Speed, Adam. *Adam Out of Eden, or An Abstract of Divers Excellent Experiments Touching on the Advancement of Husbandry*. London, 1659.

Spufford, Margaret. *Contrasting Communities: English Villagers in the Sixteenth and Seventeenth Centuries*. Cambridge University Press, 1974.

  The Great Reclothing of Rural England: Petty Chapmen and their Wares in the Seventeenth Century. London, Hambledon Press, 1984.

Spufford, Peter and Margaret Spufford. *Eccleshall: The Story of a Staffordshire Market Town and its Dependent Villages*, Department of Extra-mural Studies, U. of Keele, Staffordshire, 1964.

Steel, D. J., ed. *National Index of Parish Registers*, vol. 1. London, Society of Genealogists, 1968.

Styles, Philip. *Studies in Seventeenth Century Warwickshire*. Kineton, Roundwood Press, 1978.

Supple, B. E. *Commercial Crisis and Change in England, 1600–1642: A Study in the Instability of a Mercantile Economy.* Cambridge University Press, 1959.

Swain, John. 'Industry and the Economy in Northeast Lancashire c. 1500–1640'. Unpublished Ph.D. thesis, Cambridge, 1983.

Tate, W. E. *A Domesday of English Enclosure Acts and Awards*, ed. M. E. Turner. Reading, 1978.

Tawney, A. J. and R. H. Tawney. 'An Occupational Census of the Seventeenth Century', *Economic History Review*, vol. 5, 1939, pp. 25–64.

Taylor, Carl E. 'Synergy among Mass Infections, Famines, and Poverty', *Journal of Interdisciplinary History*, vol. 14, 1983, pp. 483–501.

Thick, Malcolm. 'Market Gardening in England and Wales', in *The Agrarian History of England and Wales*, vol. 5, ed. Joan Thirsk. Cambridge University Press, 1985, pp. 503–32.

Thirsk, Joan. 'Agrarian History, 1540–1950', in *The Victoria County History of Leicester*, vol. 2, ed. W. G. Hoskins. London, Oxford University Press, 1954, pp. 199–264.

'The Content and Sources of English Agrarian History after 1500', *Agricultural History Review*, vol. 3, part 2, 1955, pp. 66–79.

'Industries in the Countryside', in *Essays in the Economic and Social History of Tudor and Stuart England, in Honour of R. H. Tawney*, ed. F. J. Fisher. Cambridge University Press, 1961, pp. 70–88.

'Farming Regions', in *The Agrarian History of England and Wales*, vol. 4, *1500–1640*, ed. Joan Thirsk. Cambridge University Press, 1967a, pp. 1–112.

'Farming Techniques', in *The Agrarian History of England and Wales*, vol. 4, *1500–1640*, ed. Joan Thirsk. Cambridge University Press, 1967b, pp. 161–99.

'Introduction', in *The Agrarian History of England and Wales*, vol. 4, *1500–1640*, ed. Joan Thirsk. Cambridge University Press, 1967c, pp. xxix–xxxvii.

'Seventeenth-Century Agriculture and Social Change', in *idem*. ed. *Land, Church, and People: Essays Presented to Professor H. P. R. Finberg*, Agricultural History Review, supplement, 1970, pp. 148–77.

'The Fantastical Folly of Fashion: The English Stocking Knitting Industry, 1500–1700', in *Textile History and Economic History: Essays in Honour of Miss Julia de Lacy Mann*, eds. N. B. Harte and K. G. Ponting. Manchester University Press, 1973, pp. 50–73.

Economic Policy and Projects: The Development of a Consumer Society in Early Modern England. Oxford, Clarendon, 1978.

'Introduction', *The Agrarian History of England and Wales*, vol. 5, *1640–1750*, ed. Joan Thirsk. Cambridge University Press, 1984a, pp. xix–xxxi.

'The South-West Midlands: Warwickshire, Worcestershire, Gloucestershire, and Herefordshire', *The Agrarian History of England and Wales*, vol. 5, *1640–1750*, ed. Joan Thirsk. Cambridge University Press, 1984b, pp. 159–96.

Thirsk, Joan, ed. *The Agrarian History of England and Wales*, vol. 4, *1500–1640*. Cambridge University Press, 1967.

Land, Church, and People: Essays Presented to Professor H. P. R. Finberg, Agricultural History Review, supplement, 1970.

The Agrarian History of England and Wales, vol. 5, *1640–1750* (2 parts). Cambridge University Press, 1984–5.

Thomas, David. 'Climate and Cropping in the Early Nineteenth Century in Wales', in *Weather and Agriculture*, ed. James A. Taylor. Oxford, Pergamon, 1967, pp. 201–12.

Thomas, H. R., ed. *Sedgley 1558–1685*, Staffordshire Parish Registers Society, 1940–1.

Thompson, E. P. 'Time, Work-Discipline, and Industrial Capitalism', *Past and Present*, no. 38, 1967, pp. 56–97.

Thompson, F. M. L. *English Landed Society in the Nineteenth Century*. London, Routledge Kegan Paul, 1963.

'Horses and Hay in Britain, 1830–1918', in *Horses in European Economic History: A Preliminary Canter*, ed. F. M. L. Thompson. British Agricultural History Society, 1983, pp. 50–72.

Thompson, J. K. J. 'Variations in Industrial Structure in Pre-Industrial Languedoc', in *Manufacture in the Town and Country before the Factory*, eds. Maxine Berg, Pat Hudson, and Michael Sonenscher. Cambridge University Press, 1983, pp. 61–91.

Thorpe, Harry, 'The Lord and the Landscape Illustrated through the Changing Fortunes of a Warwickshire Parish, Wormleighton', in *English Rural Communities: The Impact of a Specialized Economy*, Dennis R. Mills, ed. London, Macmillan, 1973.

Timmer, C. Peter. 'The Turnip, New Husbandry, and the English Agricultural Revolution', *Quarterly Journal of Economics*, vol. 83, 1969, pp. 375–95.

Trainor, R. H. 'Who Married Whom? The Social and Economic Context of Matrimony in the Black Country, c. 1870–1914', unpublished paper. Keele University Centre for Regional History Seminar, 1985.

Turner, Michael. 'Arable in England and Wales: Estimates from the 1801 Crop Return', *Journal of Historical Geography*, vol. 7, 1981, pp. 291–302.

Enclosures in Britain 1750–1830. London, Macmillan, 1984.

Walter, John and Keith Wrightson. 'Dearth and the Social Order', *Past and Present*. no. 71, 1976, pp. 22–42.

Wedge, John. *A General View of the Agriculture of the County of Warwick*. London, 1794.

Westerfield, R. B. *Middlemen in English Business Particularly Between 1660 and 1760*. New Haven, Yale University Press, 1915.

Willan, T. S. *River Navigation in England, 1600–1750*, 1936, London, Cass, 1954.

The Inland Trade: Studies in English Internal Trade in the Sixteenth and Seventeenth Centuries. Manchester University Press, 1976.

Williamson, Jeffrey. 'Was It Worth It? Disamenities and Death in Nineteenth Century British Towns', *Explorations in Economic History*, vol. 19, 1982, pp. 221–45.

Wilson, Charles. *England's Apprenticeship, 1603–1763*. London, Longmans, 1965.

Wilson, R. G. 'The Supremacy of the Yorkshire Cloth Industry in the Eighteenth Century', in *Textile History and Economic History: Essays in Honour of Miss Julia de Lacy Mann*, eds. N. B. Harte and K. G. Ponting. Manchester University Press, 1973, pp. 225–46.

Wiltshire Record Office, Settlement Examinations, Wroughton (551/103), Pewsey (772/32), and Chicklade St. Sampson (1189/66).

Wood, Herbert Maxwell, ed. *The Registers of Marske in Cleveland, Co. York,* Yorkshire Parish Registers Society, vol. 16, 1903.

Wordie, J. R. 'The Chronology of English Enclosure, 1500–1914', *Economic History Review,* 2nd ser., vol. 36, 1983, pp. 483–505.

Worlidge, John. *Systema Agriculturae.* London, 1668.

Wrightson, Keith. *English Society 1580–1680.* London, Hutchinson, 1982.

Wrightson, Keith and David Levine. *Poverty and Piety in an English Town: Terling, 1525–1700.* New York, Academic Press, 1979.

Wrigley, E. A. 'Parasite or Stimulus: The town in a Pre-Industrial Economy', in *Towns in Societies: Essays in Economic History and Historical Sociology,* eds. P. Abrams and E. A. Wrigley. Cambridge University Press, 1978, pp. 285–309.

'Marriage, Fertility, and Population Growth in Eighteenth Century England', in *Marriage and Society: Studies in the Social History of Marriage,* ed. R. B. Outhwaite. London, Europa, 1981, pp. 137–85.

People, Cities, and Wealth: The Transformation of Traditional Societies. London, Blackwell, 1987.

'Urban Growth and Agricultural Change: England and the Continent in the Early Modern Period', in *People, Cities, and Wealth.* London, Blackwell, pp. 157–93.

Continuity, Chance, and Change: The Character of the Industrial Revolution in England. Cambridge University Press, 1988.

Wrigley, E. A. and R. S. Schofield. *The Population History of England, 1541–1871: A Reconstruction.* London, Edward Arnold, 1981.

Yarranton, Andrew. *England's Improvement by Sea and Land.* London, 1677.

Yelling, J. A. 'Probate Inventories and the Geography of Livestock Farming: A Study of East Worcestershire, 1540–1750', *Transactions of the Institute of British Geographers,* vol. 51, 1970, pp. 111–26.

Index

transportation, transportation costs, 107–8, 112–13, 122, 138–9, 171
tuberculosis, 163
turnips, 109, 120

vegetables, 15

wages, 17, 21–2, 29, 139, 146, 162, 174, 178
Wales, 93
Warwickshire, 5, 28, 36, 49, 54, 90–1, 153, 181, 192–3
Wash, 70–2
Weald, 83, 118, 128–9, 136, 137
weaving, 129–30, 132, 140
weddings, 17, 34, 48, 91, 131, 157
    tax on, 34
weighting, by area, 54
welfare, 170–1
west, 21, 87–8, 90, 112–13, 124, 126, 146–7, 174, 176
Westbury on Trym, Glos., 130
Westmorland, 47, 54, 140
West Country, 11, 17, 80, 83, 129–30, 136, 146, 153
West Riding, *see* Yorkshire, West Riding
Westerfield, R. B., 101, 122
wheat, 89–93
wheat mining, 178–9
Wigston Magna, Leics., 6, 95, 149
Williamson, Jeffrey, 167
Willingham, Cambs., 25, 60

Wilson, Charles, 136, 175
Wiltshire, 25, 41, 47, 129, 193
Winestead, East Riding, 29–30, 153
winter, 15, 22, 51, 92
Winwick, Northants., 95
women's work, 17–18, 27, 129–30, 132, 138, 153–4
wool, 92
woollens, 129, 136
Worcestershire, 41, 47, 90, 193
work, seasonality of, 14–18
Worlidge, John, 19
Wormleighton, Warwickshire, 36, 49, 91
Wotton under Edge, Glos., 130
Wright, Susan, 181
Wrigley, E. A., 14, 33, 42, 46, 118, 158, 163–4, 166–7, 169, 177–8, 181
Wymondham, Leics., 94

Yarranton, Andrew, 88, 94, 100
yeomen, 9
Yelling, J. A., 6, 173
Yorkshire, 136
    East Riding, 29–30, 47, 153, 193
    North Riding, 29, 193–4
    West Riding, 42, 47, 70–3, 84, 126, 128, 151, 153, 194
Young, Arthur, 6

X-Type, *see* non-seasonal, rural industry, Seasonal Types